CAUCUS OF
CORRUPTION

CAUCUS OF CORRUPTION

THE TRUTH ABOUT THE NEW DEMOCRATIC MAJORITY

MATT MARGOLIS
& MARK NOONAN

World Ahead Publishing, Inc

CAUCUS OF CORRUPTION
A World Ahead Book
Published by World Ahead Media
Los Angeles, CA

Front and Back Cover Illustrations by John Cox
Cover Design by BorregoPublishing.com, Prescott, Arizona

World Ahead Books are distributed to the trade by:

Midpoint Trade Books
27 West 20th Street, Suite 1102
New York, NY 10011

World Ahead Books are available at special discounts for bulk purchases. World Ahead Publishing also publishes books in electronic formats. For more information call (310) 961-4170 or visit www.worldahead.com.

First Edition

ISBN 10-Digit: 0-9778984-7-4
ISBN 13-Digit: 978-0-9778984-7-3
Library of Congress Control Number: 2006936039

Printed in the United States of America

hypocrisy: 1. The practice of professing beliefs, feelings, or virtues that one does not hold or possess; falseness.

2. An act or instance of such falseness.

The American Heritage® Dictionary of the English Language,

Fourth Edition

CONTENTS

PREFACE

ON DECEMBER 28, 2003, then-presidential candidate Howard Dean said of Osama bin Laden in an interview, "I've resisted pronouncing a sentence before guilt is found." He continued, "I still have this old-fashioned notion that even with people like Osama, who is very likely to be found guilty, we should do our best not to, in positions of executive power, not to prejudge jury trials."[1]

On May 14, 2005, Howard Dean, now chairman of the Democratic National Committee (DNC), said that just-indicted House Majority Leader Tom DeLay "...ought to go back to Houston where he can serve his jail sentence."[2] The indictment of DeLay was questionable, at best, and Delay had not even been given a trial date, let alone convicted. And yet here was Howard Dean, pronouncing the verdict and issuing the sentence.

In other words: According to the chairman of the Democratic Party, terrorists deserve due process, Republicans do not.

This dual attitude is clearly shared by many in Dean's party. This is also reflected in their feigned outrage over the existence of the NSA Terrorist Surveillance Program and the Terrorist Finance Tracking Program. Allegedly because of their concern for civil liberties and privacy issues, these vital national security measures had to be given the closest scrutiny possible—but Democrats will work tirelessly to thwart all such investigation of members of their own party.

This premature guilty verdict of Republicans is coupled with a presumption of the innocence of their own party. That, above anything else, is the reason why this book had to be written. This book is our response to the Democrats' one-sided crusade against corruption.

The examples highlighted in this book were in no way secret or hard to find. It didn't take a super sleuth to uncover the patterns of corruption that are ever so present in the Democratic Party. The information was out there just waiting to be found, and we've connected the dots. This book by no means chronicles all of the corruption in the Democratic Party, let alone all corruption in government. But the examples highlighted in this book will leave no one questioning the corruption and hypocrisy of the Democrats, which have become their most prominent qualities.

Many might ask, "Why don't you talk about Republicans in this book?" This book is not meant to be a smokescreen to hide the ethical lapses of members of the Republican Party, but rather to make the debate about corruption bipartisan. The "secret" of Democratic corruption has been hidden in plain sight. Democrats are even brazen about their corruption, secure in the knowledge that the mainstream media (MSM) will put up an impenetrable fog of misdirection about it.

Time and again, newspapers and television news trumpet Republican scandals, while hardly noting much more egregious and destructive corruption on the Democratic side of the aisle.

Our purpose in writing this book is to give corruption in the Democratic Party its proper notice. Without honesty, democratic government is impossible, and honesty is only possible when the people remain eternally vigilant.

Matt Margolis
Mark Noonan
February 4, 2007

ACKNOWLEDGMENTS

FIRST, I'd like to thank my co-author Mark Noonan. We've been blogging together for a few years now, and I couldn't imagine embarking on such a project like writing a book without him. And I am especially grateful to the folks at World Ahead for believing in us and this project.

This book probably never would have happened if not for the success of Blogs for Bush, GOP Bloggers, and No Agenda, and many thanks go to Rachel, Kevin, Russ, Paul, Pat, Jonathan, and Jason, whose contributions played a big role in those successes; and to Adam for being a patient and understanding Web host. And of course, I am grateful for all of our readers and fellow bloggers who have supported us. Many thanks also to Patrick, Chuck, Katie, and Kristen, for all their help and for being great resources and to John Cox for contributing his artistic talent for this book.

There were lots of people who were helpful to me throughout the process of writing this book, and I'd especially like to thank Richard Miniter and Jason Clarke for all their advice from back when this book was just an idea in my head. This book also would have been much more difficult to write without the help of many, many cups of Starbucks Coffee.

To many friends (both Republican and Democrat), I am glad for their support.

I am also glad for the love and support of Beth, who was a tremendous help with reviewing and editing this book and whose encouragement kept me going through the entire process.

I would also like to thank my family for all their support and enthusiasm. And of course, many thanks to the Democratic Party for providing us with ample material to write a book about corruption.

—*Matt Margolis*

ACKNOWLEDGMENTS

I would like to thank my co-author Matt Margolis for first offering me the opportunity to start blogging, which eventually led to this project. I also appreciate his patience and wise counsel as we worked the past year on this book.

I would also like to thank the good people at World Ahead for the opportunity to bring this book before the public; Dani DeLay-Ferro for taking the time to help unknown authors; Dean Esmay for proving to me that a liberal can be wise; the late Steven Malcolm Anderson for doing double duty as iconoclast and patriot in the blogosphere; and all of the readers and commenters at Blogs for Bush, GOP Bloggers, No Agenda, and Battle Born Politics for ensuring that any mistake I made was held up for immediate disparagement.

Additional thanks are due to my in-laws Joe and Dolores for support, Paule and Don for friendship, Kathy for prayers, Christine and Jeremy for advice, Anna for being adorable, Avery for coming late to the show, Peter for keeping the computer functioning and retrieving the first draft after my computer crashed, Amy for literary expertise, Maria for insight, Lorraine for encouraging jokes, Karen and Wanda for allowing time off to write, Joe for being delightfully anti-Republican at every turn, my father for the stacks of books as a child, my late mother for making me understand the whimsical side of life, my brothers and sisters for teaching me tolerance, and my friend Bill for sticking with me since 1971.

None of this would be possible without the steadfast support of my wife, Cheryl, who is the love of my life and has been my sounding board, confidant, and the spark that kept me going through the good and bad days.

—Mark Edward Noonan

INTRODUCTION

"Avoid the base hypocrisy of condemning in one man what you pass over in silence when committed by another."

—Theodore Roosevelt[1]

*P*EOPLE WHO LIVE *in glass houses should not throw stones.* So goes the age-old saying. Yet for some years now the Democratic Party has been tossing boulders around their glass menagerie.

Democrats, fueled by their all-consuming desire to regain power at any price, launched a crusade against what they called a "culture of corruption" in Washington, D.C., which, if you listened to them, *only* existed in the Republican Party.

Buyer's remorse is an emotional condition whereby a person feels regret after buying something. Though generally associated with the purchase of high-value items such as cars, it can also be applied to politicians and political parties—as those who voted Democratic in 2006 are about to discover.

NO AGENDA

The Democrats' crusade against corruption during the 2006 election cycle was not only a partisan smear; it was a smokescreen for their lack of a politically popular agenda. Theirs was a campaign not to clean up government but to regain power without having to reveal any of their plans and initiatives. They had neither a program to benefit America nor a positive agenda for reform. They did, however, have a litany of complaints about how Republicans ran things—especially the war in Iraq.

This deficit of ideas is a longstanding problem in the Democratic Party. In her unsuccessful bid to become chairwoman of the Democratic National Committee in 1985, Nancy Pelosi proposed the Democrats form a "policy council" to decide what the party stood for.[2] Twenty-two years later, Democrats still wander through the desert looking for an oasis with an idea they can run on.

The Democrats have criticized President Bush and the Republicans for their handling of the war on terror, for wanting to fix Social Security, and for a host of other reform proposals. For *all* of these issues they had criticism, but for *none* did they have a plan or alternative proposal. In fact, they even distanced themselves from members of their party who broke ranks and dared to offer proposals instead of complaints.

In May of 2005, Rep. Robert Wexler (D-FL) demanded that Democrats offer their own ideas to fix Social Security. He put forth his own plan, called the Social Security Forever Act. It called for tax increases to ensure solvency of the program, but at least it was a plan. In a shocking move for a party which never met a tax increase it didn't like, leaders in Wexler's party quickly distanced themselves from him. "Congressman Wexler represents a party of one," said Harry Reid's spokesman Jim Manley. Wexler spoke with Nancy Pelosi about his plan twice, and told the *Associated Press*, "It would be wrong to assume it was a receptive conversation."[3] While Republicans disagreed with Rep. Wexler's approach, they applauded his effort to offer a proposal, rather than only criticism.

In fact, during the 2006 elections, Democrats *celebrated* their lack of an agenda. When Nancy Pelosi declared the Democrats would not have a position on Iraq in their "agenda" for the 2006 elections, she actually found a way to spin this lack of a plan as something positive, asserting that lack of a Democratic plan was nothing compared to the Democrats' ability to complain about President Bush. Meanwhile, Pelosi's colleague, Rep. Rahm Emanuel (D-IL) was saying, "As for Iraq policy, at the right time, we'll have a position."[4] After all of their rhetoric that President Bush should "have a plan," they reveled in their own hypocrisy. Even after President Bush publicized his plan for victory, the Democrats continued to carp and continued to refuse to provide one of their own.

Democrats, however, haven't always eschewed putting forward ideas about how America should be governed. Even in the recent past, they have created and attempted to advance positive political agendas. However, they met with little success.

Following the Democrats' defeat in the 2004 elections, liberal columnist E.J. Dionne, Jr. wrote that the Democrats were "determined to apply the tactical lessons Newt Gingrich taught when he offered a Contract with America in 1994. There was a collective rush to the nearest thesaurus as Democrats considered a Compact with America and a Covenant with America."[5] Imitation may be the sincerest form of flattery, but what the Democrats have done in response to their past electoral losses doesn't even come close to imitating the Contract with America.

In January 2005, shortly after President Bush's second inaugural address, new senate majority leader Harry Reid presented a ten-point plan called "The American Promise," which is now a faded memory. In June 2006, House Democrats unveiled "A New Direction for America,"[6] which quickly became a slogan rather than an agenda.

These "agendas" failed to capture the American imagination, and silence doesn't win elections. The Democrats needed something to help them reverse the losing trend that started when Republicans took congress back in 1994. Consequently, they turned to their last, best hope: scandal-mongering.

THE DEMOCRATS' STRATEGY IN 2006

Back in April of 2005, Senate Minority Leader Harry Reid said it would "take a miracle" for the Democrats to regain a majority in the Senate in 2006, but changed his mind after several months, concluding that Republicans would be doomed by the indictments of Tom DeLay, "Scooter" Libby (Cheney's chief of staff), and the investigation into Senate Majority Leader Bill Frist's stock sales.[7]

And of course, the Mark Foley House page scandal in the fall of 2006 became the icing on the cake for the power-hungry Democrats. With Republicans already on the ropes from more mundane scandals, the emergence of a sex scandal was just too much for the Republican Party to overcome before Election Day.

The first time this strategy bore fruit was the ousting of former House Speaker Newt Gingrich, the man who led the GOP into a Congressional majority for the first time in decades. The Democrats' battle against Gingrich was not fought out in the realm of ideas, but in the cauldron of slander. *Eighty-four ethics charges* were filed by Democrats against Newt Gingrich over a four year period. Out of this, they managed to only get *one ethics action*—a payment to the House Ethics Committee of $300,000 by Gingrich for *inadvertently* giving inaccurate information to the Committee. But that was, after all, beside the point—the main thing was that this relentless campaign of slander made Gingrich politically toxic, and his own fellow Republicans forced him out of power when the going got too politically rough.

Twelve years and numerous electoral defeats later, they renewed their ethics war strategy and set their sights on the majority in Congress, not simply the ouster of one Tom DeLay.

On an almost daily basis throughout the 2006 campaign season, Democrats repeated their message to the media, hoping to fire up their base and dispirit Republican voters. The list of alleged Republican crimes was endless; the Democrats pointed their fingers at the entire Republican Party and charged it with cronyism, corruption, sexual misconduct, ethics violations, anything they thought would stick. *Anything* would do, and it wasn't necessary for facts or basic decency to play a role.

The Democrats hoped that the concept of "absolute power corrupts absolutely" would resonate with voters during the 2006 midterm election, and according to election night exit polls, it did.

The important thing to remember is that their strategy was not to get themselves voted *in*, but to get the Republicans voted *out*. The template for this campaign was the Democrats' 2002 campaign for governor in California. In that race, the Democrats had an unpopular incumbent, Gray Davis, who was forced to carry the albatross of failed, ultra-liberal Democratic policies.

Knowing this was a sure recipe for defeat, the Democrats decided that their best chance was to lose by a smaller margin than the Republicans. They engaged in a horrific campaign of slander against the Republican candidate. By Election Day most Californians were so disgusted with the whole mess that they stayed home and allowed Davis to slip into victory on the backs of hyperpartisan Democratic votes. While the Democrats' 2002 victory in California was short-lived due to Davis being recalled from office, the concept of winning by slander struck a chord among Democratic Party strategists.

In contrast, when the Republicans took back Congress in 1994, they had an agenda, they had vision, and they had leadership. And Democrats responded not with an agenda of their own, but a smear campaign against Newt Gingrich.

In 2006, armed with a twelve-year grudge and a lust for power, Democrats took their negative message to press conference microphones and to the television airwaves and sought to link Republicans to any and every scandal they could.

And it worked, but not as well as the Republican takeover in 1994. In 1994, Republicans gained fifty-four seats in the House and eight seats in the Senate. Looked at objectively, the Democrats' 2006 takeover mirrored historical precedent:

> Since WWII, the party of the incumbent president has typically lost more than thirty seats in the House of Representatives and six seats in the Senate during the second midterm. In addition, in the five wartime congressional elections since 1860, the president's party has lost an average of thirty-two House seats and five Senate seats.[8]

The ethics war brought Democrats no greater success than what is common for a second midterm. Americans respond to agendas, not ethics wars. Perhaps Democrats would have seen greater success had they simply told Americans their plans for the war on terror, the economy, and other important issues.

THE DEMOCRATS' CULTURE OF HYPOCRISY

Chutzpah is an excellent Yiddish word that has become common in the English language. It is a word that *sounds* like what it stands for—brazen audacity. *Chutzpah* fittingly describes DNC Chairman Howard Dean's statement following the indictment of Tom DeLay, "[Texas] is doing what the Republican-controlled federal government has failed repeatedly to do, which is hold Republicans in Washington accountable for their culture of corruption. This alleged illegal activity reaches to the highest levels of the Republican Party."[9] He added, "America can do better than leaders who use their power to promote their own personal interests instead of the interests of the American people who elected them. We simply must change the way business is done in Washington." Dean, leading a party hip-deep in politicians who seem to do nothing other than promote their personal interests, defined *chutzpah* in 2006.

Democrats even used Tom DeLay's indictment to raise money for their party. By claiming the moral high ground on corruption, the Democratic National Committee set a fundraising goal of

$340,000—double the amount of money Tom DeLay was accused of laundering—to prove "the Democratic Party's commitment to doing things differently."[10]

After DeLay turned himself in on October 20, 2005, Nancy Pelosi claimed to feel sorry for him. But she had an odd way of showing this sympathy; she posted a link to DeLay's arrest warrant on her congressional Web site, though it was later taken down after complaints. Pelosi even managed to make a nasty, partisan jab. "I even feel sadder for the American people who've had their lives affected by the culture of cronyism and corruption that exists in Washington, D.C., because of the impact on their lives, because of a special-interest agenda in Washington, D.C., at the expense of the middle class in America."[11]

Any leader of a political party is the natural target of the opposition party. This comes with the territory. But in Tom DeLay's case, the normal desire to bedevil the other side came with an extra incentive. As House majority leader, DeLay was worse than just a partisan for his own side; he was a remarkably effective leader. During an interview with Fox News, President Bush credited Tom DeLay for a "remarkable string of legislative victories" on Republican priorities, including close votes on tax relief and lawsuit reform.[12] Just like Newt Gingrich, Tom DeLay paid for his effectiveness to the Republican Party.

DeLay and Gingrich share something else. They were both forced out of power by way of ethics charges and scandal-mongering from Democrats who couldn't find "ethics" in a dictionary.

When Newt Gingrich was targeted by the Democrats, many senior House Democrats had genuine ethical troubles of their own. Among these flawed Democrats were then-House Minority Leader Rep. Dick Gephardt and long time left-wing workhorse Rep. Jim McDermott.

An ethics complaint was filed against Gephardt, "questioning whether [he] evaded federal taxes and violated House rules on a profitable seaside land deal."[13] The House Ethics Committee was also asked to investigate Gephardt's use of campaign funds to "benefit a company owned by a land developer who lent him money to buy an $800,000 vacation home on North Carolina's Outer Banks."[14] Gephardt eventually received a letter of reprove by the House Ethics Committee for misreporting a personal investment.[15] Barely a slap on the wrist.

While Republicans have too often paid an unjust price for Democrat slanders, they have shown themselves to be better at taking responsibility for their actions. Republicans remove the criminal and corrupt elements of their party. Democrats, however, have a history of holding on to them tighter, keeping them in the inner circle, and then pointing fingers at Republicans.

For instance, Senator Trent Lott was falsely labeled a racist for making laudatory comments about Strom Thurmond. Senator Robert Byrd's past membership in the Ku Klux Klan has never been a political liability, even after he used the word "niggers" during a television interview in 2001. Byrd remains in high regard in the Democratic Party and managed to avoid judgment with a simple apology.

On the one hand, black Republicans called for Lott to step down from his leadership position, which he ultimately did. On the other hand, freshman Senator Barack Obama, the only black member of the U.S. Senate, helped Senator Byrd raise over $1 million for his successful 2006 reelection campaign.[16]

Democrats *claim* to have higher ethical standards than Republicans, but, the *opposite* is true. Their corruption is as profound as their hypocrisy. Yet, holding Republicans accountable for corruption was the Democrats' favored strategy for victory in 2006. And with the media's help, their strategy worked.

The Republican Party actually holds itself to *higher* ethical standards than those required by law and custom. To this day, Democrats defend Bill Clinton, despite his countless scandals, lying under oath, and refusing to go after Osama bin Laden in the 1990s. Richard Nixon, however, will always have a blemished legacy because of Watergate.

THE ROLE OF THE MEDIA

The Democrats had created their narrative for the 2006 elections. According to them, the Republican Party had unchecked powers and had built a "culture of corruption." The only way to end it was to vote for Democrats. This mantra was readily repeated by their mainstream media cheerleaders, who are always eager accomplices in portraying the Republican Party as the epitome of corruption.

Corruption in politics is a serious cancer in the body politic, and it must be rooted out. To betray the public trust cuts right at the very heart of our democratic republic. Freedom is secure only as long as honest men and women are in charge. Of course, any campaign against corruption should be genuinely nonpartisan. All Americans agree that anyone in government who is a crook should pay a very high price—and it doesn't matter what party they belong to.

That said, any campaign to oust any specific individual from power should be done with care and motivated by a true desire to clean up Washington. The accuser must be certain of his charge and be entirely uninterested in wringing partisan political advantage out of the issue. Once an accusation is made, the accused is dogged forever by it. Even if completely exonerated, as long as that person is alive, there will be news stories referring to his or her "ethics issues."

In 2006, an allegation that George Allen used racial slurs on a regular basis in college surfaced on the left-leaning Salon.com[17] and was trumpeted by his opponent Jim Webb. Even after evidence surfaced proving the allegations false,[18] Allen's alleged racism prevailed as a favored talking point of Webb's supporters, and a national story. Meanwhile, when George Allen was revealed to have Jewish ancestry, Webb's campaign attempted to exploit that for political gain in a manner described by some Jewish congressional leaders as anti-Semitic.[19] But such contemptible tactics were never given the same attention as Allen's alleged use of racial slurs in college, or his infamous "macaca" incident.

Many lives and reputations have been destroyed by a false or exaggerated accusation. Back in the 1980s, a special prosecutor investigated Ronald Reagan's Labor Secretary, Raymond Donovan, twice. Accusations flew back and forth and the media frenzy caused most people to assume he was guilty. When it went to trial, however, Donovan was acquitted. Rising after the verdict was announced, Donovan asked, "Which office do I go to to get my reputation back?"[20]

Similarly, Texas Republican Kay Bailey Hutchison faced charges of misusing her treasury office by Travis County DA

Ronnie Earle. The charges against Hutchison were eventually dropped, but not until the day before the trial.

Earle's indictment was undoubtedly caused by Texas Democrats' desire to save the senate seat being vacated by Lloyd Bentsen, who had been appointed Treasury Secretary in the Clinton administration. Increasing the outrageousness of the false charges against Hutchison, Earle was simultaneously refusing to indict then-Governor Ann Richards.[21] Richards, a Democrat, was accused of having her staff shred long distance phone records at the governor's office. Oddly enough, the phone records in question covered the time period when Earle prepared to indict Hutchison. What was said in those records will never be known.

The Richards affair highlights how Democrats have received a free ride for far too long. Republicans are indicted right, left, and center and the media treats it as natural. This is because the media is biased against the GOP. Major news outlets seem pre-disposed to believe Republicans are sinister and corrupt, while stories about Democrat corruption are played off as the well-intentioned actions of people whose hearts are in the right place.

WHY ALL THE CORRUPTION?

In times past, the Democratic Party may have been wrong, but it stood for things broadly supported by the American people. From the reforms of the "progressive era" early in the twentieth century, to Wilson's fight to make the world safe for democracy, to FDR's restoration of American's faith in the dream of their country, to JFK's tax cutting and stout anti-communism, Democrats were firmly in the mainstream of American political life. When John F. Kennedy said, "Ask not what your country can do for you, but what you can do for your country," he struck a chord with all Americans.

But at some point, the Democrats lost this positive vision for America. Instead, they became entrenched as an opposition party, firmly devoted to defeating Republican ideals, rather than advancing their own. The days of Wilson, FDR, and JFK are long gone.

Nature, it has been said, abhors a vacuum. A vacuum exists in the realm of Democratic ideas and though it is speculation, it seems the absence of a strong and persuasive vision for America has in part contributed to the corruption within the Democrat party. While Democrats in the past emphasized the common good—"ask what you can do for your country"—today's Democrat leaders seem more interested in their own good. Lobbyists padding the pockets of politicians, cronyism, and travel to exotic places have replaced enacting policies to help the American people as the goal of Democrat politics.

Democrat leaders have lost their sense of what it means to pursue the common good, the good of America. They lack the ideas and vision that most Americans find persuasive. Consequently, they are left using what political power they have to pursue their own good, and to pursue what is politically expedient for them. That sort of culture lends itself to the corruption that pervades the Democrat party.

At the same time, the prosperity and personal gain of leaders doesn't poll well. They need a message, but they found in 2006 that their best message was to not have one. Instead, Democrats decried the corrupt practices of their political opponents, while diverting attention from their own unethical behavior. And while it was moderately successful in 2006, it is not clear that it is the long-term winning strategy Democrats will need to stay in power.

BRINGING BALANCE TO THE DEBATE

Deep and effective reforms need to be enacted to discourage the matrix of money and power that corrupts the political process. There are corrupt elements in both parties, but for far too long only members of one party have been held accountable.

If the Democrats want to talk about ethics and corruption, then the only way to have a legitimate, open, and fair discussion is for them to acknowledge the corruption within their own party. They need to be interested in doing some serious housecleaning for the benefit of the American people. They must recognize the ethical cloud that hangs over their heads. The free pass the Democrats have received must come to an end.

Had the media done its job or had Democrats rediscovered basic decency, this book might not have been necessary. But neither did, and with the Democrats in the majority again, the need for this book is greater now than ever.

Corruption does not exist *only* within the Democrat party. But the imbalance of what has been reported needs to be corrected.

Everyone in government who is corrupt should be removed and see justice. Yet removing *everyone* who is corrupt is *not* the objective of the new speaker of the House, or any of her fellow Democrats, no matter how much they claim it is. It is time, and past time, to bring balance to the debate.

This book tells the side of the story that Democrats ignore and the mainstream media refuses to tell. It is the story of a political party that has long been given a free pass by the media for their illegal and unethical ways. It is a story of influence peddling, character assassination, and hypocrisy. It is a story that must be told if real reform is to happen. The truth will come out, much to the distress of the dishonest Democrats who have tried to pass off their alleged moral and ethical superiority as conventional wisdom.

And we're starting at the top, with our new House speaker, Nancy Pelosi.

CHAPTER ONE

NANCY PELOSI

*"Every day we see a culture of corruption, incompetence,
and cronyism in Washington, D.C."*

—Nancy Pelosi, September 27, 2005[1]

THE DAUGHTER OF a former Maryland congressman and mayor of Baltimore, Nancy Pelosi was born into politics.

In keeping with the family business, Ms. Pelosi moved to San Francisco after marrying the brother of a San Francisco city councilman, but did not become active in politics until her children reached high-school age. Nancy Pelosi's introduction to the national stage began with her appointment by President Carter to a committee sent to Italy to dispense $50 million in earthquake relief.[2]

Her work in politics eventually brought her to the post of Democratic Party Chairwoman for Northern California. This position, in turn, brought Pelosi for the first time into conflict with campaign finance laws. At issue was more than $90,000 in printing done for the California Democratic Party for the 1980 campaign[3]—the union which did the printing reported it properly as an in-kind donation, but somehow, Pelosi's Democrats forgot to mention it in their financial reports—the perfect prologue to Pelosi's long climb to the top of the political heap. The state party was fined $7,000, teaching Pelosi a valuable lesson she would never forget: Sometimes the fines are so small it's worth it to break the law.

In addition to learning how to take taxpayer-funded trips and how to circumvent campaign finance laws, Pelosi discovered a passion for the political attack. At a conference in mid-1981, Pelosi demanded much more vigorous opposition to President Ronald Reagan's policies.[4] At the time, Reagan had only been in office a few months, so none of his policies had taken effect. Pelosi had no evidence that the policies weren't working; she opposed them simply because of the source. This visceral reaction to all things Republican casts some doubt on Pelosi's stated desire to work with Republicans in a bipartisan way after the Democrats' take-over of the House in November of 2006.

PELOSI'S RISE TO POWER

As chairwoman of the California Democratic Party, Pelosi was involved in changes to the selection of delegates to the Democratic National Convention. These changes required the selection of more Party leaders and elected officials as delegates, thus ensuring the convention against too much direct pressure from the people.[5] Acting in line with her growing desire to suppress opposition, Pelosi led the fight to prevent a straw poll of 1984 presidential prospects at the California Democratic Convention in January of 1983.[6]

During the 1984 election, Ronald Reagan's ambassador to the United Nations, the late Jeanne Kirkpatrick, famously warned America of the "blame-America-first San Francisco Democrats"—a rather appropriate, if too early warning, of the threat constituted by the ultimate San Francisco Democrat, Nancy Pelosi.

Pelosi was head of the San Francisco Host Committee for the Democrats' 1984 convention in San Francisco. At that time, and for many long years afterwards, it was considered impossible for a San Francisco Democrat to rise high in American politics—after all, at that 1984 convention a transvestite named "Sister Boom Boom" became a prominent emblem of liberalism in general and the Democratic Party in particular and played a part in Reagan's complete crushing of the Democrats in November of 1984.[7]

From that defeat in 1984 came Nancy Pelosi's determination that the Left never again be allowed to cause its own defeat. From the prominence of "Sister Boom Boom" was born the Democrats' desire to present a moderate face to the world; to hide their Far Left agenda behind bland statements and to rely upon scandal-mongering and fear tactics to carry the day for them. This is doubly important for a Party which has been unsure since 1985 what it stands for—other than a desire not to be Republican.

As a Californian and national Democratic Party activist, Pelosi remained the ally and protégé of long-time congressman Phillip

Burton, who represented San Francisco. When Burton died in 1983, the seat went to his widow. When Mrs. Burton came down with cancer, she was instrumental in getting Pelosi to run for the seat. Mrs. Burton's endorsement secured Pelosi the Democratic nomination.

Representing a constituency that is only 13 percent Republican, Nancy Pelosi had no worries about the outcome of the election. Still, Pelosi took nothing for granted and spent about one million dollars on the race—which she eventually won by a margin of 62 percent to 30 percent. Pelosi, upon winning, stated that her primary goals were to de-fund the liberation of Nicaragua from the communist Sandinistas and to increase AIDS research and education.

By 2002, it was public knowledge that Pelosi wanted to be the next Democratic leader in the House when Minority Leader Dick Gephardt announced he would retire in 2004. So, just how does a Democrat coming from an extraordinarily safe seat with no experience in working across the aisle convince her fellow Democrats to support her leadership bid? With money, of course. Bags of it.

Our country's campaign finance laws place limits on how much can be donated to a candidate or political action committee (PAC) in a given campaign season. Pelosi ignored the limits. She created two similar political action committees: PAC to the Future and Team Majority PAC. She then used the money made from the PACs to support other Democrats and thus buy their loyalty in the pending leadership battle. In total, Pelosi's two PACs donated to 132 House Democrats in the 2002 cycle, and all but three of them received equal to or above the $5,000 legal limit.[8]

Even Leo McCarthy, treasurer of both of Pelosi's PACs (and former Lt. Governor of California) admitted that the intention of Team Majority PAC was to circumvent limits on campaign contributions. "The main reason for the creation of the second PAC, frankly, was to give twice as much hard dollars," he said.[9] At least he was honest about why they broke the law. Eventually, the National Legal and Policy Center (NLPC) filed a complaint with the FEC on October 25, 2002.[10]

In March of 2004, the FEC ruled that Nancy Pelosi's political action committees "failed to identify themselves as affiliated with each other when they registered with the FEC, and both PACs made contributions to several candidates for the 2002 General Election, which, when aggregated, exceeded their shared $5,000 contribution limit. The PACs also received contributions from individuals that exceeded their shared $5,000 contribution limit and did not refund the excessive portion of contributions within 60 days."[11] Pelosi was fined $21,000 for funneling more than $100,000 in illegal donations to various Democratic candidates. Those candidates were ordered to return the dirty money.

Did Pelosi stop her involvement with the political action committee after receiving the fine? According to campaign finance reports, the political action committee was not dissolved. Instead, Team Majority PAC, which had $140,000 left, was used to help pay the $300,000 annual salary of her chief fundraiser and for renting a luxury box at a Simon and Garfunkel concert.[12]

It is the ultimate irony that Nancy Pelosi felt she had the moral high ground to wage a campaign against Tom DeLay when illegal contributions may be responsible for putting her in her party's leadership. Ken Boehm of the National Legal and Policy Center (NLPC) stated, "No Member of Congress has ever set up a second leadership political committee to evade contribution limits. Rep. Pelosi has been a strident supporter of campaign finance reform yet she's been caught violating the clearest and most basic law of all, the limits on contributions."[13] The sad epilogue to this story is that she is now Speaker of the House while Tom DeLay was forced into retirement.

If you've just been reelected to Congress and chosen by your party to be leader in the House, you might think that your elevated position places a requirement of increased discretion upon you. If, on the other hand, you live in an impregnable left-wing political fortress like San Francisco, then you can and will do whatever you please. For instance, Pelosi managed to get a $1 million grant to a San Francisco think tank headed up by her longtime advisor and treasurer, Leo McCarthy.[14] In a delicious bit of irony, the think tank is called the Center for Public Service and the Common Good. Perhaps the organization was named on the theory that financial rewards for political cronies are for "the common good."

Representing her San Francisco district, Pelosi became unused to opposition. In fact, she seems determined that any opposition shouldn't be debated, but destroyed. As she said on March 17, 2005, when asked what the Democrat's plan is regarding President Bush, "Why should we put a plan out? Our plan is to stop him. He must be stopped."[15] This might be the key to why Nancy Pelosi would be so bold as to complain about cronyism and other alleged forms of Republican corruption; when you believe your opponent is evil and "must be stopped," you stop at nothing—certainly, you don't stop at hypocrisy.

A PENCHANT FOR CRONYISM

Nancy Pelosi was one of former House majority leader Tom De-Lay's most outspoken critics. If there was a story in the press about alleged Republican corruption, you could bet your last dollar that Pelosi would publish a press release decrying not just that particular Republican, but all Republicans everywhere. As Tom DeLay proved an ever more effective Republican leader in the House (and started convincing more and more Democrats to vote for Republican-sponsored bills), Nancy Pelosi's criticisms waxed strong. Nancy Pelosi presented herself as the scourge of all corruption and cronyism in Congress. But, as is all too typical of public moralists, Pelosi's own actions do not match her rhetoric.

For Pelosi to lead any charge against cronyism is as laughable as it is hypocritical. Soon after becoming House minority leader, Pelosi handed out coveted committee assignments to Democrats who supported her leadership bid.[16] One was Rep. Max Sandlin of Texas, who was picked by Pelosi for a highly coveted seat on the House Ways and Means Committee. Sandlin had been romantically involved with Rep. Pelosi's daughter, Christine Pelosi. Naturally, Pelosi denied there was any connection between Christine's relationship with Sandlin and his plum committee assignment.[17] However, Sandlin did not even ask for the spot on the committee, but was given the assignment over Rep. Shelley Berkley of Nevada. Berkeley not only wanted the assignment, but was unhappy about being passed over and reportedly raised questions about the romantic *quid pro quo*.[18]

Pelosi's penchant for cronyism does not end there.

On February 7, 2005, it was reported that Pelosi was "reserving the remaining slot on the exclusive Rules Committee for Doris Matsui, the widow of her close friend, the late Rep. Bob Matsui (D-CA.),"[19] who died while in office.

The House Rules Committee is the legislative gatekeeper for the majority party. This committee decides which bills will come to the floor for a vote and when. This is about as "inside baseball" a committee assignment as you can get in Washington, D.C., and you'd think that both parties would put the best and most experienced people on it possible.

Not Nancy Pelosi.

While this is a position highly coveted by lawmakers "who seek the floor time given Rules Committee members,"[20] Pelosi oddly claimed to have had some difficulty filling the position. In our media-driven age in which the most dangerous place in America is between a politician and TV camera, it seems bizarre that there were no takers for positions on the Rules committee.

Bizarre and untrue, as it turns out.

Representative Sheila Jackson-Lee of Texas, a congresswoman of manifestly more seniority and experience than Doris Matsui, was reportedly interested in the position. The other three Democrats on the Rules committee had thirteen, eleven, and eight years of seniority. Lee had twelve years of service in the House. Doris Matsui, who could not claim any seniority, won the plum committee assignment.[21]

Whatever Pelosi's excuses for her cronyism, few would have the audacity to cast themselves as cronyism's number one enemy when actually being closer to its bedfellow. But this is standard operating procedure for Nancy Pelosi, who would let nothing— even a national tragedy—get in the way of her hypocritical crusade against corruption.

After Hurricane Katrina, Pelosi launched scorching criticism of the federal government's response. "The Katrina response," according to Pelosi, was "plagued by cronyism; cronyism that gives jobs to the friends of the Bush administration without qualifications for those jobs and cronyism that gives contracts to their corporate friends without bidding."

But criticism of the president wasn't enough for Pelosi, so she and Representative Henry Waxman introduced the Anti-Cronyism and Public Safety Act on September 27, 2005, which, in their own words, "would prohibit the President from appointing unqualified individuals to critical public safety positions in the government." The bill established minimum standards for public safety appointees by the president.

- Proven credentials relevant to the position;

- A superior record of achievement in one or more areas relevant to the position;

- Training and expertise in one or more areas relevant to the position.[22]

Pelosi's standards for her own cronies are far less severe, even when it comes to such important issues as our nation's intelligence community.

On January 26, 2005, Pelosi appointed Representative John Tierney of Massachusetts to serve on the House Permanent Select Committee on Intelligence (HPSCI). The HSPCI, as described by John Tierney's press release, "has principal responsibilities over our intelligence community and confronts the most challenging national security issues currently facing the United States."[23]

The HPSCI is another plum committee assignment. Its members receive full intelligence clearances, and many aspects of their work are classified. It is one of the most sensitive positions in the House. Tierney's qualifications on military and intelligence matters are virtually nonexistent. Even Tierney's fellow Democrats recognized that Tierney had a "light resume on military, intelligence and foreign-policy issues."[24] However, at the time of his appointment he had a more important qualification: His chief of staff was Christine Pelosi—the same daughter of Nancy Pelosi who was dating Rep. Sandlin when he was given his highly coveted committee assignment by her mother.

Pelosi's appointment of John Tierney to the HPSCI wasn't the only time she prioritized rewarding friends over our nation's security. The *Washington Post* reported on September 27, 2005, (ironically the same day Pelosi introduced her anti-cronyism bill) that Pelosi planned to replace Rep. Jane Harman of California, the ranking Democrat on the House Intelligence Committee, with Representative Alcee Hastings of Florida.[25] (Hastings is one of only six federal judges in American history to be impeached.)

But Pelosi wasn't done.

After the Democrats won control of the House in November 2006, Pelosi favored Hastings as the new *chairman* of the Intelligence Committee, never giving due consideration to Jane Harman, who had seniority. After questions were raised about Hastings' suitability for the position, Pelosi settled for Silvestre Reyes (D-TX).

Coveted committee assignments are not the only reward for being Pelosi's friend. In Congress—where trillions of dollars are spent each year—Pelosi has been quite effective at helping her political donors acquire millions of dollars.

In April 2005, the *Washington Times* reported that in 2004, Pelosi "helped secure $3 million...for a nonprofit transportation-research organization whose president gave money to her political action committee as the group was paying for a European trip for one of her policy advisers."[26]

According to the *Times*, the nine-day trip to Spain and Germany, taken by Pelosi's transportation advisor Lara Levison in April of 2004, cost $4,475 and was paid for by WestStart-CALSTART. WestStart-CALSTART announced only days earlier that Pelosi "had helped the nonprofit group secure $1 million from the Federal Transit Administration for a bus rapid-transit program. A month after the Levison trip, the group sent out a press release thanking her for a $2 million grant for a fuel-cell program."[27]

Campaign records show that the CEO of WestStart-CALSTART, John R. Boesel, had also given $1,000 to one of Pelosi's political action committees in 2003 and another $1,000 to the Democratic Congressional Campaign Committee (DCCC).

While similar actions by former House majority leader Tom DeLay sparked criticism from Nancy Pelosi, Pelosi said there was no link between the staffer's trips and grants.

It seems that no matter what Pelosi does, we're always expected to believe that her actions are honorable, even when she uses her leadership status to help members of her family.

That is what we're expected to believe about the Hunters Point Naval Shipyard's deal with the Navy to transfer ownership of the shipyard to the City of San Francisco. The agreement, which Pelosi worked on for over a decade, was finally signed on March 31, 2004, thanks to the help of Rep. Jack Murtha.[28] Also indebted to Nancy Pelosi and Jack Murtha for their efforts in finalizing the deal was Laurence Pelosi, Nancy's nephew, an executive at the time with the company that had rights to the land.

This is a rather stunning coincidence, and the media was curiously silent about it. In response to queries about this rather sweet deal, Pelosi's spokeswoman naturally said there was nothing improper about the arrangement.[29]

This incident must have made Pelosi feel indebted to Murtha. After the 2006 midterm elections, Murtha sought the position of House majority leader. Even though this position was long expected to go to Rep. Steny Hoyer, Pelosi attempted to use her new clout as the undisputed next Speaker of the House to support Murtha's bid. This decision dumbfounded many.

After making corruption a big issue during the campaign, Pelosi had the gall to support Murtha, whose involvement in the ABSCAM scandal (See Chapter Eleven) in addition to his role in the Hunters Point Naval Shipyard deal, should have made him the *last* person she supported. Although Murtha was ultimately defeated, we still learned much about Pelosi. Even after becoming Speaker of the House, she had no qualms about exercising cronyism.

TRAVEL AND DISCLOSURE

In 2005, Nancy's crusade against Tom DeLay almost backfired when she and her fellow Democrats made privately-funded trips an issue. In a statement released April 13, 2005, Pelosi said:

> Media stories are raising new questions about the conduct of Majority Leader Tom DeLay. In recent weeks, newspaper articles have detailed trips DeLay took to Russia and Scotland that he had reported were funded by nonprofit organizations, but which were directly or indirectly paid for by lobbyists or foreign agents. House rules prohibit members from taking trips funded by such entities. In both cases, lobbyist Jack Abramoff, who is under investigation by the U.S. Department of Justice and the Senate Indian Affairs Committee, was involved in these trips. Tom DeLay's extensive ties with special interest lobbyists are raising serious questions about his conduct.[30]

Back in 2001, Nancy Pelosi took a trip with other House members, including Stephanie Tubbs-Jones, to Puerto Rico. Jones, an Ohio Democrat, was on the House Ethics Committee at the time. With that in mind, one would think that everything about the trip would be on the level.

Not quite.

According to documents filed by Jones' office with the House clerk, the trip was paid for by a registered lobbyist firm, which violates House ethics rules.[31] A spokeswoman for Jones said that D.C. lobbyist firm Smith, Dawson & Andrews was "incorrectly" named as having paid for the trip. "The invitation came from Todo Puerto Rico con Vieques," said Jones spokeswoman Nicole Williams, "They hired Smith Dawson to handle logistics for the trip."

A legitimate excuse it may have been; however, the *Washington Times* noticed this was the same sort of discrepancy that made Tom DeLay a target:

> The irregularities mirror some of the ethics questions dogging House Majority Leader Tom DeLay, Texas Republican. Various investigations into casino lobbyist Jack Abramoff revealed that at least one of Mr. DeLay's trips was paid for by Mr. Abramoff rather than the private entity listed by Mr. DeLay. Mr. DeLay says he was unaware of Mr. Abramoff's connection.[32]

Only *after* the original *Washington Times* story did Jones provide records of the trip, a request that had been previously refused. She provided a sworn statement and canceled checks "as proof that a trip she took to Puerto Rico wasn't improperly paid for by [Smith, Dawson & Andrews], as her official paperwork initially stated"[33] and blamed the previous discrepancy on "human error." Nancy Pelosi had originally listed Todo Puerto Rico con Vieques (TPRV) as the sponsor, but Republicans noted "the discrepancy in travel disclosure forms raised questions about the funding of everyone's trip."[34]

House Republicans Patrick T. McHenry of North Carolina and Lynn Westmoreland of Georgia, in a letter to Pelosi, wrote, "We would hope that you would come forward with any and all documentation your office has proving that in fact the group, Todo Puerto Rico con Vieques, initiated and paid for your trip." Pelosi refused to provide any more documentation.[35] Though she called for full investigations into Republicans over paid trips, she was unwilling to be forthcoming when it came to her own involvement. For Nancy Pelosi, one party's "culture of corruption" is another party's "human error."

As Pelosi led her party in attacking Tom DeLay, many Democrats scrambled to get all their overdue travel paperwork filed.

On April 26, 2005, Ed Henry revealed on CNN's *Inside Politics* that Nancy Pelosi's office had been conducting their own internal review:

> HENRY: To give you an idea of how serious it is getting, CNN has learned that House Democratic leader Nancy Pelosi's office has been very quietly conducting a thorough internal review of all the Democratic leader's travel and her staff travel. Now, her office maintains the leader's travel has been on the up-and-up. It was all funded by private sources. They have canceled checks showing that lobbyists did not pay for it.
>
> But they have found problems with many of the trips conducted by Leader Pelosi's staffers. In fact, CNN has gotten an exclusive copy of this internal review. It shows that in the last several years, in fact, there were 42 trips by Pelosi staffers. They've found problems with 12 of them, where they were not reported promptly, and one of those trips, in fact, was to the tune of $9,000 from a Pelosi staffer who went to South Korea. Now, beyond the fact that it was not reported in a timely fashion, the significance is that it was funded by the very same nonprofit group that funded a controversial trip for Tom DeLay.
>
> So, the bottom line is, this is beginning fodder for Republicans already who are saying Democrats have been very critical of some of Tom DeLay's trips, but the more people start digging, it looks like Democrats may have some problems, too.[36]

They certainly do.

The trip to South Korea was paid for by U.S.-Korea National Exchange Council (KORUSEC). Eric Pfeiffer of National Review Online's "The Buzz" highlighted Pelosi's hypocrisy for attacking Tom DeLay's trip to South Korea, while her own staffer was a part of the same group:

Literally days before DeLay's trip, KORUSEC had changed its legal status and registered as a foreign agent. Under House rules, members of Congress and their staffs are not allowed to accept trips from such organizations. However, KORUSEC admits failing to report the changes to DeLay and other trip participants.

As last week's *Times* report[ed], the coverage on this topic failed to mention the number of Democrats who also participated in the trips. This did not stop House Minority Leader Nancy Pelosi, whose own staff member had traveled with KORUSEC, from attacking DeLay. When questioned directly, Pelosi acknowledged it was virtually impossible for trip participants to know of KORUSEC's changed status. It took nearly a week of reporting from NRO and other sources before major media outlets began reporting Pelosi's connection.[37]

But Pelosi saw things differently. *Roll Call* quoted her as saying: "It is not an issue of members of our Caucus having the same sort of a problem ... Make no mistake—there is a drastic difference between the timing of reporting things and ethical behavior."[38] Based on her behavior, the only difference is party affiliation. To her, an ethical violation is not an ethical violation when a Democrat does it—then, it's an issue of timing. Pelosi, however, has had a few more such "timing issues."

On July 1, 2005, Pelosi's office finally got around to filing reports for trips that took place in the 1990s. Those trips, worth $8,580, were paid for by "outside sponsors." According to the *Washington Post*, "[t]he most expensive trip was not reported on Pelosi's annual financial disclosure statement or on the travel disclosure form that is required within 30 days of a trip."[39]

The unreported trip was a week-long 1999 visit to Taiwan, paid for by the Chinese National Association of Industry and Commerce [CNAIC], for "meetings with government, military and business officials," according to a filing Pelosi signed June 30. The flights cost $3,400 each for Pelosi and her husband. The hotel cost was $940. The sponsor, which has picked up trips for leaders of both parties, paid $300 for meals.[40]

Perhaps Pelosi felt with her reports arriving with the flood of other travel documents being filed in a rush, that it wouldn't be noticed that her trip was paid for by CNAIC. CNAIC considers itself a Taiwanese nonprofit organization, making it a foreign agent.[41] According to House ethics rules, members cannot accept trips paid for by foreign agents.

TUNAGATE

With so many past ethical lapses, it is hardly shocking that Nancy Pelosi would be quickly corrupted by her new power as House Speaker. After shutting out Republicans from the legislative process during the first "one hundred hours" of the new Congress, House Democrats (and a number of Republicans) passed a minimum wage hike, the cornerstone of the Democrats' new legislative agenda. The passage of this signature Democratic bill was marred by the fact that a company in Nancy Pelosi's district benefited from an exemption in the bill.

While the bill passed by the House included such overseas American territories as the Northern Mariana Islands, it exempted American Samoa. Del Monte Corp., which is headquartered in San Francisco, is the parent company of StarKist Tuna, which employs 75 percent of American Samoa's workforce.[42] Because Democrats wanted to rush bills through the House with little debate during their "first one hundred hours," many Republicans were unaware of the provision. After learning about it, they recognized that there was something fishy about it. [43]

> "I am shocked," said Rep. Eric Cantor, Virginia Republican and his party's chief deputy whip, noting that Mrs. Pelosi campaigned heavily on promises of honest government. "Now we find out that she is exempting hometown companies from minimum wage. This is exactly the hypocrisy and double talk that we have come to expect from the Democrats."[44]

Naturally, Pelosi's spokeswoman *claimed* that Pelosi hadn't been lobbied by StarKist or Del Monte. But Republicans questioned this explanation.

Arizona Republican Rep. John Shadegg called the exemption unethical and declared that the Democrats were corrupted by power within the first five days of being in the majority. "Simply put: it is unethical to provide a special benefit to a company in any member of Congress' hometown. For Democrats to act in such a manner so early on in their tenure is hypocritical at best and criminal at worst."[45]

THE PARAGON OF CORRUPTION AND HYPOCRISY

During her battle to become Speaker of the House, Pelosi apparently believed harping on the Republicans' so-called "culture of corruption" would achieve better results than developing a positive agenda for change. Her actual agenda of gay marriage, abortion on demand, and surrender in the war on terror having been tossed down the Orwellian memory hole, the only thing she had to run on was this mendacious theme.

Worse yet, Nancy believed that taxpayers should be funding that campaign...and she succeeded in having them do so.

When Nancy Pelosi tried to use the term "culture of corruption," in a newsletter distributed to her constituents, she attempted to have the mailing covered under her franking privileges. House rules required her to first get approval from the Franking Commission. The commission initially turned down her request, arguing that the phrase "culture of corruption" was clearly a campaign slogan. Pelosi offered a number of alternatives and settled on "climate of corruption," and "environment of corruption," which the Franking Commission ultimately approved—paving the way for taxpayers to fund Pelosi's smear campaign.[46]

Nancy Pelosi is, as noted, a liberal's liberal. She is "for the little guy"—the champion of the people, who works her fingers to the bone to ensure that the poor and helpless are protected against the rich and predatory. In fact, she was quoted in the communist newspaper *People's Weekly World*:

> We have two oilmen in the White House. The logical follow-up from that is $3-a-gallon gasoline... Where have you been, Mr. President? You take a trip outside of Washington, see the fact that the public is outraged, come home and make a speech. Let's see that matched in your budget ... in your policy. Let's see you separating yourself from your patron, big oil.[47]

There was something odd about this stern denunciation of Big Oil: in the 2006 election, which elevated Pelosi to the Speaker's chair. Big Oil's Occidental Petroleum was Pelosi's largest single donor,[48] giving $17,000 for her efforts to, presumably, fight against the nefarious influence of Big Oil.

No one can speak of Nancy Pelosi's integrity with a straight face. In almost every aspect of her life we see her saying one thing and doing another. But there is one area in which she's never hypocritical—she's always looking out for her own interests. Pelosi fights against Big Oil (and gets paid handsomely by Big Oil to do it). She fights against Big Tobacco—going so far as to claim that American tobacco companies are deliberately hoodwinking poor third-world residents into buying their hellish product.[49] But what of Big Alcohol? Alcohol kills far more people than tobacco does in any given year—does Nancy Pelosi fight against that? No. She can't—it would cost her too much money.

As Peter Schweizer revealed in his book *Do As I Say (Not As I Do)*, Nancy Pelosi is more than willing to accept the Cesar Chavez Award from the United Farmworkers Union while simultaneously using non-union workers on her family's Napa Valley vineyards.[50]

But let's give her some credit…she wasn't *totally* hypocritical. After all, she is a supporter of illegal immigration, and the Pelosis have been more than willing to give illegal immigrants work on their vineyards. As if hiring illegal immigrants for their cheap labor isn't bad enough, according to author Joseph Klein, there is an "obvious conflict of interest every time that she votes on an immigration security bill because she and her husband personally benefit from the influx of cheap labor…"[51] Klein asks:

> Is Pelosi looking out for her own financial interests, calculating how a law imposing strict penalties on employers of illegal aliens might affect her vineyard business instead of focusing on how porous borders will affect the security of everyday American citizens?[52]

And as per usual for a senior Democrat, the fact of Pelosi's abuse of illegal immigrants does not prevent her from hypocritically attacking Republicans for being soft on border security. On July 27, 2006, Pelosi issued a scathing attack on President Bush that made her sound like a charter member of the border security watchdog group The Minutemen.[53] This attack came from a woman who has profited heavily from immigrant labor and who has voted repeatedly to encourage illegal immigrants to come to America and obtain benefits from American taxpayers.

In the final analysis, what a politician gives the people is their word. None of us get our food from a politician, or our house, or our medical care—we merely get the politician's word that we shall be able to obtain food, a home, and medical care. While during the election Pelosi and the Democrats were mum about their plans for post-victory action; now that Pelosi is Speaker, she tells us she'll do all sorts of wonderful things for the American people. But what assurance do we have they'll be forthcoming?

From Pelosi's past, we see that she has rewarded her family, her friends, and her political cronies. She has also been friendly to various well-heeled special interests. What she hasn't been is loyal to her claimed Catholic faith (in her support for abortion), nor have we seen actions which match her high-sounding and self-righteous rhetoric about befriending the "little guy."

Essentially from the start of Pelosi's leadership of the House Democrats, she has been on the frontlines of an unremitting war against the Republican Party. While it might suit Pelosi's self-image to think of herself as a crusader for truth and justice, the reality is that Pelosi is the bought-and-paid-for defender of entrenched special interests. There is no position she has proven prepared to defend if such a defense conflicts with a selfish, self-serving, narrow, bigoted left-wing worldview.

HARRY REID

*"I believe this is the most corrupt Congress
in the history of this country."*

—Harry Reid[1]

NEVADA political historian Michael Green joked that while former Senator Richard Bryan of Nevada "woke up in the morning wondering if he'd shaken everybody's hand, Harry Reid wakes up in the morning wondering if he's gotten back at all his enemies."[2]

Harry Reid is as tough as the Nevada desert he grew up in. Born in Searchlight, Nevada in 1939, Reid, son of a hard-rock miner and a mother who took in laundry to make ends meet, had to scramble to get ahead. Harry Reid is one of those who could truthfully tell stories of walking miles to school.

In spite of the obstacles of poverty and obscurity, Reid earned his law degree from George Washington University in 1964. Reid worked as an attorney in Nevada for a few years until he found his true calling, politics. He was elected to the Nevada State Assembly in 1968. From then on, hard work wasn't as necessary for Harry Reid to get ahead, though he retains his iron-edged determination.

REID'S RISE TO POWER

After less than two years in politics, Reid was elected lieutenant governor of Nevada. Reid rode on the 1970 ticket of Democratic gubernatorial candidate Mike O'Callaghan, his former high school history teacher, friend, mentor, and leg-up in Nevada politics.

Reid experienced a temporary setback in his climb to the top when he lost a bid for the U.S. Senate in 1974 by less than six hundred votes, in spite of O'Callaghan easily winning reelection and a large infusion of last-minute campaign cash from unions.[3] Instead of returning to the private sector where genuine results are required, Reid got himself appointed to the Nevada State Gaming Commission, which regulates gambling in Nevada. This kept Reid busy until, due to its ever-increasing population, Nevada went from a one-representative state to a two-representative state in time for the 1982 elections.

Fortunately for Reid, the state was split in two by making Democrat-heavy Clark County the Nevada 1st congressional district and making the entire rest of the State (very Republican-heavy) into the Nevada 2nd congressional district. Reid won election easily to that seat in the 1st congressional district and held it until being elected to the Senate in 1986.

Reid, a convert to the Church of Jesus Christ of Latter Day Saints, has the Mormon reputation for social conservatism, which serves him well as he campaigns for office in the red state of Nevada. While he almost always votes with liberals in Washington, Reid is forced to talk conservative when he's back at home.[4]

So careful is Reid about keeping the two halves of his political life apart that when he ran for reelection in 2004, none of his campaign material even mentioned his being a member of the Democratic Party, let alone his senior leadership in it. Instead, he was an "Independent for Nevada." The narrative for his campaign sounded much more like one of a Republican candidate. It stated that Reid is opposed to gay marriage, is pro-life and anti-gun control.

His prominence, combined with his spending $7,595,323 against his opponent's $645,586 and running on a conservative platform, allowed Reid to crush his Republican opponent in 2004 by 61 percent to 35 percent.

After winning that tremendous victory masquerading as a conservative, Reid found himself climbing the ranks of the Democratic Party. When Republican John Thune defeated Senate minority leader Tom Daschle (D-SD), Reid was chosen to take Daschle's place. In spite of Reid's allegedly conservative credentials, upon becoming minority leader, he assigned himself the task of obstructing Republicans at every turn.

While hypocrisy has long been a major ingredient of politics, it is astounding that a supposedly socially conservative Reid would take the leadership of a Party committed to defeating Republicans on social conservative issues.

GIVE 'EM HYPOCRISY, HARRY!

Along with the purely political fights against the Republicans, Reid engaged in the ultimately successful Democratic campaign of smearing the GOP as the party of corruption and cronyism. Reid hasn't been shy in this regard at all—repeatedly decrying the Republican's "culture of corruption" and darkly hinting about the horrific things Republicans do behind the scenes.

Appearing on *Fox News Sunday* on December 18, 2005, he told host Chris Wallace that this Congress is the "most corrupt Congress in the history of the country."[5]

Reid's bold statement was not meant to include himself or his party; otherwise he wouldn't have said that he felt that "we should get rid of the corrupt leadership we have."[6] Does anyone believe he was advocating that he or other leaders in his party should be "gotten rid of"? Does anyone believe he was demanding equal accountability on both sides of the aisle?

Don't count on it.

Reid couldn't have been clearer that when it comes to corruption, he's not suggesting ousting the ethically challenged members of his own caucus. No, he was just cluing us in to his party's strategy for 2006. "[B]y the time the elections roll around in 2006, the American people will understand better—they already understand, but they will understand better the difference between Democrats and the corrupt Congress we now have,"[7] Reid announced.

As it turned out, the American people may have been convinced that there was corruption among the Republicans, but they certainly didn't understand the truth about the difference between Republicans and Democrats. If they had, then far more Democrats would have fallen to the wrath of the voters than did Republicans.

CONNECTIONS TO JACK ABRAMOFF

When Reid was confronted by Chris Wallace about $68,000 in campaign contributions from convicted lobbyist Jack Abramoff's tribal clients, a highly defensive Reid told Wallace "don't lump me in with Jack Abramoff. This is a Republican scandal. Don't try to give any of it to me."[8]

Abramoff, who pleaded guilty to various crimes involving his lobbying activities, was mostly tied with Republicans when he was discussed in the media. It remains a fact, however, that while Democrats were not the beneficiary of *personal* donations from Jack Abramoff, Democrats did receive very large donations at the direction of Jack Abramoff from his tribal clients, and Harry Reid is among the top beneficiaries of these Abramoff-orchestrated donations.[9] In addition to these large tribal donations, Reid also "received $6,500 from Abramoff's associates at the Greenberg Traurig law and lobbying firm from 1999 through 2004."[10]

Greenberg Traurig is America's eighth largest law firm (and in Reid's top twenty donors for the period 2001 through 2006[11]) and is rather emblematic of how lobbying and political donations work in the United States. Given that Abramoff has earned a reputation as a Republican lobbyist, it might surprise people to learn that Abramoff associates at Greenberg Traurig donated to the 2004 campaigns of such Democrats as Senators John Kerry (D-MA), Chuck Schumer (D-NY), Blanche Lincoln (D-AR), former Senator Tom Daschle (D-SD), senatorial candidate Betty Castor (D-FL), and, of course, Harry Reid.[12]

Senator Reid has repeatedly said with a straight face that he's untainted by Abramoff money and that involvement with Abramoff was a Republican scandal, but the reality is that most lobbying firms donate to both sides of the aisle because that helps them gain access and influence, which is all that lobbyists really want. Jack Abramoff was no exception.

Naturally, Reid ignored his own connections to Abramoff while he saw even the most tenuous Republican connections to Abramoff as proof of corruption. A spokesman for Reid contends that Reid does not know Abramoff, and that Reid's connections to the tribes were independent of the convicted lobbyist. But Reid's connections to Abramoff don't stop with tribal donations. One of Abramoff's lobbyists, Edward P. Ayoob, assistant finance director for Reid's 1998 reelection effort, held a fundraiser for Reid at the Greenberg Traurig offices.[13] Ayoob represented eight of Abramoff's tribal clients while working at Greenberg Traurig, and

Harry Reid acted on behalf of or moved legislation benefiting six of them.[14] And just in 2001 alone, documents show Abramoff lobbyists meeting in Reid's office as many as twenty-one times.[15]

Like other Democrats who have received donations from Abramoff clients, Reid's defense is to claim he "does not recall" meeting Abramoff, nor apparently remember that he had Abramoff's minions in his office *twenty-one times*. Reid also makes the claim that he received donations from tribes and other Abramoff clients only prior to Abramoff's lobbying for them. "I've said that I received money from Indians in the past and will continue to do so," Reid said in early February 2006. Leaving aside the fact that Abramoff lobbyists were having meetings in Reid's office on a regular basis, we have already seen how it doesn't take a close, personal relationship with a lobbyist to be corrupted by him.

When dealing with lobbying, we're hardly ever confronted with neat, easily understood events. It's not like a politician writes in his diary, "met lobbyist for lunch, took $50,000 bribe, called mother on birthday." The true nature of events is always a matter of detective work. For this, it is always best to look at the sequence of events.

Reid says he didn't have anything to do with Abramoff—implying that even if there were donations from an Abramoff client, it was routine and had nothing to do with how Reid acted. If this were the case, then Reid never had anything to worry about—even the most hyper-partisan Republican wouldn't fault Reid for such an event. But Reid's problem is that at least four American Indian tribes started giving Reid campaign donations only after they hired Jack Abramoff.[16]

Between 1991 and 2000, neither the Agua Caliente Band of Cahuilla Indians of California, the Coushatta Tribe of Louisiana, the Mississippi Band of Choctaw Indians, nor the Saginaw Chippewa Indian Tribe of Michigan gave any contributions to Reid. After these tribes became Abramoff's clients, it was a different story. They not only started donating to Reid, they donated big. Reid received a total of nearly $68,000 in campaign contributions from them over a five-year period. Picking up $68,000 is not something a person does casually. This isn't paying for a twenty-dollar dinner. It takes a lot of discussion and logistical work. With this fact, we can see why Abramoff's people were in and out of Reid's office as it if had a revolving door for lobbyists.

Reid and his supporters spun an entertaining fairy tale. We were supposed to believe that a group of non-Nevada Indian tribes altruistically started giving large amounts of cash to Senator Reid and that it is mere coincidence that they all started doing it at roughly the same time.

Such revelations make it harder and harder for Reid to spin this as some sort of exclusively Republican scandal. Additionally, given the way Reid has attempted to paint any connection with Abramoff as scandalous, the legality of these donations is neither here nor there. If Democrats applied to themselves the same standard they applied to Republicans, Harry Reid would have been ousted from his leadership position by his own party. But Reid certainly has never felt that his leadership position was in jeopardy. The fact that certain tribes didn't donate to Reid until *after* they became Abramoff's clients, is, to Democrats, entirely irrelevant. In the world of the Democrats, corruption is something that only Republicans do.

If your plan is to run against your opponent's alleged corruption, then it always helps if you can find things which at least appear to be a *quid pro quo*. Something, that is, which appears to be a service rendered for a donation or other benefit received. It would certainly help Reid if there were something like that involving Republicans. It might, after all, take some attention away from Reid and the donations he's received from Abramoff's tribal clients. Unfortunately for Reid, his fellow Democrats made things rather difficult, as well as exceptionally embarrassing.

So intent were Democrats on their story of a Republican "culture of corruption," that there appears to have been a lack of message coordination. Given the universal nature of the Democratic message about GOP corruption, one would think that everyone at least asked the question, "So, do any of our people have a problem on this issue?" Such a question was either never asked or never answered truthfully. When DNC Chairman Howard Dean said that any Democrat who wrote letters on behalf of Jack Abramoff's tribal clients would "be in trouble,"[17] whether he realized it or not, he was talking about the top Democrat in the Senate.

Of the nearly $68,000 in campaign contributions, one $5,000 donation came from the Coushatta Tribe and went to Reid's non-profit Searchlight Leadership Fund. This donation was made one day after Reid wrote a letter to Secretary of Interior Gale Norton on behalf of the tribe.[18] Harry Reid would sign four letters on behalf of Abramoff's tribal clients.

The Coushatta letter sent on March 2, 2002, urged Norton to dissolve an agreement between the Jena tribe of Choctaw Indians and the state of Louisiana that would have allowed the tribe to open a casino in the state.[19]

While it might seem odd that a Nevada senator would be opposed to opening a casino, it is also in the interest of very wealthy and influential Nevada gaming bosses to have as little competition as possible. Reid had a choice between helping poor tribal citizens get ahead and helping rich people who donate to his campaigns. There was really no contest at all.

Not only has Reid received donations from some Indian tribes only *after* they became Abramoff clients, but on at least one occasion he has been rewarded with a $5,000 donation for apparently acting on their behalf.

Even the most partisan Democrat would be hard-pressed to assert there was no *quid pro quo*, especially given that his fellow Nevada senator, Republican John Ensign, signed that very same letter to Gale Norton but didn't take a dime from the Coushatta tribe. Additionally, unlike Harry Reid, John Ensign returned all of his Abramoff-connected donations.

In another letter, this one jointly signed by Reid and California Democratic Senator Dianne Feinstein, Norton was urged to reject a proposal of Cuyapaipe tribe to start their own casino which would have competed with the casino of one of Abramoff's clients.[20] Perhaps the Cuyapaipe should have done more than make a few measly donations to Republicans.

Prior to President Bush's 2006 State of the Union Address, Senator Reid signed a letter sent to President Bush containing a specific request for answers on whether Jack Abramoff had improper influence within Bush's administration. The letter declared there is "no reason to wait for indictments or convictions"[21] before the White House informs the American people of Abramoff's contacts within the administration, and "official acts that may have been undertaken at his request."[22]

Keep in mind that Abramoff's crimes revolve around his lobbying activities, not his personal donations. While it was Abramoff's dealings with his clients that lead to his undoing, Democrats claimed Abramoff was entirely criminal, all the time. Abramoff's personal donations were a red herring, but that didn't stop Democrats like Harry Reid from using harsh rhetoric targeting Republicans who had received Abramoff donations. In the Democratic story line, Abramoff was a criminal and anyone who dealt with Abramoff was guilty of a crime. As the mainstream media was relentless in insinuating rank criminality in each and every Abramoff dealing, the Democratic narrative stuck in the public mind. Meanwhile Reid himself hung on to every dime of Abramoff-connected money.[23]

Politics, of course, can put all sorts of pressure on a person, and Harry Reid's rhetoric about Abramoff and the Republicans has resulted in calls for him to return all Abramoff donations. There is no indication that the donations have been returned, but, as the *Arizona Republic* reported on December 23, 2005, Reid would "take a look over the holidays" at whether to return the Abramoff-connected donations.[24] Reid did not return any of the money. Senator Ensign—whose Abramoff contributions totaled one-third less than Reid's—returned the money in October 2005, two months after Abramoff was indicted.[25] At this point, even if Reid returned the money, it would be for political reasons, not to rid himself of tainted contributions.

It took a week after the Democrats' takeover of Congress (when Abramoff reported to federal prison) for ABC News to report Abramoff had divulged his dealings with members of Congress and their staff to investigators. Abramoff's dealings included "six to eight seriously corrupt Democratic senators."[26] Harry Reid "was one of the senators Abramoff had allegedly implicated in his cooperation with federal prosecutors."

> A source close to the investigation says Abramoff told prosecutors that more than $30,000 in campaign contributions to Reid from Abramoff's clients "were no accident and were in fact requested by Reid."

Abramoff has reportedly claimed the Nevada senator agreed to help him on matters related to Indian gambling.[27]

Conveniently for Reid and the other "seriously corrupt Democratic senators," they never had to answer for their connections to Abramoff during the 2006 campaign season.

REID'S CORRUPT FRIENDS

For a Nevada politician to run into ethics trouble is no great stretch. The confluence of money, gambling, prostitution, and politics makes for too rich a stew for political corruption to not rear its ugly head. Indeed, Harry Reid had his personal brush with ethics trouble when he faced attempts to bribe him while he was on Nevada's Gaming Commission. He did the right thing and reported the effort to the FBI, which then engineered a sting with Reid's cooperation to arrest the miscreant. All's well that end's well, but there's still plenty of dirt in Las Vegas, and Reid hasn't been able to keep all of it off.

An example of this is the case of Dario Herrera. Herrera was a Reid *protégé* and once considered not just a rising star in Nevada politics, but *the* rising star. Herrera's rise was meteoric. He rose from being a mere financial aid administrator at a community college in 1996 to fundraising for Hillary Clinton in 2000. This is going to number one like a bullet.[28] The world was seemingly at Herrera's feet, and so close was Reid to him that his son, Rory, donated $1,000 to Herrera's political campaign.[29]

To some observers, Herrera was the man to save the Nevada Democratic Party from increasing Republican strength in the state. Herrera is articulate, with movie star good looks and a winning personality. And just like Harry Reid, Herrera was elected to the Nevada State Assembly at a very young age partially on the strength of his political connections. Herrera then gained a prestigious seat on the very powerful Clark County (NV) Commission. But Herrera's political stardom fell as fast as it rose when he got caught in a massive bribery scandal that rocked not only Clark County, Nevada, and the Las Vegas city government, but extended all the way to San Diego, California.

During Herrera's run for Nevada's new 3rd congressional district in 2002 the roof fell in on him.[30] In a federal criminal probe with the voluptuous popular name of "Operation G-Sting," indictments were handed down against various politicians and striptease club owners.[31] The involvement of these "bump and grind" joints, as they are known in Las Vegas, added that extra element of spice to what was otherwise just a run-of-the-mill bribery scandal. Dario Herrera's primary problem was that he had accepted illegal campaign contributions from two strip club owners.

Herrera obtained a large number of $1,000 donations from Las Vegas developer Jim Rhodes and his employees.[32] This looks bad in the news regardless of whether Rhodes had reimbursed employees for donating to Herrera. Herrera apparently forgot the old standby of politics—before you do anything imagine how it will look on the front page of the newspaper.

As a construction firm, Rhodes has massive business before Nevada's governing bodies, and given that 90 percent of Nevada is owned by the federal government, Rhodes also has a lot of business before the federal government. It is therefore natural that Harry Reid, a very important player in the federal government, should become a major recipient of Rhodes' donations. And no more surprising is the fact that Rhodes would also become a major backer of Reid's protégé. There is a phrase in politics: "pay to play."

Paying to play can get a person in trouble. As Rhodes discovered, even the might of Harry Reid isn't proof against federal law enforcement.

Rhodes' donations to Herrera and Reid did raise some eyebrows. On March 10, 2006, the story broke that Rhodes admitted to illegally funneling some $37,000 in illegal donations to both the Reid and Herrera campaign efforts.[33] The initial complaint about the strangely large number of donations from Rhodes, his family, and employees resulted in a complaint by the National Republican Campaign Committee in September of 2002 and, just like lightning (for the FEC), the investigation was concluded two and a half years later. Rhodes agreed to pay a fine of $148,000.

What does it all mean? That is hard to say, especially when a senior Democrat is involved. Rhodes paid a fine, Herrera is in jail. As for Reid, he's now Senate majority leader, with many new and improved opportunities to do more of what he did when he was minority leader.

CONFLICTS OF INTEREST

On October 11, 2006, it was revealed that Reid had made a $700,000 profit on a land sale in 2004.[34] The real estate market in Nevada was booming at the time, so a big profit wasn't remarkable. What *is* remarkable are the details of this particular deal.

The deal originated in 1998, when Reid purchased land with his long-time friend, Nevada political wheeler-dealer Jay Brown. Nothing improper so far—but Reid then sold the land, for the original purchase price, to a limited liability company headed up by Brown, "and took a financial stake in that company."[35] Brown then had the residential land re-zoned for commercial purposes. Normally, changing land from residential to commercial use is difficult, and when the land in question is part of a master development plan designed to preserve a high quality of life, it is downright impossible. But Brown managed it.

With the land safely re-zoned, sold, and turned in to a shopping center and Reid's bank account nicely fattened, all was well for Reid—provided no one found out. The discovery, coming, as it did during a campaign season when Reid was accusing every Republican of being corrupt, was inconvenient, to say the least.

But that wasn't the end of Reid's odd land deals. Bullhead City, Arizona, is just across the Colorado River from Nevada and not very far from Reid's hometown of Searchlight. In Bullhead, depending on location (as always in real estate), vacant land can sell for $10,000 to $250,000 per acre. Given this, it is surprising that Reid managed to gain control of 160 acres of vacant land for $10,000.

In 2002, Reid paid $10,000 to Clair Haycock, a long-term Reid friend and the owner of a lubricant distribution business. Curiously, six months later Reid introduced legislation to protect lubricant distributors from order cancellations by their suppliers.[36] Of course, Reid's staff, and his friend, assert that there was no *quid pro quo*.

But as they say in television commercials, there's more:

The *Associated Press* revealed on November 13, 2006, that Senator Reid had been instrumental in getting earmarked federal funding for a bridge spanning the Colorado River between Laughlin, Nevada, and Bullhead City, Arizona.[37] There is nothing too remarkable about that in the normal course of events—but for Reid, there are some problems.

First, Reid leads a political party which ostensibly just won majority power because of their campaign against corruption—one of the corrupt things Reid and his Democrats ran against was the practice of earmarking federal funds for pet projects. Second, if you are going to fight against corruption, then you probably don't want the bridge your earmarked funds will build to benefit you personally.

Another problem for Reid is that he now owns 160 acres of undeveloped land just a couple of miles away from the bridge he got the taxpayers of the United States to fund. Once the bridge is built, Reid's property value should increase remarkably, especially as the Laughlin/Bullhead City area is already experiencing a real estate boom. Confronted with this revelation, Reid's office issued a statement asserting that Reid's support for the bridge had nothing to do with the rather large property he owns near it.

Of course it didn't.

When you see the vehemence with which Harry Reid decries the influence of lobbyists on an allegedly corrupt Republican Party in Congress, you would think that Reid has a strong distaste for lobbyists. Nothing could be further from the truth. As it turns out, one man's wicked lobbyist can be another's saintly advocate. Or, in some cases, another's family member.

In one of the many ironies of American politics, Harry Reid's four sons and his son-in-law are or were lobbyists and, according to the *Los Angeles Times*, "they represent nearly every major industry in [Nevada]."[38] As is stated in his official Senate biography, Reid makes it a priority to "open the door of opportunity for our children."[39] No one realized just how proprietary Reid was when he said "our children."

On June 11, 2002, Harry Reid introduced the Clark County Conservation of Public Land and Natural Resources Act of 2002,[40] which, under the guise of environmentalism, promised extraordinary benefits for real estate developers, corporations, and local institutions "that were paying hundreds of thousands of dollars in lobbying fees to his sons' and son-in-law's firms,"[41] as well as providing thousands of dollars in donations to Reid's Searchlight Leadership Fund.[42] Though Reid claims he's never used his position of power to deliver business to members of his family, his record tells a different story.

Reid's son-in-law, Steven Barringer, has lobbied for several companies and interests that benefited from legislation sponsored by Reid. The Howard Hughes Corporation received nearly one thousand acres of "prime Las Vegas real estate through a federal land swap," from legislation sponsored by Reid. He also sponsored legislation that freed four thousand acres of federal land for development for Henderson, Nevada, and eighteen thousand for Las Vegas and North Las Vegas.[43]

Reid's son Rory is on the Clark County (NV) Commission, while other of Reid's children have managed to obtain excellent employment opportunities. One of Reid's children actually obtained a position as a lobbyist. Most people would see at least a slight conflict of interest when you're being lobbied for government money by your own children.

Being the son of a powerful man can be a big advantage. Leif Reid, second oldest son of the senator, landed a job at the powerful law firm of Lionel, Sawyer and Collins where, among other tasks, he led the way in fighting a claim to ownership of most of Reid's hometown of Searchlight.[44] A man named Ed Seggerson produced a series of documents showing him to be the owner of most of Searchlight, and he was demanding $13.45 million. While the story caused a bit of a splash in late 2000, nothing more was ever heard about it. In a contest between a seventy-nine-year-old local eccentric and Harry Reid's son, who do you think came out on top?

Obviously, any person who is the child of a powerful and prominent person will find doors easily opened—but Harry Reid should have advised his sons that becoming lobbyists would give such a strong appearance of conflict of interest that they should seek other employment as long as Reid is an elected official.

That would be the honorable thing to do. A small matter of simple decency.

It could be said that Reid is just being a good father. But the people of Nevada voted for Harry Reid, not his sons. Harry Reid is supposed to keep his personal and political lives strictly separate. But Harry Reid is not honorable enough to refuse to use his position of power to help his friends, his family, or himself.

We're all supposed to believe that Reid is a decent man. After all, he lavished $3,300 in Christmas bonuses on his staff.[45] The only problem is that the money came from his campaign coffers, some-thing that is clearly illegal. A politician can pay his staff whatever bonus he wishes, but it has to be his own money. It seems that Reid has been playing with other people's money for so long that he's got only a hazy notion of what is his and what isn't.

For Reid, looking after the interests of the Democratic Party is the most important thing of all. And why not? After all, the Democratic Party is the agency of Reid's rise from nobody to one of the highest positions of power in the most powerful nation on earth. The party has also been the means by which Reid amassed a large fortune and secured lavish futures for his children. Not only does one not bite the hand that feeds, one takes care that the hand is safe from all harm.

The only trouble with this dog-like loyalty on the part of Reid is that it puts the people of the United States dead last in all things.

Reid would most certainly contend that he is unblemished since he's not directly involved with the criminal doings despite his strong connections to those who are clearly guilty. Reid would be correct to make such a contention. After all, who among us, especially politicians, isn't connected to tainted friends and/or relatives? Perfection is not to be found in this world. But mean-while, Reid is the man who is saying that even the slightest ap-pearance of impropriety by Republicans such as Tom DeLay makes all Republicans part of a "culture of corruption," which, of course, only a Democratic congressional majority can clean up.

The least we should expect from Senator Reid is that he will live up to the standards he sets for others. But that is not the way for a liberal political leader to behave. For liberals, it isn't so much what you do, but what you say you are doing it for and whether or not you are doing it to a Republican. Say you are doing it for the little guy, and even if it is kicking a Republican when he's down, then it's okay.

Unfortunately, the small matters of such things as simple de-cency and whose money belongs to whom don't seem to cut much ice with Harry Reid. Much more important for Reid is personal power, nice deals for friends and family, and the ability to bedevil Republicans at every turn.

CHAPTER THREE

CHUCK SCHUMER

"We are prepared to bring an end to the Republicans' corruption, cronyism and incompetence."

—Chuck Schumer[1]

SENATOR CHARLES SCHUMER (D-NY), as head of the Democratic Senatorial Campaign Committee (DSCC) during the 2006 election cycle, joined Nancy Pelosi and Harry Reid in leading the charge against the alleged Republican "culture of corruption" in government.

Born in Brooklyn, New York in 1950, Charles Schumer got his college degree and went on to law school, but never worked a single day as an attorney. He got himself elected to the New York state assembly at the age of twenty-three and has never looked back.[2]

Schumer early on proved himself a man wedded to political expediency. Taking note of the theory that some people didn't register to vote because voter rolls were used to select jurors, Schumer proposed ending the practice of using voter rolls as a jury pool.[3] More important than overall civic responsibility was Schumer's desire to mine the ranks of the apathetic for votes.

It isn't just a matter of Schumer looking out for number one— after all, politicians have to be at least in some measure egotistical. It takes a fairly large ego to put one's self forward as the *one person* who can do a particular elective job. Even given that, however, there are wise politicians who understand that being at the center of attention at all times isn't necessary. Schumer isn't one of these—the limelight seems to call him, and he's like a moth to a flame whenever some new, hot, and fashionable issue comes up.

A politician who likes the limelight and gets involved in every fashionable issue inevitably becomes a person who is deathly afraid of losing it all. The gnawing fear that one day it will all end drives such a person to do just about anything to keep on top. As money is a vital ingredient in politics, such politicians start to look upon the acquisition of campaign money as the be-all and end-all of existence. This is why Schumer has had an amazing ability to run afoul of campaign finance laws and regulations.

In 1980, Schumer made a successful run for Congress, winning the seat of Elizabeth Holtzman, who made an unsuccessful attempt at winning a Senate seat that year.[4] Things were looking good for his political career, but the honeymoon was short-lived.

CAMPAIGN SCANDALS

In December 1980, the *Village Voice* published a story entitled "Chuck Schumer's Staff Scandal," alleging that Schumer had misused public funds to pay staffers from the Assembly Committee on Oversight, Analysis and Investigation, which he chaired, to work on his campaign.[5] Ironically, the committee is responsible for tracking down abuse of state funds. This prompted U.S. Attorney General Edward R. Korman to launch an investigation.[6]

As many as six people allegedly worked on Schumer's congressional campaign while on the payroll of the Assembly Committee. The grand jury also investigated charges of mail fraud in connection with checks and vouchers mailed to state employees while they were actually working on Schumer's campaign. The only charges in federal jurisdiction were the mail fraud charges, and the Justice Department eventually decided the case was inappropriate for federal action and chose not to prosecute Schumer.[7] The case was referred to the Federal Election Commission by Schumer's House predecessor, Elizabeth Holtzman, who had become the Brooklyn district attorney.[8]

The investigation took five years, with the Federal Election Commission agreeing that there was no reason to believe Schumer had violated federal laws. However, the commission vote was split 3-3 on whether Schumer's campaign committee did commit violations.[9] No further action against Schumer was taken on this matter. Schumer survived, but he would find himself in trouble with the Federal Election Commission once again, when he ran for the U.S. Senate.

In 1998, Schumer ran successfully against Republican incumbent Senator Alfonse M. D'Amato, who had beaten Holtzman in 1980. This victory sparked new hope for the Democrats following Rudy Guiliani's 1993 victory over New York City mayor David Dinkins and George Pataki's 1994 victory over Governor Mario Cuomo.[10] Schumer was the only Democratic senate candidate who was on record opposing the impeachment of President Bill Clinton. Schumer was rewarded when President Clinton and First Lady Hillary campaigned for him, helping him collect over $2 million.

Schumer's successful fundraising may have been crucial to his victory. D'Amato's past opponents had run out of money, and he was counting on Schumer to do the same.[11]

But once again, Schumer found victory tarnished by scandal.

On April 20, 2001, a Federal Election Commission report claimed Schumer's 1998 Senate campaign took $1 million in "excessive contributions" and ordered Schumer to refund over $850,000 in contributions.

The FEC also identified nearly three hundred expenses amounting to $6.4 million that were improperly disclosed. According to the FEC, Schumer's violations were the largest since 1991.[12]

The FEC audit "identified 836 apparent excessive contributions from 789 individuals, 36 partnerships and 11 political committees totaling $999,879. ... Of this amount, excessive contributions totaling $97,050 were reattributed, re-designated or refunded, but not in a timely manner." Schumer's spokesman downplayed the FEC's findings and blamed them on bookkeeping errors.[13]

Schumer's campaign attorney Lynn Ulrecht wrote off the ruling as trivial, since Schumer's campaign had yet to be ordered to refund the money. "Nothing in here is an order from the FEC to do anything ... It's a recommendation from the audit committee that the $854,404 should be refunded. If the commission takes it up, we would discuss with the commission the legal situation."[14] Ulrecht advised Schumer not to return the donations. Schumer anticipated the FEC would levy a fine significantly smaller than the amount of money they were urging him to return.[15] He was right.

In 2003, Schumer agreed to a settlement under which he would pay a $130,000 fine and refund contributors. Schumer's office did not indicate how much would be returned to donors.[16] Schumer's spokesman said the fines resulted from technical errors. "The most common example of the errors...was when a donor contributed $2,000 and failed to declare that $1,000 went to the primary election and $1,000 went to the general. Another example was when a husband and wife contributed using one check and failed to specify that they were jointly contributing." The Campaign Finance Reform Act, which took effect on November 5, 2002, eliminated the requirement that contributors specify whether their donations were going to the primary or general election. It is no wonder Schumer was a supporter of campaign finance reform.

In campaign finance reform Schumer found his "perfect" issue. Campaign finance reform (CFR) has never been a popular issue with the public, but it is very popular with those who inform, or misinform, the public—the mainstream media (MSM). Depending on one's point of view, the MSM support for CFR is either a cynical ploy to gain control of the terms of public debate, or a selfless desire to reform our body politic. Be that as it may, the issue was ready-made to ensure that Schumer didn't have to answer too many MSM questions about his campaign finance irregularities.

Schumer's advocacy of CFR is in keeping with the primary rule of the MSM in our modern world: For the MSM, it isn't at all what a person does but what a person *advocates* that determines the sort of media coverage they'll receive. There is no sin too great to be forgiven a public figure provided that said public figure will bow before MSM pieties. For the MSM, corruption isn't doing wrong, but being on what the MSM deems the wrong side of a particular issue.

TIES TO ABRAMOFF

Schumer, with three other Senate Democrats, signed a letter to Bush administration officials and cabinet members asking them to reveal any contact they had with embattled lobbyist Jack Abramoff. "As more and more Republican officials in and out of Congress are implicated in this scandal, it has become increasingly important that the record be cleared and that any contact you or others in the administration have had with Mr. Abramoff be fully explained to the American people,"[17] the letter stated. The fact that most Republicans so "implicated" were connected to Abramoff via innuendo and guilt by association made no difference. For Schumer, it was a chance to get out in front of a story popular with the media and help himself in the bargain. Honor and decency didn't rate too highly at the moment.

Schumer, while demanding Republicans reveal their ties to Abramoff, was not equal to the task of revealing his own Abramoff ties. Schumer was one of twenty-eight Democrats who signed the letter who had received Abramoff-affiliated funds. Schumer was able to claim at least $29,000 from Abramoff's tribal clients and affiliated lobbying firms.[18]

In 1999 Chuck Schumer considered laws intended to hamstring independent counsels in their investigations of Executive Branch officials; on February 16, 2006, however, Schumer was one of thirty-one Democrats who signed a letter asking Attorney General Alberto Gonzales to remove himself from the investigation of the Jack Abramoff scandal because "the appearance of conflict looms large as the investigation has potentially widened to include Administration officials."[19]

Schumer said Gonzales could "avoid any appearance of impropriety by recusing himself. If there was ever a case that was both sensitive and rife with potential conflict—it is this one."[20] For Schumer, as for too many Democrats, what is right is whatever helps a Democrat and harms a Republican. Independent counsels are evil when addressed to Democratic presidents, necessary when addressed to Republican presidents. As long as Schumer is useful to the Democratic Party, it and the media will do whatever it takes to protect him.

SLEAZY FUNDRAISING

If there's any way that Schumer has been tremendously useful to the Democratic Party, it is not by legislation or by developing new ideas to lead the Democrats out into bold, new political territory. Schumer's value to the Party is more mundane than that.

Charles Schumer, as it turns out, is one of the all-time champion political fundraisers. While Senator Schumer does not face the voters of New York again until 2010, he had $9,984,296 in campaign cash as of September 30, 2005, in the bank—and he has raised a total of $22,179,440 since 2001. In January of 2006 alone, Schumer raised $187,281. So intense is Schumer's love for cold, hard campaign cash that he didn't even let a national tragedy get in the way of a good fund-raising pitch.

While Democrats were blaming President Bush for the government's response to Hurricane Katrina, Senator Schumer attached a plea for donations to the Democratic Senatorial Campaign Committee to a petition demanding the removal of then-FEMA head Michael Brown.[21] Brian Nick of the National Republican Senatorial Committee called it "a disgrace to exploit Hurricane Katrina to raise political funds."[22] However, only after the story reached the press was the plea for money removed.

Schumer spokesman Phil Singer admitted asking for donations in that manner was a mistake and said they would donate any contributions raised as a result of the petition to the Red Cross.[23]

While Schumer and his DSCC enjoyed a fundraising advantage over the Republican counterpart during the 2006 election cycle, Schumer knew that it would take more than money to secure a victory. Normally, it would also take a carefully crafted message of change and an excellent political strategy to play up Democratic strengths while minimizing those of the Republicans. The Democrats in 2006 must have found that their message didn't poll well in focus groups, because talking about a plan or an agenda seems to have been a forbidden act.

Speaking at a breakfast sponsored by the *Christian Science Monitor* in April 2006, Schumer said that a unified Democratic policy agenda is "necessary but not sufficient" to triumph in the 2006 midterm elections. What else would it take? According to *The Hill*, which reported on the speech:

> Schumer said that several themes would carry Democrats at the polls, including their "culture of corruption" message, labeling Bush and Republicans as incompetent after the government's response to Hurricane Katrina and the prolonged war in Iraq. Democrats, he said, will focus on issues that "help the average middle-class person."[24]

This was the same recipe for victory we had heard before from Pelosi and Reid. It was not about the Democrats and why they *should* be in power. It was about the Republicans and why they *shouldn't* be in power. And the so-called Republican "culture of corruption" was the not-so-secret ingredient that made the Democrats taste their upcoming victory more than anything else.

As head of the DSCC, Senator Schumer certainly wanted to see his party make gains in the November 2006 elections, especially in the Senate. Taking over the Senate would be an exceptionally bright feather in Schumer's cap, and he saw early on that 2006 was the year to make it happen. "Senate Democrats are looking at a political landscape wide open for victory," he wrote in *The Hill* on November 3, 2005.

Schumer also believed that the Democrats' crusade against corruption would be their ticket to victory. "[The 2006] election cycle is about bringing back an honest, responsible and competent government that is focused on average Americans."[25]

As a lawmaker whose every step up the ladder of success in politics has been dogged by accusations of campaign finance irregularities, Schumer's charge can only be described as ironic.

SCANDAL AT THE DSCC

Chuck Schumer considers himself a champion of privacy rights. Following a security breach at consumer data company Choice-Point, Inc. and the theft of data from Lexis-Nexis in early 2005, hundreds of thousands of Americans faced the risk of identity theft. Schumer declared "[t]he new rise in identity theft cases nationwide is approaching epidemic proportions and Congress must act quickly to bolster privacy protections."[26]

He was right, and that epidemic eventually spread to the Democratic Senatorial Campaign Committee.

In the fall of 2005, federal prosecutors began investigating two of Schumer's staffers at the DSCC: research director Katie Barge and Lauren Weiner.[27] The two staffers illegally obtained the credit report of Maryland Lieutenant Governor Michael Steele, an African-American and rising star nationally in the Republican Party. Apparently this was part of their opposition research on the Republican, who was preparing for his Senate bid.

Steele's social security number was found on a public court document and was subsequently used to obtain his credit report illegally.[28] Schumer's tough talk on ensuring privacy for consumers apparently does not apply to ensuring privacy for political adversaries. But then again, the issue of privacy is just another in the popular issues of the day; anything Schumer ever said on the subject would have been fodder for the cameras and entirely unrelated to Schumer's real desire—power and prestige for himself.

Dan Ronayne of the National Republican Senatorial Committee (NRSC) said, "When you speak with such zeal about the importance of respecting privacy and an organization you head has violated someone's very personal credit information, that speaks for itself."[29] Yet DSCC spokesman Phil Singer quickly dismissed criticisms made by the NRSC and conservative commentators. "The idea that one can equate a single incident involving two twenty-somethings that the DSCC reported immediately to the authorities with the pattern of ethical problems experienced by the House majority leader is laughable."[30]

This was no laughing matter. Singer would like to write off the incident as the indiscretion of young and inexperienced staffers, but before working for the DSCC, Barge headed the research staff at David Brock's liberal media watchdog organization Media Matters and is "highly regarded in the tight-knit community of Democratic researchers,"[31] according to friends and associates. She's also worked as a researcher for a number of campaigns.

Even though the DSCC said this was an isolated incident, Lt. Governor Steele has not received an apology directly from the DSCC. Steele told FOX News in early December 2005, "I'm still waiting for an apology, I've not received a letter or a phone call or any contact from the Chairman, Chuck Schumer, or any member of the DSCC." Steele explained that even though the DSCC told them that they've apologized, they had not apologized to him, and since it was his social security number and credit report they stole, their apology was misdirected.[32]

But no apology to Steele has ever been made, and such an apology from Schumer or any member of the DSCC is unlikely, considering how they handled the situation. While Barge and Weiner were suspended after admitting they illegally obtained

Steele's credit report, they were suspended *with pay*.[33] Instead of being fired, they were given a paid vacation.

Newsday reported that the DSCC even picked up the hefty tab for their legal defense.[34] Ironically, Barge's attorney was William Lawler III, who represented former New Jersey governor Jim McGreevy during his sex scandal in 2004.[35]

Black conservative leaders suspected racism played a role in Steele being targeted by the DSCC. "They are trying to prevent any [black] Republican from forging ahead," said nationally syndicated talk-radio host Rev. Jesse Lee Peterson, who is also the founder of the Brotherhood Organization of a New Destiny. "If a black Republican sets the tone, it is going to have a huge impact on young blacks. It is going to show them that Republicans are not trying to hold you back, they are not trying to stand in your way."[36]

Niger Innis, a spokesman for the civil rights group the Congress of Racial Equality argued he didn't believe it was a coincidence that Democrats targeted "the highest-ranking, statewide black Republican elected official," and said that the reception Steele is getting from black voters in Maryland scares not only Maryland Democrats, but Democrats on the national level as well.[37]

On September 26, 2005, a letter was sent to Senator Schumer from Republican senators Olympia Snow, John Ensign, Rick Santorum, Trent Lott, and Lincoln Chafee expressing how troubled they were to learn about what Schumer's staffers had done:

> While the DSCC press secretary and counsel have publicly denied that the DSCC accessed the personal credit reports of any other Republican Senators or candidates, the security of our families' finances is too important to rely on the assurances of the professional political staff and consultants whose primary focus is defeating us next November.
>
> Therefore, we are seeking your personal assurance, as a colleague, that employees or agents of the DSCC did not access our personal credit history or the personal credit history of any of our family members.[38]

The DSCC responded that they had not accessed any of their personal credit histories.

The *New York Times*, after ignoring the story for weeks, finally mentioned the scandal, but derided Republican criticisms as mere exploitations. According to the *Times*, "National Republicans, who face an uphill battle in their efforts to capture the open United States Senate seat in heavily Democratic Maryland [in 2006], are trying to exploit potential legal problems that Democrats are now suddenly facing in that race."[39] This is a means of turning the story around on the Republicans. The story, as far as the *New York Times* is concerned, wasn't about Steele's illegally obtained credit information, but appalling attempts by Republicans to smear Democrats. In the topsy-turvy world of the Democrats and their MSM partners, it is simply bad manners to bring up Democratic immorality.

On March 24, 2006, Lauren Weiner pleaded guilty "to a misdemeanor charge of fraud in connection with computers,"[40] avoiding any jail time, but was required to do 150 hours of community service within a year. Barge was never charged with a crime. Conveniently left out of the *Associated Press* story and the plea agreement was any reference to Chuck Schumer, for whom Weiner and Barge were working.[41] Thanks to the media, Schumer would once again come out of a scandal unscathed.

Did Schumer have anything to do with this incident? Perhaps not. However, despite his championing of privacy rights, Schumer did not immediately fire Barge and Weiner after the incident; instead, they got paid leave and legal services on the DSCC's dollar.

Steele would again futilely demand an apology from Schumer and other Democratic leaders after he discovered a Democratic operative secretly videotaping a conversation between him and two mothers of soldiers killed in Iraq. The videotaping took place during a homecoming ceremony for the Army National Guard 243rd Engineers on September 30, 2006... a *non-political* event:

> While speaking with two mothers whose sons had died in Iraq, I noticed the ever present Democrat operative filming our conversation. A conversation with parents who have lost a loved one in combat is private in nature and has no place in partisan politics, and certainly not in the smear campaign you have waged against me even before I entered the race for United States Senate. The filming of this conversation demonstrates a callous disregard for families who have lost a loved one and is an indefensible invasion of privacy.[42]

Schumer's silence on the matter was deafening.

It is a strange dance Republicans have to participate in. Republicans have to adhere to an impossibly high standard at all times, and any failure on the part of any Republican taints the whole party. Meanwhile, Democrats don't have to adhere to any standards, and any scandal involving Democrats is just a sad event and probably the fault of Republicans. It allows a senator like Chuck Schumer to anoint himself a champion of privacy rights, even when he refuses to accept responsibility for gross privacy violations committed by his own staffers against his political opponents.

After being out of power for over a decade, Democrats like Schumer were willing to do anything for political gain. For them, desperate situations required desperate measures. Even illegal ones. For someone with Schumer's history and unique talents in the fields of obfuscation, innuendo, character assassination, and media manipulation, this was a perfect job. And he did it very well, as the results of the 2006 midterm elections show.

CHAPTER FOUR

RAHM EMANUEL

"We're going to talk about cronyism, corruption and abuse of power and how it ties to everything that's gone wrong."

—Rahm Emanuel[1]

PRIVATE SECURITY firms reputedly hire a large number of ex-cons because "it takes one to know one." Who better to make a house safe from burglars than a former burglar who knows the tricks of the trade? It seems the Democrats used the same logic when they selected Representative Rahm Emanuel to head the Democratic Congressional Campaign Committee in 2005. Emanuel's recruitment of conservative Democrat candidates helped Democrats take control over the House of Representatives in 2006 and earned Emanuel a reputation as the architect of the Democrats' takeover of the House.

Rahm Emanuel was born into the crucible of Chicago, Illinois, in 1959. He joined his first political campaign—for Democrat David Robinson of Chicago—while still in college. During this race, Emanuel showed signs of being a first-rate fundraiser. Sometimes, when a donor would provide, say, $250 for the campaign, Emanuel would call him up later and say, "That's not enough."[2]

Chicago is well-known as a place of deep political corruption. It is the place where juries make strange decisions and dead people show up in droves on Election Day. It is also one of the last big cities in America to be run by an old-fashioned political machine.

This political machine, fashioned in days gone by Richard Daley, Sr., has so locked up control of Chicago for the Democratic Party and its beneficiaries that the chances of a Republican winning anything in Chicago are virtually zero. In the 5th congressional district, the Republican candidate only managed 24 percent of the vote in 2004.

Chicago is a rather rough and tumble city. It certainly isn't for the faint-hearted. Ever since the days when Al Capone terrorized the citizens of Chicago with massacres and gang wars, Chicago has been known as a place where only the tough can get ahead. Significantly, Emanuel was once known as being "Al Capone-esque" in the way he does business. After one particularly rough campaign season, Emanuel sent a letter to a colleague saying, "It's been awful working with you." Attached to the letter was a rotting fish.[3]

Emanuel—unlike a lot of politicians—has some private sector experience. He worked as a professional ballet dancer before joining the backroom political operations of Illinois politics. While working as a professional ballet dancer might not seem the best training for the knee-to-groin politics of Chicago, it actually requires the perfect balance and grace needed by Emanuel. After all, while Emanuel had long experience slandering his fellow Democrats, Republicans were more of an unknown quantity for Emanuel. For Emanuel to crawl out of the muck of Chicago politics and accuse Republicans of being sleazy took a lot of courage, but he proved he was up to the task.

Emanuel's first break into national politics was in 1985, when he was still at the tender age of twenty-six. He was tapped by then House majority whip Tony Coelho[4] to set up and run part of the national field campaign for the Democratic Congressional Campaign Committee.[5] In this capacity, Emanuel helped the Democrats gain two seats in the increasingly conservative Midwest.

Emanuel's early political activities also included a position as senior advisor to, and chief fundraiser for, Chicago mayor Richard Daley, Jr., during his victorious campaign in 1989. Emanuel helped Daley raise $7.5 million for that campaign—an astounding sum for a city mayoral election even today.

It was after that successful campaign that Emanuel turned his talents towards smear tactics. Deciding that negative campaigning is the best way to go all the time and everywhere, Emanuel founded a company called Research Group that helped politicians strategize for their campaigns—and if strategy didn't work, Research Group would also rake over a man's past to see if there was any dirt that could be used against him.[6]

After dancing and Illinois political activity, Emanuel came to the attention of Governor Bill Clinton of Arkansas and was hired in 1991 to be part of Clinton's fundraising efforts for the 1992 primary season. Whatever else can be said of Bill Clinton, he certainly picked the right man for the job. When you are a deeply flawed candidate, it is a saving grace to have a cutthroat political operative who can both raise bags of money and work out smear tactics against opponents.

Emanuel was instrumental in getting Clinton to fundraise massively and this might have made the difference, as Clinton's main Democratic opposition in 1992, Paul Tsongas of Massachusetts, eventually had to drop out due to lack of funds. At any rate, Emanuel's work on the campaign was rewarded with the post of senior advisor in the Clinton White House.

In 1998 Emanuel left the White House to take a job with the investment banking firm of Dresdner Kleinwort Wasserstein—yet another one of those corporate bodies who donate massively to both political parties, though Dresdner seems to give a bit more to Democrats than to Republicans.[7] It should also be noted that while Emanuel has a long and interesting *résumé*, "investment banker" doesn't show up anywhere on it.

Emanuel left Dresdner in 2002 to run for Congress in Illinois' 5th congressional district, which includes northern Chicago and part of Cook County. He won the seat handily in a heavily Democratic district once held by convicted House Democrat Dan Rostenkowski[8] and later by Rod Blagojevich, who went on to become a highly investigated governor of Illinois.

In 2005, Emanuel was named chairman of the Democratic Congressional Campaign Committee (DCCC). Now sometimes called "Rahmbo" due to his penchant for aggressive politics, Emanuel has stated that in his position, "winning is everything." What happened to that old fashioned value of it all being about how you played the game?

Emanuel joined Pelosi in making corruption and ethics the centerpiece of their efforts to regain the majority in the House.

If politicians are to make cleaning up corruption the center-piece of their campaign to win Congressional seats, it stands to reason that they would have to exemplify moral and ethical integrity. Being squeaky clean is always difficult for politicians from the Chicago area, and perhaps too much to ask. Some bare minimum of probity, however, should be demanded. It is unfortunate that Emanuel is seemingly no different from the common run of Chicago pols.

The supreme irony of Emanuel's participation in the ethics war to regain power in Congress in 2006 is that Emanuel wouldn't be in the position he is in today had it not been for a corrupt political machine operating on his behalf.

HIRED TRUCK SCANDAL

Federal court documents released May 2, 2005, revealed that Chicago City Hall officials ordered Donald Tomczak, the city water department boss, to "to marshal his political army of city workers" for a number of politicians, including Congressman Rahm Emanuel.[9] Tomczak had been running the city water department since Daley was first elected mayor in 1989, with the help of Emanuel. Tomczak pleaded guilty on July 29, 2005, and admitted that he "took bribes, solicited political contributions and helped rig the city's hiring and promotion process."[10] Not exactly the sterling character you want backing up your anti-corruption bid. But it gets even worse than that.

On December 20, Robert Mangiamele pleaded guilty to charges of mail fraud and paying bribes to get work in the city's Hired Truck Program. Between 1998 and 2003, he paid bribes to Tomczak's bagman, city supervisor Roger McMahon, who has also pleaded guilty to his role in the scandal. The bribes got him an average of $175,000 a year in business from the city water department. According to his plea agreement, he was also hit up for campaign contributions, which he always gave.[11]

Gerald Wesolowski, the director of finance and administration for the water department between late 1998 and at least January 2004, took over performing functions and tasks related to the Hired Truck Program following Roger McMahon's retirement. Wesolowski reported to First Deputy Commissioner Tomczak.[12] At Tomczak's direction, Wesolowski "performed and authorized official Department actions to benefit the financial interests of certain favored trucking companies that participated in the Hired Truck Program."[13] These companies in return "provided cash, campaign contributions and other things of value" for the benefit of Wesolowski, Tomczak, and political campaigns associated with Tomczak.

Wesolowski's signed plea agreement said that in exchange for campaign work for Rahm Emanuel, Tomczak rewarded employees of the water department with promotions, raises, and overtime.[14] The field activity included handing out literature and door-to-door activities and typically occurred on weekends during election cycles.

However, when Tomczak learned of campaigns selected by city officials, Wesolowski, Tomczak, and between five and ten department employees met on city premises, during normal business hours. "Following the meetings, [Wesolowski] was aware that Tomczak's political coordinators, who were Department employees, contacted individual department employees to obtain 'volunteers' for the field activities."[15] Wesolowski himself, on behalf of Tomczak, "participated in certain field activities with department employees on behalf of the campaigns affiliated with Jeff Tomczak," including the campaign of Rahm Emanuel.[16]

It is an unfortunate fact of life that this is the normal run of events in Chicago. Chicago, of course, has been essentially under exclusively Democratic Party rule for decades, and the long-term affect of this one-party rule has been rampant corruption. There is nothing wrong with wanting to fight a political battle to root out corruption and cronyism in politics, but there is something very wrong in the tainted product of a corrupt political machine leading the charge against corruption. If we are to run against a "culture of corruption," then it should be against *all* corruption.

EMANUEL'S PAID TRIPS

About two weeks before the 2004 elections, Rep. Emanuel took a trip to Paris sponsored by the Jean Jaurès Foundation, a group named for the famed French socialist leader assassinated at the start of the First World War.[17] The organization is dedicated to advancing a socialistic view of government around the world.

According to the *Chicago Tribune*, "The [Jean Jaurès Foundation] paid $4,823 for transportation fees and lodging for Emanuel and his wife, Amy Rule. They listed no expenses for meals but hired a translator for $1,190." It might seem curious that right before a vital American election a member of the United States House of Representatives should travel to a French socialist organization, but given that the Jaurès Foundation clearly backed the Democrats in America's 2004 election and has been disparaging of America's effort in the war on terror, it perhaps isn't as strange as it initially seems.[18]

In August of 2004 Emanuel received $2,194 to fly to Los Angeles as a guest on Bill Maher's television show, *Real Time with Bill Maher*.[19] At prevailing rates, $2,194 could buy the average American at least six flights between Los Angeles and Chicago.

DIRTY MONEY

As chairman of the Democratic Congressional Campaign Committee (DCCC), Rahm Emanuel was a loud critic of Republicans who didn't return contributions they received from Tom DeLay's political action committee, ARMPAC. The DCCC began an online campaign demanding Republicans return "DeLay's dirty money" after he was *indicted*.[20] The online petition declared, "[t]he least House Republicans can do is run their 2006 campaigns without continuing to capitalize on the culture of corruption DeLay has cultivated."

Like Nancy Pelosi, Harry Reid, Chuck Schumer, and many others, Rahm Emanuel knows all about capitalizing on corruption.

It became abundantly clear that Democrats were attempting to use their crusade against corruption to gain seats in Congress in 2006, using not only a smear campaign, but a shame campaign to wring money from Republican candidates in front of the election. They didn't just want to get rid of Tom DeLay, they wanted to get rid of the money he'd raised for his fellow Republicans.

But what did the DCCC chairman do when Chicago attorney and former national Democrat Party finance director Joseph A. Cari, Jr., who donated $5,000 to Emanuel's campaigns, was indicted on federal charges on extortion? Considering Emanuel's rhetoric about Republicans returning dirty money, one might assume that Emanuel would have returned the tainted contributions without hesitation. He did not.

It is quite the nasty scandal, after all. An Illinois businessman used Cari in schemes to defraud the state's Teacher's Retirement System.[21] The meat of the scandal is that Cari and others received bogus "finders fees" for directing Retirement System investments to companies with ties to Cari and others.

After Cari's indictment on August 3, 2005, Rahm Emanuel said he would *not* return Cari's contributions to his campaign—he would only return the money if Cari pleaded guilty! Cari pleaded guilty on September 14, 2005, and Emanuel claimed he then donated the $5,000 to Hurricane Katrina relief efforts.[22] However, later stories revealed that Emanuel kept the $5,000, asserting that since it was donated prior to the indictments, it was clean money.[23]

Yet Emanuel insisted Republicans return contributions they received from Tom DeLay within hours of DeLay's indictment on September 28, 2005—*before* being found guilty of anything! More than that, Cari has also donated to Emanuel's fellow Democrats John Kerry, Debbie Stabenow, Barbara Boxer, Tom Daschle, Hillary Clinton, Howard Dean, Wesley Clark, and Chris Dodd.[24] Where was Emanuel's call for those donations to be returned?

Cari's contributions didn't become "dirty money" until after he pleaded guilty; Tom DeLay's contributions became "dirty money" immediately after he was indicted. Apparently, Rahm Emanuel felt a different, looser standard applied when it came to contributions that filled his campaign's coffers. The DCCC still claims to have tough standards when it comes to donations.[25] Just not as tough as the standards they apply to Republicans.

One of the many Republicans targeted by the DCCC's campaign to force Republicans to return contributions from DeLay's PAC was John Boozman, who received $15,000 in campaign donations. The chairman of the Arkansas Democratic Party, Jason Willett, also criticized Boozman, despite the fact he was simply applying Emanuel's standard to himself. "Congressman DeLay was indicted, but he hasn't been [convicted] of anything. If he were convicted then I would return it," he said.[26] And, really, when you think about it, Boozman is holding himself to a higher standard—Emanuel didn't even return the genuinely *tainted* money (even if he did allegedly donate it to Katrina relief), while Boozman said he would do so if DeLay were ever convicted.

Nothing happens in a political vacuum, and it should be noted that Cari also donated $7,500 to the Democratic Senatorial Campaign Committee.[27]

Emanuel's love for dirty money doesn't end there.

On October 12, 2005, former Congressman Frank Ballance was sentenced to four years in prison, after pleading guilty to using a charity (that he helped create) to funnel over $2 million in taxpayer dollars to his law firm and to members of his family.[28] Yet Emanuel's DCCC chose not to return $29,500 balance contributed to their campaign, and, even when Ballance began his prison sentence, they had no intentions of returning the contributions.[29]

Given Emanuel's background of shady deals and political backstabbing, it was no surprise that he held nothing back in his goal of Democratic victory in 2006. Highly partisan Democrats might be pleased with a man who fights it out tooth and nail, but wiser heads must wonder if such a victory would be worth it.

As head of the DCCC, Emanuel refused to return thousands of dollars in dirty money from convicted felons. So while money from the political action committee of a Republican congressman who has not been found guilty of any crime must be returned, Democrats saw nothing wrong with keeping contributions from individuals who actually did plead guilty for their crimes.

Everyone likes it when their side wins. For those who are most interested in politics, the cut and thrust of a good political battle is like nectar to a bee—it is the thing that makes political life worth living. But standards must be maintained. Winning really isn't everything—and it is worth nothing if it is won by skullduggery.

It was a sad day when Rahm Emanuel was picked as the coming man in Democratic politics. Can we trust such a man to tell the truth? To work in the best interests of America as a whole? Mendacity and vulgarity have carried Emanuel to the heights of political power, and there is no indication that power and success will change him into something better than a political hatchet man.

CHAPTER FIVE

DISHONORABLE MENTION

"…if the facts are such that there is an ethical violation or there is a criminal violation, then I think it is appropriate for the ethics committee and for perhaps the Congress to act, period, whether it is a Democrat or a Republican."

—Rep. Steny Hoyer[1]

CORRUPTION is clearly rampant within the Democratic party. While we so far have focused on the Democratic leadership, there are numerous scandals, ethical breaches and other problems deserving of mention in this book. This chapter features the stories of those Democrats who have earned "dishonorable mentions" for their lack of scruples.

NEW JERSEY POLITICIANS

While most politicians view fundraising as a distasteful necessity, others take to it like a duck to water. A prime example of such a duck is one of the all-time champions at raising money, former Senator Robert Torricelli (D-NJ).

After a long career as a backroom political operative, Torricelli leveraged his political contacts into a seat in the U.S. House of Representatives, and then, in 1996, into the U.S. Senate. From his Senate position, Torricelli became the champion of fundraising for the Democratic Party. So effective at this was Torricelli that he was made head of the Democratic Senatorial Campaign Committee in 2000, where he led the Democrats to their best Senate showing since 1986. Things seemed bright for Torricelli, except that from the moment he was elected to the Senate, Torricelli was dogged by stories of campaign finance scandals.

The 1996 political season, headed by the match-up between President Clinton and Senator Bob Dole, was a bit of a snoozer. President Clinton was never really in danger of being defeated, and a political shift at the Congressional level was improbable.

But the Democrat campaigns provided their own intrigue. It was in 1996 when the Democrats, from the Democratic National Committee (DNC) all the way to the Clinton/Gore reelection effort, ran into problems such as there being "no controlling legal authority"[2] over whether a vice president should accept envelopes stuffed with cash from Buddhist monks who have taken a vow of poverty.

As a premier fundraiser for the Democratic Party, Senator Torricelli couldn't avoid the various campaign finance controversies surrounding the Democrats' 1996 effort. For example, Torricelli slipped a little-noticed amendment into a massive spending bill that killed the construction of two dams. The dams in question were opposed by a major Torricelli donor.[3] This caused a stir, but was only one part of a number of campaign finance irregularities that ended up haunting Torricelli's Senate term.

After a long period of investigations, accusations and stout denials by Torricelli that he had done anything wrong, it was revealed that he had taken bribes in the form of cash and gifts.[4] In spite of his having been "severely admonished"[5] months earlier by the Senate Ethics Committee, it took the actual revelation of bribe-taking to put Torricelli's reelection effort in jeopardy. In keeping with the public perception about corruption, only a "smoking gun" proved sufficient to get a Democrat in political hot water. More importantly for Democrats, as Toricelli's popularity cratered, it became vital to save the seat.[6]

It was decided that Torricelli would bow out of the race and fellow Democrat and former senator Frank Lautenberg would replace him. Objections by Torricelli's Republican opponent that it was unfair to change the ballot a month before the vote were calmly brushed aside by the New Jersey Supreme Court, which oddly held that voters deserve to have two major party candidates on the ballot—if one of them drops out, regardless of when, another *must* be allowed to replace him. This was a bitter pill for

Torricelli to swallow, as Lautenberg had been his arch-political nemesis for years. But Party loyalty is Party loyalty, and, for Democrats, some times you have to do unsavory things when you are protecting your Party. And New Jersey Democrats have a lot of experience in this.

When New Jersey Governor Jim McGreevey resigned as a result of his adultery (see Chapter Twelve) it became vital for Democrats to save the governorship. The fact that McGreevey was not only immoral, but had also endangered the people of New Jersey by placing his lover in charge of New Jersey's homeland security didn't matter. All that mattered was working things to best ensure that Democrat would follow Democrat in the governor's office. To do this McGreevey delayed resignation his resignation until after the fall elections, avoiding a special election and making it possible for New Jersey State Senate President Richard Codey, a fellow Democrat, to serve the remainder of the term, which ended January 2006... That was plenty of time for the anger and resentment over McGreevey's actions to subside, reducing the risk that fallout from the scandal could result in a Republican upset in the next gubernatorial election.

All the Democrats needed was a man who had a clean reputation. The ability to pour massive amounts of his own money into the campaign was also a plus.

Jon Corzine (D-NJ) had some money to spend on politics. When he was elected to the U.S. Senate in 2000, he spent $60 million of his own money on the campaign. That worked out to $39.70 per favorable vote in his narrow win over an under-funded GOP candidate. That also worked out to spending $10 million per year for a six-year Senate term—if Corzine had served a full term. Before completing his first term, he ran for governor of New Jersey.

A bit of housecleaning was required before taking on the task of running for governor. Just days before he announced his candidacy for governor of New Jersey in 2004, Corzine forgave a $470,000 mortgage loan made in 2002 to his then-girlfriend Carla Katz, who also happened to be the president of the Communications Workers of America (CWA), New Jersey's largest union. When not defending union members against allegations of criminal negligence,[7] Ms. Katz spent time with Senator Corzine at places like the Sundance Film Festival.[8] Additionally, as head of a major union with a lot of business before the government of New Jersey, Ms. Katz kept a keen eye on New Jersey political developments. As Corzine's bid for governor went forward, he received the CWA's enthusiastic endorsement.[9] When you've spent $60 million on a Senate seat, you have to figure that getting a major endorsement for a mere $470,000 is a bargain.

When word of the forgiveness of the loan came out, Corzine claimed that there was nothing odd about it. It was all just an innocent matter of Katz facing some financial issues; and both Katz and Corzine firmly asserted that there was no *quid pro quo*, and that there wouldn't be any conflict of interest should Corzine win the governorship.[10] All of this was given out straight-faced by all concerned, and the media reported it without so much as a raised eyebrow.

But not everyone agreed that there was no conflict. Sherry Sylvester, the campaign and communications director of Corzine's Republican opponent Doug Forrester, told *National Review Online* that there was no question there was a conflict. "A half-million-dollar loan to the state's largest labor union is a conflict. Imagine the outrage if Tom DeLay gave half a million dollars to the U.S. Chamber of Commerce."[11]

In fact, Corzine failed to disclose the loan-turned-gift on his Senate expense reports, which was the basis for an ethics complaint that was filed against him on September 1, 2005, by New Jersey public interest lawyer Carl Mayer, who says the forgiving of the loan amounts to a bribe. "The only difference between this case and the Torricelli case is that Robert Torricelli was caught taking bribes and not disclosing them and Jon Corzine has been caught giving bribes and not disclosing them," he said.[12] Ironically, it was Torricelli who introduced Corzine and Katz. New Jersey politics is the proof that truth is stranger than fiction.

Corzine's ethical problems did not begin with forgiving a large loan—and they did not end there, either.

Corzine broke Senate rules when he "voted to give himself and a select set of fellow millionaire investors a lucrative tax break from their controversial takeover of [the Shinsei Bank Ltd. of Japan]"[13] in March of 2004. The complaint, filed by Carl Mayer and Bruce Afran, alleges that Corzine concealed his financial interests in the bank to members of the Senate Foreign Relations Committee. A carefully written clause in the treaty gave a tax break to a small group who invested in failing banks that were subsidized by the Japanese government. This tax break saved Corzine and his partners millions of dollars.

Corzine naturally pled ignorance, saying that his focus on his gubernatorial campaign contributed to his being unaware of the tax break. It's obviously ironic that he remembered a $470,000 loan while focused on his gubernatorial campaign, but "forgot" that he had invested millions in a bank. According to Bill Allison of the non-partisan Center for Public Integrity, there is no clearer conflict of interest than voting on bills you have a direct financial stake in. "I don't think you're going to find a clearer case of somebody voting their own pocketbook."[14] Allison said.

Corzine's claim that he didn't know the clause was in the treaty does not absolve him. "If he said he didn't know, then he's just not doing his job. It's just appalling. That's hardly any kind of excuse," according to Allison.[15]

Despite the ethical cloud hanging over Jon Corzine, he won the New Jersey gubernatorial election in November 2005 against his Republican opponent, Doug Forrester. New Jersey, despite being a Democrat stronghold, became a heavily competitive and closely watched race, along with the only other gubernatorial race that year in Virgina, which was won by Democrat candidate Tim Kaine.

In the aftermath of these two victories, Democrats on the national level cheered and credited both President Bush's low approval ratings and the Republican "culture of corruption" for these victories and claimed this was a sign to come of Democrat victories in the midterm elections of 2006. DNC Chairman Howard Dean claimed that the voters of New Jersey and Virginia rejected Republican "dirty-tricks politics," and the "culture of corruption and incompetence."[16] It is odd how the rejection involved electing a corrupt man to replace a corruptly incompetent man. Perhaps the voters of New Jersey were satisfied that it was at least an incremental improvement.

Corzine certainly didn't improve his behavior now that he was in office. When lobbyist (and former Corzine campaign worker) Karen Golding was arrested on February 6, 2006, for stalking a New

Jersey state assemblyman, she new exactly where to turn for bail money: her recently inaugurated governor, Jon Corzine.

Golding had been accused of breaking in to the government-issued car of Assemblyman Joseph Cryan (who had also been recently appointed as NJ Democratic Party Chair by Corzine) and writing threatening letters. Corzine defended his actions, claiming to have not asked Golding any questions about her predicament. He would also claim that, in retrospect, he would not have lent her the money, declaring in a statement "...in light of my position as governor, I realize this was a mistake."[17] Apparently, Corzine learned nothing from his earlier problems surrounding the $470,000 loan-turned-gift to his former girlfriend Carla Katz.

Despite Corzine's own admission of wrongdoing, the governor's Advisory Ethics Panel (ironically created by former Governor James McGreevey) later ruled that he had done nothing wrong, but did "recommend that [Corzine] consider whether, in order to avoid even the *appearance* of impropriety, the Governor's office should refrain from dealing with Ms. Golding as a lobbyist" until her legal problems were settled.[18] Left unclear was whether a settlement by guilty verdict would make Golding *persona non grata* in Corzine's administration.

It is clear that Corzine is set in his corrupt and unethical ways. Whether in the United States Senate or in his home state of New Jersey, he continues to bring shame to his name and public distrust in government officials with his poor decisions.

Leaving the Senate provided Corzine with the opportunity to appoint a successor who could restore faith in government. With the political climate as it was, such an act would have been a wise decision. Instead, when Corzine left Washington, D.C. for New Jersey, the Senate said goodbye to one of its most disreputable members, only to say hello to another New Jersey politician with skeletons in his closet: Senator Robert Menendez.

Following the eruption of the McGreevey scandal, Menendez joined a group called "Leave Now," designed to force McGreevey out in time for a special election to be held in 2004. The purpose, as far as Menendez was concerned, was to get McGreevey out of office, and Corzine in. This would leave the path clear for Menendez to take Corzine's Senate seat.

McGreevey loyalists were not going to stand for that and revealed that Menendez had had a long-term affair with his former chief of staff, Kay LiCausi,[19] a lobbyist and political consultant nearly twenty years his junior. In addition to the allegations of an extramarital affair, Menendez was also accused of steering over $200,000 in fundraising and political consulting contracts to LiCausi, who also lobbied Menendez on behalf of her clients. In 2003 and 2004, Menendez paid LiCausi more than $50,000 just for "fundraising consulting."

But that's not all. According to a July 2005 *New York Times* profile of LiCausi, it was her "swift climb up the ladder" that was really suspicious.

> ...what has struck many seasoned politicians and consultants in New Jersey is the speed of Ms. LiCausi's ascent and the scope of her work, even in the state's forgiving political culture. She had little experience on Capitol Hill or in Trenton. In her highest position, she supervised a half-dozen members of Mr. Menendez's Jersey City staff.

> "This woman starts out as a midlevel staffer and then, all of a sudden, she's the greatest lobbyist on the East Coast?" said Bobby Jackson, the publisher of a small newspaper in Jersey City, who supported Glenn Cunningham, the former mayor of Jersey City, a political opponent of Mr. Menendez.

> [...]

> The tale of her swift success, however, is complicated by the widespread belief among elected officials and political consultants in Hudson County and former members of Mr. Menendez's staff that she and the congressman had a romantic relationship.[20]

LiCausi started K.L. Strategies after helping Menendez win reelection "in a typical landslide for him." K.L. Strategies consists of LiCausi and one associate. With an influx of clients with connections to Menendez, LiCausi's infant firm was making lots of money, while LiCausi was still making money as a paid political consultant and fundraiser for Menendez.

That wasn't the only example of Menendez having a tangled relationship.

On March 7, 2006, it was revealed that back in 2003, while Menendez was still serving in the House, he had written a letter of recommendation for Hindsight, Inc.,[21] a major campaign contributor. In an action that reeked of *quid pro quo*, five days after the letter was dated, Menendez received $4,000 in contributions from Hindsight. Some months later, Hindsight, in spite of bidding $850,000 above the low bidder, was awarded a $4 million contract by Hudson County.

It would be easy, at this point, to think that Menendez' whole purpose in life was personal enrichment, but Menendez wasn't appointed to Corzine's Senate seat simply to give his girlfriend and other associates a leg up in the political world. Menendez's primary job was to hold the seat for the Democratic Party— especially as 2006 looked like a year in which the Democrats had a shot at winning a Senate majority, something which would be complicated if a "safe" Senate seat fell to the Republicans. Unfortunately for the Democrats, Bob Menendez's one-man culture of corruption became an ever larger millstone around his neck.

By September of 2006, things began to look extremely bleak for Menendez. When it was revealed that a federal investigation had been launched to investigate the fact that Menendez was receiving $3,000 a month in "rent" from North Hudson Community Action,[22] a nonprofit group Menendez had brought millions of dollars in federal grants while still in the House, polling started to show Menendez on a path to political destruction in November.

Menendez's troubles continued when tapes were released revealing that one of his close friends and associates, New Jersey lawyer Donald Scarinci, back in 1999 at the behest of Rep. Menendez, asked Oscar Sandoval, a psychiatrist with contracts with Hudson County, to rehire Dr. Vicente Ruiz, a friend of Menendez, in order to "protect" his contracts with the county at a time when Sandoval was in danger of losing them.[23] According to tapes made of the exchange, Scarinci told Sandoval, "If you can deal with Dr. Ruiz and make him happy, Menendez will consider that a favor. If you can't, then that's okay ... you can't."[24]

As if this wasn't bad enough, The *Associated Press* reported that according to court documents, Ruiz "believed some of the money from the government contract would be kicked back to Menendez."[25]

Menendez had been linked to the scandal since the end of March 2006, when the *New Jersey Journal* first reported on the scandal.[26] But it was only after the tapes were released in September that Menendez actually distanced himself from Scarinci.

As soon as the tapes were released, the Menendez campaign cut its ties with Scarinci, who had been among Menendez's closest advisers and fundraisers. A Menendez spokesman also denied that Scarinci had been acting on Menendez's behalf. But the state GOP was quick to point out that all the allegations about Scarinci had been made public in the spring when Sandoval filed court papers revealing the nature of the tapes. When asked why Menendez waited until the release of the tapes to sever ties with Scarinci, a Menendez spokesman noted the distinction between the court papers and the tapes: "That's a big difference."[27]

Menendez was also tied to another scandal in April 2006, when the *New York Times* reported that a number of New Jersey politicians, including Menendez, were linked to a political patronage scheme at New Jersey's state medical school. According to the report, "Patronage hiring was so pervasive ... that job applications were marked with a numeral indicating the potency of the applicants' political connections." Candidates recommended by Menendez received the highest ranking.[28]

As might be expected of someone with Menendez's background, his campaign funds were also highly suspect.

Charles Kushner, a gigantic source of funding for Bob Menendez,[29] pled guilty to federal charges back in 2004. Despite the conviction, Menendez decided that Kushner's dirty money wasn't too dirty for him and decided to keep most of it.

U.S. Sen. Robert Menendez had received at least $159,000 since 1997 from Kushner, his real estate partners, and their relatives. He donated just $6,000 of that—the amount the FEC said had been given illegally—to charity after the developer's conviction.[30]

Menendez spokesman Matthew Miller defended keeping the remaining Kusher contributions because they "were raised legally before anyone had any knowledge of Mr. Kushner's bizarre and criminal behavior," and had nothing to with his illegal activity.[31] But even Jon Corzine returned Kushner's cash. All of it.

But Menendez has the company of many Democrats and Democrat committees that have received campaign cash from Kushner, but have decided to keep all or most of it.

Since 1997, the Democratic National Committee received $2.1 million in Kushner-connected cash and only returned $149,000.[32] The Democratic Senatorial Campaign Committee (DSCC) received $722,500, but didn't return any of it.[33]

In the end Kushner contributed at least $5.1 million to Democrats and Democrat committees (including Charles Schumer, Hillary Clinton, Ken Salazar, and the Kerry/Edwards campaign). $4.7 million of that dirty money was kept.[34] The hypocrisy here is breathtaking in scope: Democrats demanded that any donation to Republicans even remotely connected to Abramoff, even if legal, be returned, and yet they justify keeping even questionable Kushner donations!

Menendez had been touched by scandal so much that a few months before the midterm elections, party insiders were talking about a possible Torricelli-switch, but Democrats eventually promised not to replace him.[35] Still, ethical questions were raised about Menendez even to the last days of the campaign. With just over a week before the election, the *New York Times* ran a story about a waterfront development project called the Peninsula at Bayonne Harbor that "produced considerable work for some of his chief political supporters,"[36] adding to the already lengthy list.

The first major contract to develop the site went to a company that hired a Menendez friend and political confidant, Donald Scarinci, to lobby for it. That developer later took on Mr. Menendez's former campaign treasurer, Carl Goldberg, as a partner. Bonds for a portion of the project were underwritten by Dennis Enright, a top campaign contributor, while Kay LiCausi, a former Menendez Congressional aide and major fund-raiser, received lucrative work lobbying for the project.[37]

Menendez denied having any role in securing the contracts for his friends and associates. Despite all the scandals plaguing Menendez, he handily won a full term to the U.S. Senate.

The litany of allegations against Menendez reads like someone attempting to see if they can violate all Ten Commandments and still remain politically viable. Either that or it is a test to see just how much Democratic voters will swallow in the name of keeping the dreaded Republicans out of office.

From the romantic relationship between Menendez and Li-Causi, with her strange and virtual overnight success, to stories of Menendez exerting pressure for favored groups and individuals, examples of shady political fundraising, and a slew of other scandals and accusations under his belt, it is quite clear that New Jersey lost one corrupt senator only to gain another. And Menendez will be serving in the Senate for at least another six years, or until he gets indicted.

"BAGHDAD" JIM MCDERMOTT

Most Democrats like to cast themselves as the defender of the little guy. They are very self-congratulatory about how they "speak truth to power" and fight for the poor and oppressed. So ingrained is this self-image that it sometimes gets Democrats in a bind.

One particular Democrat who knows all about that is Rep. Jim McDermott of Washington.

In 1996, a Florida couple, John and Alice Martin, intercepted a call on Ohio Republican Rep. John Boehner's cell phone and recorded it. Illegally.

The call was a conference call between Newt Gingrich and other Republican congressmen discussing how to respond to the ethics investigation of Gingrich. The Martins gave the recording to Jim McDermott in January 1997, and he leaked it to the media.[38]

After the Martins revealed McDermott's role, he was *forced* to recuse himself from the House ethics committee, which was investigating Newt Gingrich. And by no means did McDermott go quietly. Similar to the way Democrats today blame Republicans for their ethical problems, McDermott blamed partisan maneuvering by the Republicans for forcing him to step down. "At every turn, the Republican majority on the committee has delayed, stonewalled or otherwise obstructed sensible efforts to get at the whole truth."[39]

Despite the fact that the cellular phone conversations were recorded illegally, McDermott condemned then-ethics committee Chairman Nancy L. Johnson, a Republican from Connecticut, for refusing to accept the recordings into evidence against Newt Gingrich. In a letter to Johnson, McDermott wrote, "Rather than evaluate the evidence of the breach and give it such weight as it is fairly entitled to receive, [Johnson], without committee or House approval, [has] jettisoned the evidence and willfully ignored its content."[40] Perhaps McDermott forgot about the Constitution?

As Democrats pounced on Tom DeLay over alleged ethics violations, they refused to convene the ethics committee, effectively blocking the investigation into McDermott's actions. DeLay's problems were the ones getting media attention, not McDermott's, even though DeLay was more than willing go through an ethics investigation to clear his name.

Rep. Boehner would file a lawsuit against McDermott, which, after several years going through the courts, resulted in U.S. District Court for the District of Columbia judge Thomas F. Hogan ruling that because McDermott "participated in an illegal transaction when he accepted the tape from the Martins, he is without First Amendment protection and Plaintiff Boehner is therefore entitled to judgment as a matter of law."[41]

Hogan ordered McDermott to pay a $60,000 fine and Rep. Boehner's attorney fees, which were over $600,000.[42] McDermott appealed and was heard by U.S. Circuit Court of Appeals for the District of Columbia on November 15, 2005. In March of 2006, a federal appeals court upheld the previous ruling. But McDermott wasn't done fighting, and three months later, the U.S. Circuit Court of Appeals for the District of Columbia agreed to hear new arguments in the case. McDermott said he looked forward "to presenting a vigorous defense of the First Amendment issues at stake in this case, and we believe there is precedent all the way to the U.S. Supreme Court to support our position."[43]

On November 1, 2006, the appeals court heard the arguments of both sides with a decision to be rendered in the future.[44] About a month later, the House Ethics Committee issued a report, concluding that McDermott "risked undermining the ethics process" by disclosing the taped conversation to the media (but did not violate overall House rules), leaving the issue of the legality of his actions to the courts, and took no further action.[45]

Even though the committee ruled he violated ethics standards, McDermott was pleased with the ruling. In an e-mail to the *Associated Press*, he said, "I am...pleased with the committee's acknowledgment that pending litigation in the federal court will decide the question of law over the First Amendment issues involved."[46]

For McDermott this level of hypocrisy is not surprising. He has a history of aligning himself with dictators and terrorist sympathizers, while claiming to be a defender of freedom and justice.

In April 2004, McDermott had to return a $5,000 contribution made by Shakir al-Khafaji to his legal defense fund.[47] Shakir al-Khafaji, an Iraqi-American and real estate developer in Detroit, Michigan, was financially tied to Saddam Hussein's regime (see Chapter Six).

McDermott and al-Khafaji go way back. In fact, al-Khafaji accompanied McDermott on his infamous trip to Iraq in 2002. Al-Khafaji, who was also active in the so-called anti-war movement, made the contribution after the 2002 trip. Whether it is violating the privacy rights of individual Americans, or attempting to undercut the elected government of the United States, everything for McDermott is trumped by the necessity that his left-wing ideology advance. There is no bribe he will not take or give, no crime he won't sanction or commit, as long as a Republican is on the wrong end of it all.

WILLIAM JEFFERSON

One would believe that the ethical and legal troubles of congressional Democrats during the height of their crusade against corruption should have derailed their efforts to exploit the issue of for their own political gain. If any Democrat's troubles should have prompted Democrats to quickly and quietly change their campaign theme for 2006, Rep. William Jefferson's should have done so. But the media refused to give it the same attention as the problems plaguing Republicans.

On Wednesday, August 3, 2005, federal agents carried out a series of raids on Rep. William Jefferson's homes in News Orleans and Washington, D.C.. They also targeted Jefferson's office, car, and the home of his campaign treasurer.[48] FBI agents seized a large amount of cold, hard cash in the raids on Jefferson's homes—literally, as the cash was kept in a freezer.[49]

Jefferson, a veteran member of the Ways and Means Committee, had been the subject of a year-long undercover FBI sting for allegedly agreeing to invest in a Virginia-based high-tech company that was starting up, and then use his influence in Congress to steer business to the company.[50] Subpoenas also indicated that investigators were also seeking information on a telecommunications deal he was trying to broker in Nigeria over the previous year.

The small Kentucky-based telecom company, iGate Corp., unable to compete with bigger companies in the United States, had tried to jumpstart its business in Nigeria. The *Times-Picayune* of New Orleans reported that iGate had patented technology that "can deliver voice, data and video along copper telephone lines faster and more cheaply than a digital subscriber line [DSL], which is common in many American households and businesses."

Despite this technology, iGate was unable to compete against the likes of DSL providers like Verizon, and "decided to test the waters in Nigeria, a poor nation but one of the fastest-growing telecommunications markets in the world. [...] The company was seeking financing to launch the project in Nigeria."[51]

Nigeria has long been known for being one of the most corrupt nations on earth. Nothing gets done in Nigeria without bribing someone. Given this, it was natural that anyone wishing to push a company via bribery would work the deal through Nigeria. And in Congressman Jefferson, iGate found a man who never asked *if* he should take a bribe, but only *how much* he would demand for his services.

In the iGate affair, Jefferson allegedly had demanded 5 to 7 percent of the money being gathered for the Nigerian venture, as well as the employment of one of Jefferson's children at a salary of $2,500 to $5,000 per month. One of Jefferson's daughters did the legal work in setting up the deal—and, in fact, the actual solicitation of the bribe took place in the lobby of the daughter's office.[52]

While Jefferson has been contemptible in his use of public office for personal enrichment, what is more worrisome is that the Democrat Party failed to do anything about him. While Democratic leaders like Pelosi and Reid were quick to call for resignations of Republicans hit by bogus prosecutions, Jefferson's very serious crimes have been greeted with silence, even after Jefferson's former aide Brett Pfeffer pleaded guilty in January 2006 for bribery and implicated Jefferson (known as Representative A on court documents) for his role in the scandal.[53]

Jefferson's deal with the company was to be funded via the United States Export-Import Bank. This taxpayer-funded organization is designed to help American business expand American trade for the benefit of the country as a whole.

Had this deal gone forward, then a large amount of taxpayer money would not have gone to help America's export trade, but would have gone to enrich one corrupt Congressman and his family. All Americans would suffer so that Jefferson's personal gain.

Even national tragedy can be adversely affected by the actions of the corrupt. While New Orleans was undergoing the tragedy of Katrina, Congressman Jefferson had other things on his mind. Commandeering a National Guard vehicle and its personnel, he made his way to his residence in New Orleans and retrieved "a laptop computer, three suitcases, and a box about the size of a small refrigerator,"[54] which he then had loaded up and driven out.

As the investigation into Jefferson continued, the media did not give it the same kind of attention as it did the Randy "Duke" Cunningham bribery scandal.[55]

In April of 2006, Citizens for Responsibility and Ethics in Washington (CREW) prepared an ethics complaint against Jefferson "regarding his role in a conspiracy and bribery scheme as well as for misusing federal resources in the wake of hurricane Katrina."[56]

Pressure mounted against Jefferson, but he refused to resign. In a statement, Jefferson claimed, "I would take full responsibility for any crime that I committed, if that were the case. But I will not plead guilty to something I did not do, no matter how things are made to look and no matter the risk."[57] Like William Jefferson Clinton, his claims of innocence were disingenuous.

As the investigation into Jefferson's bribery scandal continued, Democrats were curiously silent. That is until FBI agents searched Jefferson's congressional office on May 20, 2006, which had some Democrats (and even some Republicans) raising a stink about an alleged conflict of separation of powers, with Nancy Pelosi implying there was an "abuse of power by the Executive Branch."[58]

But the "abuse of power" smokescreen wasn't enough to detract from Jefferson's problems. The day after the controversial raid, the *Associated Press* reported on the existence of a videotape showing Jefferson "accepting $100,000 in $100 bills from an FBI informant whose conversations with the lawmaker also were recorded."[59]

At one audiotaped meeting, Rep. William Jefferson, (D-LA), chuckles about writing in code to keep secret what the government contends was his corrupt role in getting his children a cut of a communications company's deal for work in Africa.

As Jefferson and the informant passed notes about what percentage the lawmaker's family might receive, the congressman "began laughing and said, 'All these damn notes we're writing to each other as if we're talking, as if the FBI is watching,'" according to the affidavit.[60]

Most of the money was recovered in the August 2005 raid of Jefferson's home. Jefferson's lawyer protested that the disclosure was "part of a public relations agenda and an attempt to embarrass Congressman Jefferson," and dismissed the affidavit as "just one side of the story which has not been tested in court."[61] It was later reported that Jefferson attempted to hide documents from FBI agents when they searched his home.[62] Even as they raised a fuss about the search of Jefferson's office, the Democrats couldn't ignore the new evidence against him, and they have to do something to save face.

Clearly realizing how Jefferson's ethical problems would haunt the Democratic Party in light of their campaign against the Republican "culture of corruption," Nancy Pelosi asked Jefferson to resign from the Ways and Means Committee on May 24, 2006.[63] "In the interest of upholding the high ethical standard of the House Democratic Caucus, I am writing to request your immediate resignation," she wrote. In the spirit of the House Democratic Caucus's "high ethical standards," Jefferson rebuffed her request and refused.

Jefferson had been under investigation since March 2005. It was only *after* the *Associated Press* reported on the existence of videotape evidence against Jefferson on May 21, 2006, that his party decided to act.

So much for those high ethical standards.

House Democrats, clearly left with no choice, voted to strip Jefferson of his committee assignment on June 15, 2006.[64] Sadly, the ongoing bribery investigation mattered little to his constituents. Not only did Jefferson come in first place in his Louisiana district on election day,[65] but he went on to easily defeat his opponent in the runoff election.[66]

There's no doubt that Jefferson will make a name for himself in Nancy Pelosi's honest, open, and ethical Congress.[67]

PATRICK KENNEDY

In the summer of 1969, Senator Ted Kennedy drove off the Dike Bridge in Chappaquiddick, leaving passenger Mary Jo Kopechne behind to drown. He would eventually plead guilty to leaving the scene of an accident, and was given a suspended sentence. His son, Patrick Kennedy, is a chip off the old block.

On May 4, 2006, Patrick Kennedy found himself walking in his father's footsteps—or shall we say driving down the same path— when he crashed his car near the U.S. Capitol, nearly hitting a police cruiser and slamming into a security barricade, around 3 a.m.[68] Fortunately for the younger Kennedy, no one was killed.

Officers on the scene described him as staggering, appearing to be intoxicated, and noted "an odor of alcohol."[69] Despite these signs that Kennedy had been driving under the influence, officers on the scene were not allowed to perform sobriety tests on the congressman, and he was given a ride home by Capitol Police officials.

Kennedy claimed he had not consumed alcohol prior to driving, but a waitress at the Hawk 'n' Dove, a popular Capitol Hill bar, said she saw him drinking there hours before the incident.[70] Kennedy would later claim that his crash was a result of medications he took and quickly checked himself into rehab for an addiction to prescription pain medication. Many questions surrounded the incident, including the interference of high-ranking officers, who didn't allow field sobriety tests to be conducted and took the congressman home.

Despite the evidence that alcohol was indeed a factor in Kennedy's crash, by going into rehab, Kennedy made his cover story (that medication—not alcohol—caused his crash) sound true. And to leave as little doubt as possible, or at least make it unfashionable to criticize him, he wasted no time playing the victim, declaring at a press conference "I struggle every day with this disease, as do millions of Americans."

Kennedy's performance worked. No criminal investigation was conducted, and his drunken crash and the coverup would just become another example of a member of the Kennedy clan beating the rap. He was easily reelected.

CYNTHIA MCKINNEY

One Democrat who rightfully did not return to Congress was Cynthia McKinney. On March 29, 2006, Cynthia McKinney punched a Capitol police officer after he had flagged her down for not passing through the metal detector.[71] As a member of Congress, McKinney was not required to go through the detectors, but the officer had not recognized her. In responding to reports of the incident, McKinney naturally played the race card. "Washington, DC and local newspapers, as well as authors of books, have carried my 'working while black' stories of such encounters on Capitol Hill." She continued:

> Sadly, there are only 14 black women Members of Congress. And surely our faces are distinguishable. But why my face is continually unrecognizable can only be answered by these offending police officers. Capitol Hill Police are given face recognition instructions as a part of their official training. Capitol Hill Police are required to recognize, greet, and distinguish Members of Congress as a part of their official role and responsibilities. In fact, according to the US Capitol Police, their mission is to protect and support the Congress in meeting its Constitutional responsibilities. The US Capitol Police mission statement makes no distinction about selective application of its mission depending upon whether a Member of Congress is black, woman, or has a new hairstyle.[72]

Her message was clear. The fact that she responded with violence wasn't important. This was about race. At least, to her it was. But even members of her own party weren't jumping on that train. *The Hill* reported a few days after the incident that some Democrats were trying to distance themselves from her. After all, it conflicted with their goals of exploiting Republican ethical problems.

"There's been a lot of eye-rolling," said an aide to a moderate Democrat who spoke on condition of anonymity. "The national attention it's been getting has been unfortunate. It's becoming a distraction."[73]

As this incident erupted, another McKinney scandal came to light. WSB-TV Channel 2 Action News in Atlanta "uncovered documents showing McKinney, (D-GA), spent about $1,000 of taxpayers' money to fly singer Isaac Hayes to Georgia to help dedicate a new office in Atlanta."[74]

But the big story was her scuffle with the Capitol Hill police officer. A federal grand jury heard evidence on the case, and it was looking as if McKinney would suffer the consequences of her actions. No such luck. On June 16, 2006, the grand jury declined to indict McKinney.[75] She had officially beaten the rap. But it wasn't over.

Local and national police unions called for the House ethics committee to investigate the incident.[76] That hardly fazed her, even with a two primary challengers hoping to unseat her. In fact, she didn't seem to think she had anything to worry about in her election, as she failed to show up to *two* primary debates. Who can blame her for her complacency, when so many in her party survived scandals and still continued to have long careers in Congress?

Much to her surprise, while McKinney beat the rap in the legal system, her political career was soon to be over. She failed to obtain 50 percent of the vote in the July 18, 2006, primary election, and was defeated in the Democratic runoff election on August 8, 2006.[77] McKinney, like many in her party, would not lose with dignity.

McKinney kept true to her paranoid ways right up to the end; within an hour of the start of voting, McKinney's blog was making accusations of voting irregularities.[78] Following her defeat, there was a scuffle between her bodyguards (who were members of the New Black Panther Party) and members of the media after leaving her campaign headquarters. Members of McKinney's entourage were recorded making racist and anti-Semitic comments, blaming McKinney's defeat on Israel, calling members of the media "crackers," and referring to McKinney's victorious opponent as an Uncle Tom.[79] This was not the first time Jews were blamed for her defeat. In August of 2002, when she was defeated by Denise Majette, her father said she had lost because "Jews have bought everybody."[80] McKinney herself has been accused of anti-Semitism.

Following the release of the video, a former McKinney staffer came forward with allegations that he had been fired for being Jewish. Appearing on Fox New Channel's *Hannity & Colmes*, the former staffer claimed he regularly heard McKinney and others in her office "vilify Israel as an enemy nation, as a nation that was hell-bent on destroying other people," and after revealing he needed to take a day off to celebrate the Jewish High Holidays, he came back and was told his position was de-funded.[81]

Cynthia McKinney's defeat was unique. While neither her party, the ethics committee, nor the law saw fit to take action against her, the voters in her district sent her packing.

Soviet leaders used to refer to criminals who were pro-Soviet as "socially friendly elements." Often these criminals would get a lighter sentence, and early release. Torricelli, McDermott, Jefferson, Kennedy, McKinney et al are the Democratic version of this phenomenon. Since their heart is in the right place, they constitue "socially friendly elements" and must be given endless consideration for their sins.

CHAPTER SIX

BOTCHED JOKES

"You know, education, if you make the most of it, if you study hard and you do your homework, and you make an effort to be smart, uh, you, you can do well. If you don't, you get stuck in Iraq."

—John Kerry

TRADITION is a very important element in any human group. Some traditions are very serious, like our annual laying of the wreath at the Tomb of the Unknown Soldier; others are more whimsical, such as the Randwick Wap in Gloucestershire, England. This May festival involves a procession of local notables dunked in a pond, and cheeses rolled down a hill. What the occasion celebrates remains a bit mysterious, but as it has been going on for centuries, the tradition is best left alone.

Were such a festival as "the Wap" to take place in America, Democrats would likely picket it as insufficiently racially diverse, while some post-modernist professors would proclaim that the festival merely perpetuates the white male power structure. As a rule, if there is something people have been *enjoying* for a long time, Democrats oppose it—though if anyone comes up with a new religion or lifestyle, Democrats will immediately proclaim it an inherent human right and demand legislation to protect it.

It is unfortunate that while Democrats mostly scoff at traditions, there are some they seem to honor every waking moment. Among these is their thirty-five-year-old contempt for the United States military and all it stands for.

In the annals of political history there have been many jokes, some of them botched. Late in the 2006 campaign season, Senator John Kerry (D-MA) impugned the honor of American military personnel by implying only uneducated people get "stuck" in the military. The resulting firestorm momentarily seemed as if it would raise GOP chances on Election Day, and thus a desperate situation called for a desperate, yet typically Democratic, tactic: claim that he didn't say what we all knew he said. Kerry, after his initial defiance, claimed that the whole thing was a "botched joke," aimed at President Bush. This absurd claim was emblematic of the Democrats' entire 2006 campaign.

In truth, what Kerry actually said—study hard, or you'll wind up stuck in Iraq—accurately represented the Democrats' attitude towards the military. When Kerry came home from his short stint in Vietnam, he found that "war hero" didn't play well in politically liberal Massachusetts, so he switched to "anti-war hero," making slanderous statements before the United States Senate when he accused the American armed forces of acting like a bunch of blood-crazed savages in Vietnam. From that time until this, the underlying liberal/left storyline on the American military is that it is made up of ill-educated losers who become barbarians whenever war breaks out.

Sadly, accusing American soldiers of committing war crimes and of being lazy and uneducated are not the worst things Kerry has done.

During the 2004 presidential campaign, John Kerry rarely missed an opportunity to remind the country he is a Vietnam War veteran. Sometimes, the campaign seemed to focus more on the war in Vietnam than the war on terror. This strategy most certainly contributed to Kerry's downfall. The rise of the Swift Boat Veterans for Truth, who challenged Kerry's claims of being a war hero, caused him to backpedal on a number of claims he made about his time in Vietnam.

One of the more shocking stories to come out in 2004 was Kerry's presence at a November 1971 meeting of the Vietnam Veterans Against the War. During the meeting, the "Phoenix Project," a plan to assassinate pro-war U.S. senators, was discussed. Several anti-war activists remembered Kerry being at the meeting.[1]

Kerry adamantly denied that he attended the meeting, until new evidence (reports from FBI informants) surfaced contradicting his claim. Kerry's rhetoric changed after this new evidence came to light:

> "John Kerry had no personal recollection of this meeting 33 years ago," a Kerry campaign spokesman, David Wade, said in a statement e-mailed last night from Idaho, where Mr. Kerry is on vacation.
>
> Mr. Wade said Mr. Kerry does remember "disagreements with elements of VVAW leadership" that led to his resignation, but the statement did not specify what the disagreements were.
>
> "If there are valid FBI surveillance reports from credible sources that place some of those disagreements in Kansas City, we accept that historical footnote in the account of his work to end the difficult and divisive war," the statement said. [2]

Minutes of the meeting were provided to the *New York Sun* by Gerald Nicosia, a historian and expert on anti-Vietnam war activism, who also happened to be a Kerry supporter:

> "My evidence is incontrovertible. He was there," Mr. Nicosia said in an interview yesterday. "There's no way that five or six agents saw his ghost there," said the historian, who lives in Marin County, north of San Francisco.
>
> Mr. Nicosia said that the records show Mr. Kerry resigned from the group on the third day of the meeting, following discussion of the assassination plan and an argument between Mr. Kerry and another VVAW national coordinator, Al Hubbard.
>
> Reading from an FBI informant report, Mr. Nicosia said, "John Kerry at a national Vietnam Veterans Against the War meeting appeared and announced to those present that he resigned for personal reasons but said he would be able to speak for VVAW" at future events. Another document "describes a conversation actually a confrontation between John Kerry and Hubbard that was taking place on one of the days of that meeting," Mr. Nicosia added.[3]

Kerry did speak out against the plot at the meeting and resigned from VVAW, but what did the future U.S. senator do about it afterwards? Nothing. He never warned the authorities about the discussed plot. This should have derailed his presidential campaign, but for some people, Kerry's participating in a debate about assassinating U.S. senators wasn't bad while President Bush's deposing a brutal dictator was the worst thing to ever happen.

The comment by Kerry's spokesman about Kerry's "work" to end the Vietnam War reveals the way Democrats hide their true selves. Only rarely, if at all, will any Democrat say that the United States was defeated in Vietnam. But defeated we were—why the reticence about the word "defeat"? Because it was Democrats who created the defeat—neither while we were engaged in active combat nor when we provided support to the South Vietnamese government was there a defeat in Vietnam. Defeat came only after Congressional Democrats—egged on by the Kerrys of America—cut off support for South Vietnam. Defeat is inevitable when one side is running out of ammunition and the other isn't. Kerry's "work" was to work for American defeat, though you'll never hear Kerry—or any other anti-war Democrat—say that is what resulted from their "work."

The Democrats' war against the U.S. military started when a Republican took over the mess the Democrats had made out of the Vietnam War. While many Americans by 1968 were frustrated over the lack of progress and victory in Vietnam, the U.S. military was still respected everywhere outside the precincts of the Far Left. But just as soon as Republican Richard Nixon took over as commander in chief of the United States military in 1969, Democrats began to find glaring flaws not just in strategy and tactics, but in the very existence of an armed U.S. force. It would seem that in their desire to get at Richard Nixon, the Democrats didn't consider what effect their dishonest tactics would have on America as a whole. This might have been the first time the Democrats fell into this trap, but it certainly wasn't the last.

During the Nixon administration, the Democrats merely played with anti-military sentiment. In the Vietnam era, it was very fashionable to be anti-military, especially once the Democrats were off the hook for the conduct of the war. Hard as it may be to believe, when John Kerry first came home from Vietnam, he sought office on the strength of his alleged war heroism. Only after his war hero stance failed did Kerry denounce the American military. The Far

Left generated false accusations of war crimes by American troops, but most Democrats shied away from such things—while keeping, of course, to a general anti-military line which played well with left-wing voters. Back then, Democrats still had some strength in "red" areas of the country, and didn't wish to risk their power by adhering to their anti-military "principles."

With Ronald Reagan's election to the presidency in 1980, however, the Democrats found themselves forced to grow serious about their anti-military stance. Reagan was elected president partly on a platform of supporting military build-up to challenge the Soviet Union. Reagan held the view—at that time considered foolish by all but a few—that the Soviet Union could not only be confronted but rolled back upon itself and eventually destroyed.

It is hard for people in 2007 to remember both the threat and the apparent permanent nature of the old Union of Soviet Socialist Republics. It has, after all, been more than fifteen years since that glorious Christmas Day when the dictator of the USSR announced on television that he was dictator of nothing—that the USSR, an inhumane tyranny responsible for millions of murders in its seventy-four-year existence, was no more. Back in 1980, however, the USSR loomed large in the world. It was permanent and Americans would just have to get along with it, somehow. And if that meant concessions at the negotiating table, then so be it. Ronald Reagan thought differently.

Boiled down, Reagan's plan was to use the freedom of the United States to out-compete the communist giant into bankruptcy. Convinced that America was a good nation and that the American people, unleashed, would make short work of any threat, Reagan set to work—and a very big part of his work was defense build up. Democrats were immediately incensed and wasted no time in starting a full-scale assault on everything Reagan touched, especially the military.

All through the 1980s Democrats decried each new infusion of federal funds for defense. While the United States was faced with a USSR on the march in central America, battling for control of Afghanistan, and deploying short and medium range nuclear missiles in Europe, denouncing any increase in America's defensive capability was standard Democratic campaign rhetoric. Democrats were nearly uniformly opposed to any strong effort on the part of the United States to defeat the enemies of freedom.

Along with standard left-wing issues—back in those days, especially, increases in AIDS research funding—Nancy Pelosi made cutting defense spending one of the main issues of her first campaign for political office.[4] She also condemned Ronald Reagan's request for aid to the anti-communist rebels in Nicaragua.[5] To Far Left ideologues like Pelosi, the communists who were crushing the people of Nicaragua were the good guys, while America led by Reagan was the cause of all evil in the world.

Each and every weapons system now in the United States arsenal was condemned in the past by Democrats. Had we listened to the Democratic critics in the 1980s, our brave men and women of the armed forces would lack the M-1 Abrams tank, the F-16 fighter, the Patriot anti-aircraft missile, the Navy's AEGIS combat system, and a host of other weapons that have proved their worth again and again on the battlefields of liberty.

Invariably, the condemnations claimed that the item was too expensive, wouldn't work, and would destabilize world peace. How weapons that wouldn't work could destabilize the world was a question Democrats never answered, but they were quite certain they were right. Democrats viewed Reagan's defense buildup as a mere giveaway to corporate special interests and/or a manifestation of Reagan's messianic desire for an apocalyptic war. So desperate was the Left's desire to derail Reagan and the GOP that a United States senator evidently corresponded with leaders of the Soviet Union to coordinate ways and means of thwarting the Reagan defense build-up and defeating him at the polls in 1984.

As Paul Kengor notes in his book, *The Crusader: Ronald Reagan and the Fall of Communism*, Senator Ted Kennedy (D-MA), through an intermediary, advised Soviet leader Yuri Andropov that Kennedy, like the Soviets, thought America's defense build-up was wrong and offered to help the Soviets make their case to the American people in a manner designed to undermine public confidence in Reagan administration policies.[6] Kengor wrote:

> According to the KGB document, Kennedy's goal in reaching out to Andropov was to defeat Reagan on two fronts: He hoped to reverse the president's defense policies and foil

his 1984 reelection bid. If the memo is in fact an accurate account of what transpired, it constitutes a remarkable example of the lengths to which some on the political left, including a sitting U.S. senator, were willing to go to stop Ronald Reagan...[7]

Only in the strange and corrupt world of the Democrats would someone think that colluding with our enemies is in America's best interests. Kengor suggests that had this story made the newspapers or nightly news broadcasts at the time, "it would have been a major story of the 1984 campaign." [8] Perhaps he was giving the media too much credit.

The shocking revelations that a sitting U.S. senator may have been working to undermine American foreign policy caused hardly a ripple in the media when Kengor's book came out in 2006.

Similarly, when the details of the NSA Terrorist Surveillance program were leaked and reported by the *New York Times* in December 2005, Democrats were less concerned about the leak of the vital program than they were about accusing President Bush of spying on American citizens.

Kennedy's actions against Reagan during the 1984 campaign, if it *had* become a big story, would have likely been spun in Kennedy's favor. Now, the years have insulated him from any rebuke for his actions, which some would describe as treasonous.

Ted Kennedy, heir to a corrupt family fortune, should not be considered a tribune of moral virtue by anyone in America. While Kennedy's reaching out to America's enemies didn't succeed in making Reagan a one-term president, Kennedy remained steadfast in opposing Reagan, stooping to any low necessary to do so.

It was this same Ted Kennedy who launched a brutal verbal assault on Supreme Court nominee Robert Bork by claiming that Bork, as a justice, would turn black Americans into second-class citizens and would force women into having back-alley abortions.[9]

Ted Kennedy's whole attack on Bork was a lie from start to finish, as was the whole Democratic effort to undermine Ronald Reagan in his battle against communism—and just as the whole Democratic effort to undermine our effort in the war on terror is a lie from start to finish. But when one of your senior leaders has already gone as far as colluding with the enemies of the United

States in order to gain political advantage, the mere slandering of an honest man or slandering of the United States military is rather trivial.

Dishonesty breeds dishonesty, *ad infinitum*. By the time of the attacks of 9/11, the Democratic position was automatically that of disdain for the military, opposition to military action, and slanderous assaults on any Republican who may be in charge. Those attacks of that infamous day merely muted and delayed the Democratic onslaught; they didn't end it or even so much as modify it.

While Americans proudly waved their flag in the months immediately following the 9/11 attacks, one could easily think that here, at last, was a clear struggle between good and evil that everyone left, right and center could agree on. This attitude was only possible because most people, most of the time, are unable to plumb the corrupt depths reached by Democrats on a regular basis. But in the person of Representative Jim McDermott, the real Democratic attitude is revealed.

In the fall of 2002, Rep. Jim McDermott of Washington made headlines for going on a five-day trip to Iraq with other House Democrats, during which he criticized President Bush's call to use force against Saddam Hussein.

For McDermott, Saddam Hussein's Iraq was the "little guy" standing up to the big, bad United States of America. It was a natural for him to go to Baghdad on the eve of armed conflict. Not to do so would have destroyed McDermott's highly inflated image of himself, and there's nothing more deadly for a left-wing Democrat than to be less than the most controversial, dedicated, and "progressive" person around.

Republicans mildly pointed out that touring Baghdad as the guest of a lunatic dictator at war with the United States since 1991 just *might* constitute giving aid and comfort to the enemy, but such accusations were mostly ignored—and condemned when noticed. The media portrayed McDermott as a hero who refused to "give in" to President Bush,[10] and the whole treason angle just didn't fit in with the media narrative. McDermott remained stout in his opposition to the liberation of Iraq, even going so far as to claim that Saddam's capture was staged for President Bush's political benefit.[11] McDermott and the other House Democrats were accompanied to Iraq by Detroit real estate developer Shakir al-Khafaji, an Iraqi-American with financial ties to Saddam Hussein's regime.

McDermott argued he was unaware of al-Khafaji's ties to Saddam's regime, and, according to his spokesman, McDermott and al-Khafaji met for the first time on that trip. But back in 2003, McDermott referred to al-Khafaji as "a friend" and claimed that the two had forged a relationship on the trip. At the time, al-Khafaji claimed he was not a supporter of Saddam Hussein.[12]

Yet Seattle activist Bert Sacks, who was on the trip with McDermott, said al-Khafaji appeared to have contacts within the regime and helped make travel arrangements within the country and arranged meetings with officials of the regime.[13] Al-Khafaji admitted his acquaintance with members of the regime. "I know everybody in the regime, and they respected me a lot, but at the same time, I was not an advocate of that regime at any time."[14] We are expected to believe that McDermott had absolutely no idea of his "friend's" connection to Saddam Hussein's regime.

Since 1996, al-Khafaji has donated thousands of dollars to Democratic candidates in order to increase political support to end sanctions on Iraq, including Rep. John Conyers, Senator Carl Levin, and the Clinton/Gore Primary Committee.[15] This friend of the Saddam regime certainly seems to have plenty of friends in the Democratic Party.

The *Sunday Telegraph* of London reported on May 4, 2003 that it had obtained documents indicating Saddam Hussein attempted to bribe former U.N. weapons inspector Scott Ritter with gold jewelry, to be funneled through al-Khafaji. "The documents, which are signed by the then director-general of Iraqi intelligence, purport to reveal close links between Mr al-Khafaji and Iraqi intelligence, and suggest that the regime was making available substantial funds to offer him."[16]

Ritter confirmed on the *The O'Reilly Factor* to host Bill O'Reilly that he *did* receive the bribe. "I turned down the gifts, and I reported it to the FBI when I came back [to the United States]."[17]

Arrogant and sure of himself, McDermott views the world in very black-and-white terms (while decrying people for doing just that)—he and his "progressive" allies are always right, everyone else is always wrong. Friendship with one of Saddam's bagmen wasn't a problem for McDermott, because the bagman was on the side of the anti-American and anti-Bush angels.

Democrats's actions toward the U.S. military and American national defense show an amazing level of contempt coupled with gross negligence. Issues of vital import—issues of life and death— appear to be viewed entirely through a narrow, partisan political prism. When Representative Charlie Rangel (D-NY) introduced a proposal to re-institute a military draft, it wasn't because he wanted to ensure a stronger America in a world of enemies.[18] Charlie Rangel had nothing but politics in mind.

Rangel's purpose was twofold. In the short term, he wanted to embarrass President Bush. The idea was to get the draft issue on television news and, just perhaps, pull President Bush and his team off base—get them to maybe make ill-advised statements regarding military service that could be twisted in an anti-Bush and/or anti-GOP manner. The second, and actually more impor- tant—more sinister—motive was that since this was an officially proposed bill Democrats could use it to scare up votes during the 2004 election.

Democrats, and especially Far Left Democrats like Rangel, remember when Richard Nixon completely pulled the plug on the mass anti-war movement by terminating the draft. Nixon's move was a cynical ploy informed by his correct understanding that the anti-war movement was mostly staffed by slacker college students who were, plain and simple, afraid to do their duty to their coun- try. Once the draft was over, all those young men allegedly pas- sionate for peace became entirely disinterested in the subject. Rangel's draft proposal was a backdoor attempt at reviving the mass anti-war movement of the late 1960s and early 1970s.

With the bill officially before Congress—though with zero chance of passing—various senior Democrats, including current DNC chairman Howard Dean, began hinting to college students that a plan existed to revive the draft after the 2004 election. Anonymous messages on the Internet talked of a secret GOP plan to draft men into the army after Republicans fooled Americans into reelecting them in 2004. Excellent conspiracy theory stuff, and well-targeted towards the audience least likely to be informed on the current state of affairs: college students locked up in the left-wing enclaves of our colleges and universities. The whole program was shot down when the Congressional GOP called for a vote on Rangel's quixotic proposal, and it was speedily defeated—Rangel himself voted against the bill.[19]

Contempt for the military hasn't prevented Democrats from attempting to profit from military affairs. Viewing America as their private patrimony to be spent as they see fit, Democrats have no problem spending vast sums on national defense, provided there is a bit of pork for the Democrats in question.

The Presidio was a very old Army post in San Francisco. When the Cold War ended and America began to close military bases, the Presidio was placed on the chopping block. The Presidio included fifteen hundred acres of some of the most valuable real estate in the world, and local San Francisco residents wanted it turned into a public park. Unfortunately, there wasn't much opportunity in such a proposal for Nancy Pelosi to make political hay.

The end result was that by very hard lobbying, Pelosi managed to get the Presidio designated as America's first for-profit national park. Far Left Pelosi, she of *de-facto* socialist San Francisco, saw to it that when the Presidio transferred from military to civil use, a private entity took it over. Various real estate cronies of Pelosi were prominently represented on the board. While left-wing stalwarts like former San Francisco Mayor Willie Brown wanted to build low-income housing on the site, Pelosi's cronies opted instead for luxury condos.[20] Pelosi's giveaway of the Presidio to her cronies seems to have caused her some trouble even on the Left, though it seems that anti-capitalistic purity is the left-wing motivator here.[21]

There is always something for the left-wing Democrats to be "anti" about as regards the military. Pelosi is just one of scores of senior Democrats on record stating that America doesn't need a ballistic missile defense system.[22] Presumably this is because they trust that the dictators of North Korea and Iran would never dream of using a nuclear weapon against the United States, or against an American ally.

Of course, one might say that San Francisco is a special case; so anti-military are San Franciscans that they rejected making the USS *Iowa* a museum.[23] Faced with the prospect of honoring the thousands of brave Americans who had served on the *Iowa*, the government of San Francisco opted for the purest anti-military course.

The anti-military sentiment in San Francisco reached a level of absurdity worthy of a satirical comedy act when the San Francisco School Board voted to eliminate the Junior Reserve Officers Training (JROTC) program because, as school board member Dan Kelly put it, "The military should be separated from civilian life."[24]

Even outside San Francisco, the anti-military attitude is quite strong in the Democratic Party. As it regards President Bush and the war on terror, there isn't any conspiracy theory too bizarre for left-wing Democrats to believe. Any stroll through the left side of the Internet will show that the Left thinks that President Bush had a hand in the 9/11 attacks; that the war is being fought for oil, Halliburton profits, or the Jews; that bin Laden was allowed to escape so Bush and the GOP would have an issue to bamboozle the American people about; that Saddam's execution was rushed—after three years—in order to prevent his testifying against President Bush.

The thought that President Bush is conducting the war as best he can never enters into the mind of the Left. Another left-wing conviction is that the war is entirely about bin Laden and al-Qaeda. By concentrating on bin Laden and the fact that he's still unaccounted for, the Left mentally takes no responsibility for the larger issues America faces. This certainty that bin Laden is central—and the corresponding assertion that any efforts not directed at bin Laden are wasteful sideshows—is in spite of the fact that as early as October of 2001 both military and civilian commanders stated clearly that bin Laden wasn't the primary target.[25]

On November 19, 2005, there was an incident in the Iraqi town of Haditha. At the end of the day, a large number of Iraqis were dead, including some who appeared to be non-combatants. War is a brutal activity; as Sherman said, it is all Hell. Mistakes are made; innocent people die. But no one outside the participants knew exactly what happened in Haditha. Various accusations were made, and the military began to investigate. Long before any investigation was complete and long before any non-participant could make a determination based on the facts, Congressman Jack Murtha accused the Marines involved of war crimes.

Murtha stated the Marines had killed the Iraqis in Haditha "in cold blood."[26] This is a serious charge to make—it is a war crime, if true. But Murtha simply could not know whether anyone was murdered in Haditha. Why would Murtha, himself a veteran of the Vietnam War, make such a claim? Perhaps because, in the left-wing Democrats' world, this is "supporting the troops."

We can only surmise, of course, but it appeared to be a play for left-wing support for Murtha's prospective run for House majority leader. It is unknown whether Murtha was already convinced of Democratic victory when he made the accusation in April or whether he was just covering his bases just in case. Be that as it may, it worked like a charm for Murtha.

Here was a decorated combat veteran feeding the anti-war, anti-military Left precisely the sort of red meat it craved. Left-wing bloggers exploded with sensationalist stories and hopes for a quick conviction of all involved, including President Bush, for war crimes. The more responsible, though no less left-wing, *Nation* considered Murtha's revelation to be proof that there was a climate of impunity among the American military in Iraq. Murtha was the man of the hour.

After all, it was a stepping stone to power. For Murtha, the Marines were just a prop in a morality play—and, unfortunately, it seems that this is the only purpose Democrats have for the United States military. For Democrats like John Kerry, it is a prop to shore up national security credentials for a presidential run; for other Democrats it is a means of helping others at no cost to themselves (such as our endless mission in the Balkans); for others it is used as a strawman for "I'm such a courageous man for speaking out" sort of actions.

This is not the way Democrats have always been or, indeed, the way all Democrats are today. Once upon a time, Republicans and Democrats vied with each other to demonstrate their love of our military. In today's world, however, when you are talking to a pro-military person, you are most often talking to a Republican, while when you are talking to a Democrat, seven out of ten times you are talking to someone who has contempt for the military. What happened?

The Democrats, as a party, have become so infused with dishonesty—dishonesty about what they believe, what they want to do, etc.—that it has eaten away at their character to the point where they are at one with our enemies when it comes to accusing the United States military of being criminal and/or of being incompetent.

On December 29, 2006, Senator Barak Obama (D-IL)—riding high on a sea of positive media coverage about his prospective presidential bid—sent an e-mail to urging people to contact President Bush about the campaign in Iraq.[27] Obama, like most Democrats, wanted a U.S. withdrawal from Iraq—and, also like most Democrats, he asserted in his e-mail that there was no military solution possible in Iraq. It boggles the mind to try and comprehend that a sitting United States senator who has hopes of becoming the president of the United States asserted that the United States military—more than 1.4 million strong—could not defeat a ragged collection of terrorists in Iraq who probably numbered no more than twenty thousand. If that were true, then we might as well disband our military altogether.

Democrats like to say that while they are opposed to the war (or at least President Bush's conduct of the war), they are in favor of the troops. The endless repetition of this assertion is rather nauseating in light of the manner in which Democratic operatives have repeatedly attempted to disenfranchise military voters, many of whom tend to vote Republican.

The first time there was an overt attempt to suppress military votes on account of their feared GOP bent was during the Florida recount in 2000.

A group of Democratic voters, at the behest of the Gore campaign, filed suit to prevent the counting of twenty-four hundred absentee military ballots on the grounds that they had arrived after the election day.[28] As Bush led Gore by just a few hundred votes, and about 60 percent of those twenty-four hundred ballots were likely Bush votes, eliminating them would result in a President Gore. For the Democrats, disenfranchising men and women on active military service in defense of the right to vote was an insignificant price to pay for getting a Democrat over the finish line.

In 2004, realizing that the presidential election was going to be close and having a hard time finding their way to 270 electoral votes, the Democrats decided to try and make things a little easier for themselves by yet more attempts at suppressing the military vote. The most glaring example of this was in Pennsylvania.

Democratic Governor Ed Rendell noted that twenty-six thousand Pennsylvania military personnel were overseas and determined that nothing as trivial as votes would prevent John Kerry from winning Pennsylvania's twenty-one electoral votes.[29] Ralph Nader's quixotic campaign provided the excuse: When the Pennsylvania Supreme Court ruled that Nader could not be on the Pennsylvania ballot after absentee ballots containing Nader's name had already been sent, Rendell, obviously aware of the Republican leanings of military, refused to support a lawsuit guaranteeing that late replacement absentee ballots would be counted.[30]

The attempts to suppress the votes of the armed forces failed in both 2000 and 2004, but the fact that such attempts were made at all reveals the depths to which the Democrats have sunk.

The Democrats are generous with their statements that they support the troops, but rhetoric and reality don't match. A common talking point among Democratic activists in the 2006 campaign was how many military veterans were running as Democrats for Congress. Depending on whom you listened to, from forty to fifty-three war veterans were running as Democrats for the House in 2006. A great talking point—it looked good in the news cycles, but were the Democrats really interested in getting more veterans in to the House? The facts show they weren't.

In the Colorado 6th district race, Democrat veteran Bill Winter squared off with incumbent Republican Tom Tancredo. Winter managed to raise $801,000 in his losing bid—outspent by Trancredo by more than two to one. As any political observer will tell you, it is mighty difficult to beat an incumbent and it takes a lot of resources. While $801,000 sounds like a lot, it was less than Pelosi spent on her first campaign running as an ultra liberal in ultra liberal San Francisco against neglible opposition. Meanwhile, over in the 3rd district, Democrat John Salazar crushed his Republican opponent by 61 percent to 31 percent after spending more than $2 million dollars on his campaign. It doesn't seem that Salazar had strong opposition.

More than half of Salazar's funds came from PACs, while in Winter's case he only received 18 percent of his money from PACs.[31] A Democratic party determined to actually have military members in the House would have given some of Salazar's PAC money to Winter. But that wasn't the point of having military veterans run—the point, and the only point, was to have a talking point to use against Republicans.

The contemptible use to which Democrats put veterans in 2006 is just part of the larger issue of Democratic contempt for our military. One doesn't say they support the cops, but don't support them stopping crime and yet Democrats are trying to get everyone to believe that they support the troops, but don't support what the troops are doing. In fact, to listen to Democratic rhetoric, our troops are held to be either mental incompetents or bloodthirsty savages.

CHAPTER SEVEN

ABRAMOFF DEMOCRATS

"There's no evidence that I've seen that Jack Abramoff directed any contributions to Democrats. ... The Democrats are not involved in this."

—Howard Dean[1]

AMONG THE MANY things Democrats painted as part of the alleged Republican "culture of corruption" was former Majority Leader DeLay's "K Street Project." While we might wish to think a level playing field exists in politics, money generally flows to power. What use is it to spread the cash around the losers of the last election? Other than hedging bets about the future, not much.

During the decades of Democratic dominance in Congress, most donations flowed to the Democratic Party. After all, if you wanted a bill pushed, you talked to the relevant Democratic committee chairman. The ranking Republican could be helpful—especially when a Republican held the White House—but, on the whole, you really wanted the Democrats.

When Republicans roared—mostly unexpectedly—into Congressional power in the 1994 elections, it took a while for old habits to die. To put it bluntly, a majority of donations still flowed to the defeated Democrats. Perhaps this was understandable at first—the GOP might lose the next election, and if you were a lobbyist, you certainly didn't want Democrats taking vengeance on you. But the imbalance towards the losers could not long endure, and DeLay's K Street Project was established to bring a bit of reality to the world of politics.

To hear the Democrats talk about it, the K Street Project meant DeLay and the Republicans going door-to-door soliciting bribes. Like the famed scene in *Casablanca* where Capt. Renault closes down Rick's Cafe Americain because he is "shocked, *shocked*" to find gambling going on...right before he collects his winnings, Democrats were shocked, *shocked* to find that the Republican Party was getting donations the Democrats felt entitled to. Illustrative of the Democrats' hypocrisy is the fact that as they complained about Republican efforts on K Street, senior Democrats like Democratic Whip Steny Hoyer (D-MD) were also trolling K Street for campaign cash.[2]

How crowded would the store be if there were only one in town and everything was sold there? In large measure, this is what Washington, D.C., has become—the only store in town, and everything is for sale. You can't find any aspect of American life which does not have a federal finger stuck into it. Sometimes the finger is hardly noticeable, other times it is overwhelming, but there it is, all the time. If you want the finger to move in a way beneficial to you, you have to go to Washington. And what do you do if your busy schedule prevents you from prowling the halls of Congress looking for governmental assistance? You hire a lobbyist.

The word "lobbyist" has, deservedly, earned an unsavory conotation. There is something vaguely un-American about well-paid pitchmen going to Washington to grease representatives in favor of a person or group. Our legislative branch is supposed to represent the general will of the people, not the will of well-connected special pleaders. Still, there is a strong dose of rationality behind it—what sense could 535 representatives and senators make of three hundred million voices shouting at them? Lobbying might be evil—but it is a necessary one.

Lobbyists, as a class, might be nefarious, but each of us probably has some lobby we like. Gun owners love lobbyists from the National Rifle Association, while most NRA members probably dislike, sight unseen, most lobbyists. As a rule, people who send their pleaders to Congress don't consider their guys to be evil, but are sure that all lobbyists are evil. Another way to think of it is that one man's advocate for truth, justice, and the American way is another man's lobbyist for greedy "corporate Amerika" out to destroy all that is good in the world.

Jack Abramoff has, by all accounts, been a lobbyist's lobbyist. "Connected" doesn't even begin to describe the man. Born in Atlantic City, New Jersey, in 1958 but moving to Beverly Hills, California at the age of ten, Abramoff took early to politics. He was a college organizer in Massachusetts—of all places—for Ronald Reagan's 1980 presidential campaign. From there, things took off for Abramoff. To read a list of people connected to Abramoff is to read a list of the heavyweights in American government for the past quarter-century. And while Abramoff has had a lot to do with Republicans, Abramoff's influence has crossed party and ideological lines quite often.

A lobbyist trades on his perceived access to the movers and shakers. Thus, a lobbyist might have his own ideological bent, but few would refuse to give money to or wine and dine members of the other side of the aisle in order to achieve what they want. A lobbyist will give money to anyone to bend the ear of those he thinks can help his client. And yet Democrats like Harry Reid, Nancy Pelosi, and Howard Dean are insistent that the Abramoff scandal was purely Republican and that the problems with corrupt lobbyists do not extend beyond the Republican Party.

Abramoff has run afoul of many state and federal laws, has pleaded guilty and is now serving time in jail. The house of cards has indeed collapsed for the one-time super lobbyist. The crux of the matter for Abramoff is some allegedly illegal deals involving a floating casino and the bilking of Indian tribes via fraudulent lobbying activities.

Aside from lurid rumor, there is no evidence of any Republican Party member or leader engaging in illegal activity along with Abramoff, but Abramoff's Republican connections are highly touted in Democratic circles. Taking donations from a man, even if he turns out to be dirty, does not constitute illegal or immoral behavior. But, then again, the morality of it all is hardly the point here—Democrats want corruption issues to haunt Republicans, and Abramoff's GOP connections are too good a scandal to pass up.

The Abramoff scandal undoubtedly hurt Republicans in the 2006 elections. Tom DeLay was forced into retirement, and his seat in the House went to a Democrat. Senator Conrad Burns, once considered a shoo-in for reelection, was defeated in Montana, partly due to his receiving contributions from Jack Abramoff, his associates, and his tribal clients. The only lawmaker to actually confess to wrongdoing in the Abramoff scandal was Rep. Bob Ney of Ohio.

Republicans recognize the fallibility of their fellow Republicans. They know that men and women are no angels, and when a Republican runs afoul of the law or morality, Republicans expect that person will pay the just price for their failures, and if that means losing office and winding up in jail, so be it. Democrats may have seen Bob Ney's guilty plea as a victory for them, but the Republican Party ultimately benefited by ridding itself of one of its members who had gone wrong. But even the Democrats' attacks on Bob Ney were hypocritical in nature.

In October 2005, House Minority Leader Nancy Pelosi called for an investigation of Bob Ney because of a *Washington Post* story "showing a relationship between Jack Abramoff, Congressman Ney and a contract that was awarded."[3]

Around the same time Pelosi called for an investigation into Bob Ney's activities, a story in *The Hill* revealed a relationship between Jack Abramoff, Senator Tom Harkin (D-IA), and two fundraisers that were not appropriately disclosed to the FEC.[4] But did she call for an investigation into Tom Harkin's Abramoff connection because of that story? Of course not. Pelosi turned an evil eye on Ney, but a blind eye on her fellow Democrats.

Appearing on NBC's *Today Show* on January 26, 2006, DNC Chairman Howard Dean declared unequivocally that "not one dime of Jack Abramoff's money ever went to any Democrat," and challenged anyone to look at FEC reports.[5]

A few days later Chris Wallace asked Dean during his appearance on *Fox News Sunday* what he would say if it came out that Democrats had written letters on behalf of Abramoff's tribal clients.[6] Dean told Wallace "That's a big problem, and those Democrats are in trouble, and they should be in trouble, and our party, if the American people will put us back in power in '06, we will have on the president's desk things that outlaw all those kinds of behaviors." But Dean's words hardly mean the Democratic Party would be tough on Democrats who took actions on behalf Abramoff's clients.

Dean stoutly asserted that there were no such Democrats. "No Democrat delivered anything and there's no accusation and no investigation that any Democrat ever delivered anything to Jack Abramoff, and that's not true of the Republicans."

But those kinds of behaviors were in fact very common with Democrats and Abramoff clients.

On January 23, 2003, a letter went to the Interior Department on behalf of the Saginaw tribe. Both senators from Michigan, Senator Stabenow and Senator Carl Levin, contributed to this letter. Stabenow had previously received a $2,000 donation from the Saginaw back in March 2002 and received another $2,000 donation from the tribe six months after her letter. Levin received smaller donations from the Saginaw and Abramoff's firm in 2001 and 2002.[7]

Senator John Breaux of Louisiana wrote his own letter on behalf of the Coushatta Indian tribe. Five days later the Coushattas donated $1,000 to his campaign and another $10,000 to his library fund. Senator Mary Landrieu sent a letter a few days after Senator Breaux on behalf of the tribe and received a $2,000 donation to her campaign the very same day and another $5,000 by the end of the month. Her letter on the tribe's behalf ultimately got at least $24,000 to her campaign coffers by the end of the year.

In 2003, Senator Tom Harkin wrote at least three letters to the Bush administration on behalf of the Sac & Fox tribe, for which he received input from Michael D. Smith of Abramoff's lobbying team. Harkin's letters coincided with donations to his campaign and political action committee from Smith and his tribal clients.[8]

In addition to the letters written on behalf of Abramoff's tribal clients and the donations he received as a result, Harkin held two fundraisers in Jack Abramoff's skybox: a campaign fundraiser in the summer of 2002 and an event in December 2003 for Harkin's political action committee, To Organize a Majority. Harkin failed to report these fundraisers until the fall of 2005, following an internal audit.[9] Such in-kind donations are supposed to be reported to the FEC in monthly or quarterly reports.

Senators Levin and Stabenow contributed to yet another letter to the Interior Department on behalf of the Saginaw dated July 14, 2003. While defending her actions on the basis that the Saginaw tribe is based in her home state, Stabenow altered FEC reports from 2002 and 2003 that showed she'd receive $4,000 from the Saginaw tribe's legislative director, Christopher Petras, who worked closely with Jack Abramoff. *The Hill* reported that Stabenow "amended her reports to show that the contributions came from the tribe itself and not Petras."[10]

Montana Senator Max Baucus, the ranking Democrat on the Senate Finance Committee, used Abramoff's skybox in March 2001 and also never reported it. He received nearly $19,000 in donations from Abramoff's clients.[11]

Nancy Pelosi also received contributions from Abramoff's tribal clients. The Agua Caliente Band of Cahuilla Indians gave her $1,000 in August 14, 2002, and the Saginaw tribe donated $2,000 on November 19, 2003, according to FEC records.

While Abramoff's connections to Democratic and Republican power players have caused many a political headache, the only demands by leaders of the Democratic Party were for *Republicans* to return Abramoff-connected donations. But Abramoff and his clients didn't donate only to Republicans. As we have already seen, many Democrats also received such donations.

All told, since 1999, Jack Abramoff or associates have donated about $4.4 million, 66 percent of which went to Republicans, 34 percent to Democrats.[12] This spreading of the wealth reflects a normal mix of lobbyists' donations between majority and minority parties over the past six years and proves that the scandals involving Abramoff involved both political parties.

Being in the minority party didn't stop Democrats from getting donations from Abramoff's clients or going on trips with him. In 1997, Abramoff led a Congressional delegation to Pakistan that was attended by New York Democrat Rep. Michael McNulty.[13]

Records show that Abramoff also paid expenses for another trip that year to the Northern Marianas Islands (an American territory in the western Pacific), for which Abramoff lobbied. Participants included two of Tom DeLay's aides, as well as Mississippi Democrat Rep. Bennie Thompson, and Rep. James Clyburn, of South Carolina.[14] In yet another bit of irony, Clyburn was tapped by Nancy Pelosi to chair the Democrats' so called Clean House Task Force. Thompson's and Clyburn's travel expenses came out to about $5,000 each.

Abramoff was lobbying not on behalf of the Northern Marianas Island, but on behalf of textile interests located on those islands. While the islands are U.S. territory and the people who live there are U.S. citizens, the self-governing nature of the commonwealth exempts it from many U.S. laws, including minimum wage laws. This has been a source of conflict as unionized textile workers in the United States have difficulty competing with the Marianas textile workers, who make much lower wages. As is usual in such disputes, the textile companies have been called "sweatshops" by critics, who make endless demands to force people six thousand miles from the United States to act as if they were in Akron, Ohio.

On March 10, 2006, Byron York in *National Review Online* revealed that Willie Tan—a major Marianas textile manufacturer—and his family had donated $6,000 to Friends of Hillary, one of Hillary Clinton's PACs.[15] Willie Tan had hired Jack Abramoff to lobby against efforts to force his businesses to comply with U.S. wage laws.

But this was not the first time Hillary Clinton received money from the alleged "sweatshops" of the Northern Marianas Islands. In 1995, Hillary attended the largest fundraiser in Marianas history, as a result of which Marianas textile interests donated $17,500 to the Democratic National Committee.

That wasn't the end of the largesse from the Marianas and its textile magnates—who donated $132,000 for the 1996 Clinton-Gore reelection effort and $510,000 in "soft money" contributions for the Democratic National Committee. All of this money flowing from the tiny Marianas made it, *per capita*, the largest donor to the Democrats in the United States.

Rep. Gregory Meeks took a 2002 trip to Malaysia paid for by a group connected to Jack Abramoff. Rep. Meeks "visited Kuala Lumpur on a fact-finding mission involving terrorism and trade issues." Also on the trip were two members of Greenberg Traurig, for which Jack Abramoff had lobbied since 2001. The Institute of Strategic and International Studies, a Malaysian think tank believed to receive some funding from the Malaysian government,[16] also sponsored the trip.

Democrats have enjoyed many perks thanks to Jack Abramoff, but that doesn't stop them from denying connections to him.

Like Senators Harkin and Baucus, Senator Byron Dorgan of North Dakota held a fundraiser in Abramoff's skybox in 2001. And like Senators Harkin and Baucus, Dorgan failed to disclose the fundraiser to the FEC. Dorgan claims he did not know Abramoff. But Dorgan's connections to Abramoff don't end there. Dorgan also received contributions arranged by Abramoff in 2002 after Dorgan "took action[s] favorable to Abramoff's tribal clients."[17]

According to a lawyer for the Louisiana Coushatta Indians, Abramoff is responsible for a $5,000 donation to Dorgan's political action committee a mere three weeks after Dorgan "urged fellow senators to fund a tribal school program Abramoff's clients wanted to use."[18] Dorgan would, in the end, receive $20,000 in donations from Abramoff's firm and tribal clients.

Dorgan also received at least $11,500 in donations from Michael D. Smith, a partner of Abramoff representing the Mashpee Wampanoag tribe of Massachusetts, for arranging congressional help for the tribe. Investigators also have information suggesting that Dorgan and his staff "may have had more than twenty contacts with Abramoff's lobbying team involving the Marianas tribes and other clients over the years."[19]

Dorgan's connections to Abramoff are particularly interesting—Dorgan is the vice chairman of the Senate Indian Affairs Committee, which led the investigation in Jack Abramoff's questionable dealings with the Indian tribes.

Despite Dorgan's connections to Abramoff, he refused to recuse himself from the investigation of Abramoff's activities, even though lawmakers are required to avoid any appearance of a conflict of interest in performing official duties and accepting donations.[20] Though he claims there's no conflict of interest, Dorgan returned a total of $67,000 he received from Abramoff's tribal clients after several *Associated Press* reports on the donations were published.[21]

Unlike Dorgan and Baucus, Rep. Charlie Rangel of New York refused to return donations he received from Abramoff's tribal clients. Between 1997 and 2005, Rangel received thousands of dollars in donations to his political action committee from Abramoff's tribal clients. The Agua Caliente Band of Cahuilla Indians donated $12,000 and the Mississippi Band of Choctaw Indians donated

$35,000.[22] The Cahuilla Indians also reportedly donated $9,000 to Rangel's reelection campaign.[23]

Rangel claimed there was no connection between the tribal donations he received and Jack Abramoff; however, he did receive $2,000 from Abramoff's firm, Greenberg Traurig. That contribution, small in comparison to the contributions from Abramoff's clients, was a small sacrifice to make in order to give the appearance of sincerity. Rangel donated that small sum to the Boys Choir of Harlem, because that donation "may have been tainted by Abramoff's involvement with the firm." The larger sums of cash remain in his coffers. According to the Center for Responsive Politics, Rangel received more Abramoff-connected donations than either Bob Ney or Tom DeLay.[24]

No Democrat has collected more donations from Abramoff's tribal clients than Rep. Patrick Kennedy of Rhode Island, who received $42,500[25] over a period of five years.[26] The *Washington Post* published a graphic titled "How Abramoff Spread the Wealth" on December 12, 2005, which actually put the amount of Abramoff-connected contributions to Kennedy at $131,000 between 1999 and 2004.[27] Like several others in his party, Kennedy did not take well to the revelation and responded with a terse, one-paragraph letter to the editor declaring that he had no ties to Jack Abramoff. Indeed, Mr. Kennedy left the impression that he was victimized by Abramoff, along with the tribes.[28]

One of the problems with tracking who got what from Abramoff and his clients is the fact that so many people got so much. Taking the case of Patrick Kennedy as an example: Open Secrets, the online source for tracking political contributions, says that Kennedy received $31,000 of Abramoff-connected money, while the *Associated Press* reported the amount as $42,500.

Part of the problem is how money is classified. Abramoff was so connected with so many different lobbying enterprises that untangling the web may, in the end, prove impossible. The web is so tortured that Sean Richardson, Rep. Kennedy's chief of staff, felt he could boldly claim not a single penny of Kennedy's donations had anything to do with Jack Abramoff.

Democrats who don't return their Abramoff-connected donations justify their decision by claiming that they never met

Abramoff and/or never received *personal* donations from him. Representative Kennedy, claiming to have his own personal relationship with Indian tribes, decided to keep donations from Abramoff's clients.

Senator Patty Murray from Washington—famous for opining that Osama bin Laden is supported because he provides day care—received $40,980 from Abramoff's tribal clients.'[29] This, it should be noted, exceeds by more than $10,000 the amount of Abramoff money Tom DeLay received. Nevertheless, Murray said it would "taint" the tribes to return the contributions, so she selflessly decided to keep the $40,980 and allow only herself be tainted by the cash.[30] A tough sacrifice to make.

Senator Patrick Leahy, the ranking Democrat on the judiciary committee, also received money from Jack Abramoff's clients and associates. Leahy received thousands of dollars from attorneys from Greenberg Traurig, as well as Preston, Gates, Ellis, Meeds and Rouvelas. Leahy also received $1,000 from another Abramoff tribal client, the Saginaw Chippewa.[31]

Leahy's connections don't end there. In 2003, Leahy's campaign received donations from lobbyist Michael D. Smith and Edward Ayoob, the former aide to Harry Reid, both of whom worked with Abramoff.[32] When the *Vermont Guardian* reported this connection, Leahy's chief of staff, Ed Pagano, was eager to dismiss it. "Jack Abramoff has been a top Republican operative, a favored Republican lobbyist, and a Bush campaign 'Pioneer' who plied his trade deep in the heart of the Republican inner circle."[33] Deep in the heart of the Democratic inner circle, too, it would seem.

Since 2002, Ayoob has donated over $55,000 to Democrats and their political action committees.[34] Even with this massive flow of Abramoff money to Democrats, Bob Casey, Jr. (D-PA)—trying to achieve the moral high ground in his battle for Rick Santorum's (R-PA) senate seat—had the nerve to criticize Senator Santorum for not immediately returning contributions he received from Abramoff's clients. Santorum donated the tribal contributions to charity "because his campaign said it was virtually impossible to determine whether the money was related to Mr. Abramoff's lobbying activities."[35]

Despite Casey's grandstanding, he refused to return contributions he received from Smith and Ayoob. While the donations were made *after* Abramoff resigned from the firm, the Santorum campaign correctly called it a double standard. "Both of these gentlemen were part of Abramoff's team, and there are reports of their close connections with Abramoff... For Casey to not contribute these contributions to charity or return them is completely hypocritical," said Santorum campaign spokeswoman Virginia Davis.

Even Howard Dean can't deny ties to Abramoff. William Tate, writing at the *American Thinker*, reported that during his failed presidential campaign, Dean received a $1,000 donation from Greenberg Traurig lobbyist Ronald Platt, a member of Abramoff's lobbying team, on June 30, 2003. Tate noted, "[a]t that time, lobbyist disclosure forms show Platt as working with Abramoff on two of the controversial tribal accounts: the Coushatta Tribe of Louisiana, and the Chitimacha Tribe of Louisiana. The forms show that Platt worked on a third controversial tribal account, the Sandia Pueblo, with other Abramoff Team members but not Abramoff."[36]

In some ways, it is easier to list the Democrats Abramoff *didn't* orchestrate donations to. But, for clarity, we will list the Democrats who have received donations from members of Team Abramoff:

> Democrat Senators Clinton, Kerry, Daschle, Boxer, Baucus, Bayh, Breaux, Cantwell, Carnahan, Cleland, Conrad, Dodd, Dorgan, Feingold, Harkin, Hollings, Johnson (Tim), Landrieu, Leahy, Lieberman, Lincoln, Mikulski, Murray, Nelson, Pryor, Reed, Rockefeller, and Torricelli—who left the Senate in disgrace under the cloud of his own campaign finance scandal—as well as the Democratic Senate Majority Fund, a plethora of Democratic congressmen, and PACs that distributed funds across the Democratic Party landscape.[37]

According to Tate, each individual lobbyist in Team Abramoff donated exclusively to one political party, and during the time period Abramoff worked at Greenberg Traurig, seven of the lobbyists donated $265,203 to Democrats and nine of the lobbyists gave $255,315 to Republicans. "The numbers are so close," wrote Tate, "that one can't help but speculate that it could well be the result of forethought, a concerted effort to spread influence in both parties."[38]

It is little known to the public, thanks to some apparent MSM code of silence, that Team Abramoff members not only donated to Democrats, but they also *worked* for Democrats. Michael Smith worked for the Gore-Lieberman 2000 campaign. He also "distributed $168,000 to Democratic candidates through his Winning Margins PAC from 2001-2004, the closest reporting period to the time Abramoff was at Greenberg Traurig, according to federal records." Smith's personal donations to Democrats rival the personal donations to Republicans from Abramoff. Mr. Smith goes to Washington, indeed—but he isn't the only one, not by a long shot.

Among the Abramoff confederates who worked for the Democratic side of the aisle are: Edward Ayoob, a former aide to Senator Harry Reid; Amy Berger, former aide to Senator John D. Rockefeller (D-WV); Diane Blagman, former chief of staff to Rep. Bob Carr (D-MI); Shana Tesler Hook, a former Clinton White House official; Ronald L. Platt, a former aide to the late Sen. Lloyd M. Bentsen (D-TX); Stephanie Leger Short, an aide to former Sen. John Breaux (D-LA); and Alan Slomowitz, an aide to former Rep. Robert A. Borski (D-PA).

And we would be remiss if we didn't mention some rather substantial donations to the Democratic Senatorial Campaign Committee ($423,000) and the Democratic Congressional Campaign Committee ($354,000); these amounts, as it turns out, are larger than the amount donated to the Republican National Committee.[39]

After hearing all of this, what does the Abramoff scandal really tell us? That our politics are wide open to influence peddlers. The crux of the problem is the amount of power Washington has gained over everyday life in America.

The vilification of lobbyists, and the influence they exerted on Republicans, may have been an effective campaign theme for the Democrats—especially in light of the Abramoff scandal. But, in early fall of 2006, as the elections drew closer and the prospects of their taking over at least one House seemed inevitable, *Roll Call* reported that House Democratic leaders wasted no time in courting Democratic lobbyists and special interests to help House Democrats "close the deal."[40]

For all their rhetoric about the evils of lobbyists, common sense would lead us to believe that Democrats would have taken the road less traveled, but in fact, they took road that leads to K Street.

With power comes money. For some who have reached a high station in life, it isn't enough to be rich; they have to be kowtowed to by our political system. The greatest exemplar of a rich man confusing his money with the right to wield power is George Soros—the billionaire financial shark who has set himself up as the money-bags of every anti-American and anti-Republican group there is in the United States. Money flows to Washington in an effort to move the political system this way or that, and with money comes temptation. There is so much temptation that even honest men and women often get tangled up in webs of contributions and kickbacks.

This does not mean that anyone who has lunch with a lobbyist or takes a lobbyist-sponsored donation is guilty. But with the confluence of money and power, many people do get caught up in the system and appear guilty when they are not. On the other hand, many of those who are working the system for personal profit are able to shield themselves from consequences by *appearing* to keep everything legal.

Donations made by Abramoff personally were perfectly legal and above-board. Abramoff got himself into trouble based upon things he did to or with his clients: those he was lobbying on behalf of. And simply because Abramoff is a Republican, Democrats with the avid help of the liberal mainstream media worked this up into the scandal of all scandals. Fortunately for the Democrats, their connections to Abramoff went largely unreported during the 2006 campaign season.

For Democrats to try and paint this as a Republican-only scandal—especially with the Democrats' massive connections to Abramoff—is absurd and does a great disservice to our nation as a whole. As we've seen, Abramoff "plied his trade" deep into the Democratic Party as well as the GOP. The entire nation is affected when lobbyists corrupt our political system. To run a campaign of "evil Republican crooks" might make Democrats feel better, but it doesn't get to the heart of the problem.

We need to reform our way of lobbying. It is a pity that the Democrats, in their desperate desire for an anti-GOP club, have ignored their own taint and prevented a free and fair debate about how we fix the system Serious men and women will have to work out an equitable way to ensure that corruption is minimized while people and groups are still able to get their message across to elected officials. The worry is that the Democrats will destroy the works so badly that it will prove impossible for common sense and good will to have their way.

As a final note on the subject, it was reported on November 11, 2006, by *Bloomberg* that Democratic lobbyists "relish" the fact that they are now part of the power elite in Washington.[41] These lobbyists certainly would be happy—after all, the dean of the Democratic lobbyists, Thomas Boggs, has known Nancy Pelosi since they were four years old. Boggs was also once the classmate of Pelosi's husband.

That should make getting access to power pretty easy.

CHAPTER EIGHT

FAMILY HIRING & NEPOTISM

"The opportunity to build a better future starts with a good job."

—2004 Democratic Party Platform[1]

AFTER WEEKS of ethics accusations from Democrats, Tom De-Lay came under fire again when the *New York Times* reported on April 5, 2005, that Tom DeLay's political action committee and reelection campaigns paid his wife Christine DeLay and his daughter Dani DeLay Ferro over $500,000 since 2001.

According to the *New York Times*, advocacy groups charged that the payments DeLay's family members received were "unusually generous," and "should be the focus of new scrutiny of [DeLay]."[2] However, Mrs. DeLay and Mrs. Ferro were paid $4,000 and $3,700 respectively in the month of March, which was typical of their monthly payments through the previous two years. DeLay blasted the report and accused the media of trying to embarrass him.

JESSE JACKSON, JR.

The son of the famed civil rights leader who learned how to play the race card to shake down corporations for "donations" to his various causes, Jesse Jackson, Jr. is a Congressman from Illinois. Family connections can make quite a difference—it isn't too often that a thirty-year-old running for his first political office gets donations from Johnnie Cochran, Bill Cosby, and Maya Angelou.[3] For Jesse Jackson, Jr., however, it was just par for the course.

All parents hope for a better future for their children, so it is natural that the elder Jackson wouldn't want his son to butter his bread using shakedown tactics. In his position as an elected official, it wouldn't be proper for Jackson, Jr. to rabble-rouse outside corporate headquarters, but it is hard to have lived the lifestyle of the rich and famous from the proceeds of your father's shenanigans and then live quietly off a House member's relatively small income.[4]

House rules prohibit members from having spouses or relatives on their Congressional payroll. But in 2001, Jesse Jackson Jr. went to the Federal Elections Commission when he wanted to hire his wife as a campaign consultant. The FEC ruled that it was appropriate for a candidate to pay salaries to families as long as they were paid fair market value for actually performing campaign related services.

Who decides what "fair market value" is remains unclear. But Jackson gets the big donations, so he can add to his family income without actually looking like he is adding to his personal income.

In the 2006 election cycle, Jackson raised $1 million, spent $616,000, and ended the cycle with $1.2 million on hand.[5] With that amount of cash floating around, "fair value" can be quite high and hardly make a dent in the campaign chest.

Given that the younger Jackson got approval to pay his family members from campaign funds, entering politics has made him a functional millionaire. He certainly couldn't be raising those vast sums of money to win campaigns: he easily won reelection in 2006 with nearly 79 percent of the vote. He may not need vast amounts of cash to win reelection, but having a few thousand dollars extra in his campaign chest certainly has come in handy for paying his wife to work on his finance committee.[6]

FORTNEY "PETE" STARK

The Oakland area of California has a long-held reputation for roughness. In contrast to the more civilized city of San Francisco across the Bay, Oakland comes across as brash to those who love it, rude to those who don't. It is, after all, the home of the Black Panthers and the Oakland Raiders; two groups not noted for being invited to tea parties.

California representative. Fortney "Pete" Stark represents Oakland and other parts of the Bay Area in the House of Representatives. He's a colorful man, but quite in tune with Oakland, it would seem. Back in 2003, during a session of the House Ways and Means Committee, Stark apparently did not like the way things were going and went off into a verbal tirade—using homophobic terminology and actually challenging Representative Scott McInnis (R-CO) to a fight.[7]

That is the rough and tumble world of politics. In other areas, Pete Stark is gentle as a lamb and quite solicitous of the wellbeing of others. Especially when they are related to him. While putting himself forward as the defender of the little guy and the scourge of Republican special interests, Stark employed his wife Deborah Stark as a campaign consultant earning $2,400 per month.[8]

JIM COSTA

First-term congressmen are traditionally at their most vulnerable when they seek reelection, and as California Republican Jim Costa won with only 53 percent of the vote in 2004, he was expecting a fight in the 20th district in 2006.

Given this, it is no surprise that Costa raised nearly $900,000 for his reelection bid. Back during that 2004 campaign, Costa's cousin made $45,000 as Costa's "co-campaign manager," so Costa knew how expensive seeking office can be.[9]

Perhaps Costa just wants to make certain that, come what may, at least someone benefitted from his political career. In the end, there was no risk for Costa—he ran unopposed in 2006 (a Republican made a minor effort to challenge him in the spring of 2006, but as he only raised $6,333, his campaign never got to the general election).

LINCOLN DAVIS

Lincoln Davis (D-TN) currently represents Tennessee's 4th district in the House of Representatives. On his Web site, Davis asserts that he is working hard to improve job opportunities for the people of his district. Reading it, you get the impression that he'll leave no stone unturned to bring opportunity to the 4th district.

Given that Davis is the owner of a construction business, citizens should expect him to concentrate on profitable private enterprise to increase employment.

The business was private—very private, as it turns out. So private that only family members could be brought in. Davis hired both his sister-in-law and his daughter for his campaign. His sister-in-law has served as his campaign treasurer since 1994, and his daughter worked as his campaign coordinator in the last half of 2004.[10]

TIM BISHOP

Fairly new to politics, Rep. Tim Bishop of Long Island seems to have learned quickly what keeps politicians in office. On his Web site, he brags that he's brought $65 million in federal funding home to his district.

Bishop also brought home to his daughter Molly a nice job as his campaign finance director. Molly was paid $87,828 in salary and travel expenses between 2004 and 2005.[11] Not bad for a part time job. Naturally, Bishop saw nothing wrong with this, and he actually has a good record of finding jobs for family members. Bishop, as the former provost of Southampton College "employed a total of ten members of his extended family at the East End campus, including his wife."[12]

Bishop's fellow Long Island Democrat Rep. Steve Israel also hired family, paying his seventeen-year-old daughter $4,005 to lick stamps and stuff envelopes.[13]

HOWARD BERMAN

Democratic Rep. Howard L. Berman of California has whom he calls "one of the most talented campaign strategists" as a longtime consultant: his brother. Berman paid $205,500 to two firms headed by his brother Michael Berman.[14]

One can only wonder how many other Democrats happen to be related to "the most talented" people around. Berman, a former member of the House ethics committee, noted, "You're not supposed to use your campaign funds for personal expenses or matters unrelated to politics. The test is what kind of work they are performing. I'm getting one of the most talented campaign strategists at a pretty good price. Out on the commercial marketplace, my brother makes a lot more money."[15]

DICK GEPHARDT

Former Rep. Dick Gephardt might have announced his retirement from Congress with high hopes of actually gaining the Democrats'

2004 presidential nomination, but by the time early 2004 came around, it was clear that Gephardt's chances were in line with those of a snowball in the Sahara. Still, it wasn't a complete loss: Dick Gephardt's daughter, Chrissy Gephardt, was paid $3,500 a month working full time for her father's presidential campaign.

JOE LIEBERMAN

Senator Joe Lieberman's two eldest children, Matt and Rebecca, worked on their father's failed 2004 presidential campaign as fundraisers and were paid six-figure salaries. The campaign defended the Lieberman children, arguing that they were important to fundraising efforts.[16]

JOHN KERRY

Senator John Kerry also brought his daughters, Alexandra and Vanessa Kerry, on the campaign trail. Rumor has it that to Kerry campaign insiders, the girls were more of a liability than an asset to the campaign. Alexandra, a filmmaker, had a five-person entourage that followed her everywhere, racking up expenses for the campaign, despite the fact that "she didn't exactly do anything," according to one Kerry confidant.[17]

BARBARA BOXER

During the 2002 campaign cycle, California Senator Barbara Boxer funneled nearly $119,000 in fundraising consulting fees from her political action committee, PAC For A Change, to Douglas Boxer & Associates. As the name implies, this consulting firm is run by her son. It must be presumed Pelosi was satisfied with her son's work, as she tossed another $25,000 in consulting fees his way during the 2004 cycle,[18] and $85,000 more during the 2006 election cycle.[19]

MAXINE WATERS

When it comes to using one's position to help family, few can compare to California Rep. Maxine Waters. Waters, originally a poor girl from Missouri, perhaps more than anyone has learned how financially beneficial a House seat can be.

Most famed for her advocacy of the theory that the CIA started the "crack" cocaine epidemic as a deliberate plot to harm African-Americans, Waters has spent her whole career as a provocative political nuisance, using her political influence to benefit family members. Waters' family seems to have made over $1 million dollars between 1996 and 2004 "by doing business with companies, candidates and causes that the influential congresswoman has helped."[20]

Her daughter, Karen Waters, "has charged candidates for spots on her mother's 'slate mailer,' a sample ballot that many voters in South Los Angeles use to guide their choices." For candidates to guarantee themselves a spot on Waters' sample ballot, they first need "to get her endorsement."[21] According to the candidates, they then "received a call from Karen Waters telling them the cost of advertising it."[22] Karen *claimed* she did not consult her mother when deciding on the fee.

Karen's brother, Edward Waters, made about $115,000 for his involvement in the L.A. Vote slate mailer.[23] Edward, a high school basketball coach, allegedly also works as a political consultant and was paid $4,129 in 2004 by his mother's campaign.[24]

The L.A. Vote mailer has benefited the Waters children in many ways, including consulting work with candidates who "earned" the Congresswoman's endorsement by paying to get put on the mailer.

Karen Waters has also been paid by a nonprofit organization she and her mother both set up, which receives funding from special interests aided by Rep. Waters.

Maxine Waters' husband, Sidney Williams, has gotten a piece of the action, too. The congresswoman's husband "was paid nearly $500,000 for consulting work with Siebert, Brandford Shank and Co., a municipal bond company, and with politicians whom his wife supports."[25]

Melanie Sloan of Citizens for Responsibility and Ethics in Washington, a liberal watchdog group, says, "It looks like congresswoman Waters is using her position to financially benefit her family members, and that is at the very least unethical." [26]

This is the sort of thing you can get away with when you represent a highly gerrymandered House district. As is common for California Democrats, Waters represents a district with relatively few voters. Taking advantage of what turns out to be a loophole in the United States Constituiton (which requires that all House members represent roughly the same number of persons), the raw number of people of her district is as high as any other, but the number of actual voters is only about two-thirds that of districts held by Republican House members from California. Having fewer voters to answer to gives Waters all the time she needs to both spin her tinfoil hat conspiracy theories and ensure her family members live very high indeed.

JOHN MURTHA

Rep. John Murtha, who made headlines in November 2005 for advocating a cut and run policy from Iraq within six months, did not make the front pages for his close ties to his brother's lobbying firm, KSA Consulting, which several Republicans believe merit an investigation by the House Ethics Committee.

The *Los Angeles Times* reported on June 13, 2005 that at least ten companies KSA Consulting lobbied for received over $20 million in funding in the FY2005 defense appropriations. KSA directly lobbied Rep. Murtha's office on behalf of seven companies and employs a former longtime aide to Murtha.[27]

Murtha, at the request of Nancy Pelosi, also urged Navy officials to transfer the Hunters Point Naval Shipyard to the city of San Francisco when Pelosi's nephew was a top executive at the company that owned the rights to the land (see Chapter One).

In response to queries about this rather sweet deal, Pelosi's spokeswoman naturally said there was nothing improper about the arrangement, calling the allegations of impropriety "absolutely ludicrous, and an attempt to divert from the real issue that Mr. Murtha is attempting to engage in debate on a critically important topic—U.S. policy in Iraq. The real story here is the Republican strategy to try to discredit Congressman Murtha."[28] But Murtha's ethical lapses cannot be written off as Republican smears. Even some Democrats conceded at the time that an investigation of Murtha was possibly warranted.

PAUL KANJORSKI

As the ranking Democrat on the Defense Appropriations Committee, Murtha added earmarks into defense bills that brought millions of dollars in federal research funds to companies owned by the children of fellow Pennsylvania Democrat, Rep. Paul Kanjorski.[29] But Kanjorski hasn't always let Murtha do the dirty work for him.

In 1999, Kanjorski managed to insert a line into a defense appropriations bill that that brought millions of dollars in federal funding to Cornerstone Technologies, a company run by Kanjorski's daughter and four nephews, in violation of federal law and House ethics rules. Kanjorski absurdly claims that the only reason his child and other family members were involved with the company is because no other company would take on the job. It was, according to Kanjorski, a "last resort." Kanjorski still serves in the House. Meanwhile, without government funding Cornerstone went belly up, leaving creditors holding the bag.[30]

DIANNE FEINSTEIN

Senator Dianne Feinstein, the new chairwoman of the Senate Rules Committee, has always opposed the war in Iraq, but hasn't let her opposition stop her from financially benefiting from the war:

> As chairperson and ranking member of the Military Construction Appropriations subcommittee (MILCON) from 2001 through the end of 2005, Feinstein supervised the appropriation of billions of dollars a year for specific military construction projects. Two defense contractors whose interests were largely controlled by her husband, financier Richard C. Blum, benefited from decisions made by Feinstein as leader of this powerful subcommittee.[31]

Metroactive reported, "from 1997 through the end of 2005, with Feinstein's knowledge, Blum was a majority owner of both URS Corp. and Perini Corp." Michael Klein, a top legal adviser to Feinstein and business partner of her husband, "routinely informed Feinstein about specific federal projects coming before her in which Perini had a stake."[32]

Such knowledge should have prompted her to explicitly avoid acting on any legislation affecting both Perini and URS. Unfortunately she did not. For years Feinstein lobbied Pentagon officials to support her favored defense projects, "some of which already were or subsequently became URS or Perini contracts." [33]

Making the situation even odder, the Senate Ethics Committee secretly made contradictory rulings about the conflicts of interest:

According to Klein, the Senate Select Committee on Ethics ruled, in secret, that Feinstein did not have a conflict of interest with Perini because, due to the existence of the bid and project lists provided by Klein, she knew when to recuse herself. Klein says that after URS declined to participate in his conflict-of-interest prevention plan, the ethics committee ruled that Feinstein could act on matters that affected URS because she did not have a list of URS' needs. That these confidential rulings are contradictory is obvious and calls for explanation.[34]

According to Wendell Rawls, executive director of the Center for Public Integrity in Washington, D.C., Senator Feinstein "has had a serious conflict of interest, a serious insensitivity to ethical considerations." [35]

"...The very least she should have done is to recuse herself from having conversations, debates, voting or any other kind of legislative activity that involved either Perini Corporation or URS Corporation or any other business activity where her husband's financial interests were involved.

"I cannot understand how someone who complains so vigorously as she has about conflicts of interest in the government and Congress can have turned such a deaf ear and a blind eye to her own. Because of her level of influence, the conflict of interest is just as serious as the Halliburton-Cheney connection."[36]

At least Vice-President Cheney sold his stock in Halliburton. Feinstein, on the other hand, has seen her family income increase substantially as a result of the appropriations she lobbied and voted for.

In her annual Public Financial Disclosure Reports, Feinstein records a sizeable family income from large investments in Perini, which is based in Framingham, Mass., and in URS, headquartered in San Francisco. But she has not publicly acknowledged the conflict of interest between her job as a congressional appropriator and her husband's longtime control of Perini and URS—and that omission has called her ethical standards into question, say the experts.[37]

There is such a thing as "conflict of interest," and most politicians try to steer clear of anything that resembles it. It is just too handy a club for an opponent to beat you with.

DEMOCRATIC FAMILY VALUABLES

While Americans are at times amazed that a mere representative earns $165,200 per year, the fact is that living in D.C. is very expensive, and there is a large cost associated with being in Congress. Given the costs, it would be hard to get rich being a congressman, and there is the added risk that every two or six years you can be voted out of office.

It is hard to plan a future in that situation; hard, that is, to set children up in a style pleasing to a powerful parent. The temptation to put the children on the gravy train becomes, for some people, irresistible. While it is illegal to, say, make a spouse a legislative aide, it is quite possible to make a spouse a campaign manager. The funding for the job comes from donations and thus isn't covered by any nepotism statutes.

The possibilities are endless, and most have been exploited. Hiring family members for campaign work; getting grants for organizations they work for; getting them employment as lobbyists; having them start up companies that you can appropriate money for—it's all been done and largely accepted.

The love of money is the corrosive acid which distorts values and causes otherwise sensible men and women to do things that only a fool would normally do. Our country has become so rich and so powerful that it is hard for an elected official who doesn't have access to a private fortune to feel fairly treated if he or she has only their official salary to live on. When you are courted by the rich and famous, it is impossible to remain middle class. The burning desire to compete with billionaires and movie stars is a hard temptation to resist, and some are not equal to the task.

It is the rare Democrat who doesn't have his or her hand out, trying to cage some personal profit from a bloated and wasteful political system largely created in the past by Democrats and now to be run by them again for at least the next two years. For all too many Democrats, there is a sense of entitlement to the life of wealth and privilege. Some Democrats were born to wealth, like Senators Ted Kennedy or Jay Rockefeller; others managed to marry in to it like John Kerry (more than once). But as most Democrats don't have a fabulously wealthy father or access to a rich widow, they have to build their swanky lifestyle by other means.

We have seen in the few examples cited in this brief chapter that Democrats are not immune to using their position as a means of personal and family enrichment. The sad fact of the matter is that there was no lack of material for such a chapter.

This situation must be brought under control—we must make it as nearly impossible as we can for an elected official to profit, either personally or through family and friends, from the immense power that attends office holding in the United States. Unfortunately, as long as we have our current Democratic leadership and their lapdogs in the MSM, we are unlikely to have a new direction for our government.

CHAPTER NINE

PRIVATELY FUNDED TRAVEL

"I believe every member of Congress should have to explain why they don't travel at least once a year to an important place."

—Dick Durbin[1]

ONE GETS the impression from the Democrats' rhetoric on ethics and corruption that they support a comprehensive plan to clean up government. Complaining about corruption when it can be directed against your opponent is all well and good, but rhetoric and reality don't necessarily have to agree.

Everyone likes to see new places and new people. Travel broadens the horizons and refreshes the mind. It can also, if you like, keep you from being tied down to the drudgery of work.

There are plenty of groups that are interested in influencing public policy, and what better way to "educate" lawmakers about an issue than by picking up the tab for a congressional trip? These trips are legal,[2] but must be "related to some kind of official business, a meeting, a conference, or a fact-finding mission."[3] As one lobbyist put it, it is much easier to lobby a congressman when he is away from D.C.[4]

Lawmakers can be easily enticed to participate in such trips when the destinations appeal to them, according to Jim Albertine, the former president of the American League of Lobbyists:

> "...The nicer the setting, the more relaxed they are. Of course you have to look at their interests. Some members like to play golf, some like to fish, some members like to hunt. Everybody has different tastes. So you have to iden-

tify what those interests are and what those tastes are and coordinate a trip that might be more acceptable, or something they might like."[5]

Even though such trips are acceptable according to ethics rules and are not funded by taxpayer dollars, it wasn't difficult for Democrats to cast them in a dark light and launch an ethics war against Republicans over the practice. This makes great political theater. The only risk is a public demand for reform, which would jeopardize every politician's ability to take swank vacations.

The public did demand reform.

In the spring of 2005, Nancy Pelosi brought the issue of privately funded congressional travel into the forefront by calling for an investigation into a trip taken by Tom DeLay and reportedly paid for by a lobbyist.

This sparked a firestorm that sent both Republicans and Democrats into a mad rush to get their travel disclosure forms in order. While Democrats claimed Republicans were inappropriately influenced by trips paid for by lobbyists and other groups, they didn't see anything improper with their own globe-trotting on someone else's dime, even when the dime belonged to a lobbyist.

In May of 2005, the *Chicago Tribune* reported on the extensive travel of Illinois' representatives in Congress. Senator Dick Durbin took seven privately funded trips in 2000, sometimes accompanied by his daughter or his wife.

"[The Aspen Institute] paid expenses for the senator and his daughter Jennifer—about $8,400—to travel to Rome in late spring 2003 for a 'conference on the global environment.' In 2001, the Institute paid for a trip to Florence, Italy, for Durbin and his wife, Loretta—about $8,600—for a conference on 'national security and the global environment.'

'These are nice places to visit—I won't mislead you—but we do serious work there,' Durbin said, noting that no lobbyists were at the conferences. 'They are one of the few occasions we have for bipartisan meetings among senators away from Washington to discuss issues, and I really find them valuable.'"[6]

Durbin admitted that the trips gave him an opportunity to spend time with his wife.

Jesse Jackson Jr. took a $19,500 trip to Dubai, in the United Arab Emirates, and Qatar in April 2001, which was sponsored by the Islamic Institute.[7]

Over the past several years Representative Danny Davis has gone to Nigeria, Taiwan, Israel, China, Hawaii, Ukraine, Grand Cayman Island, St. Kitts, and the Virgin Islands. Despite the disclosure forms to prove it, he declared in May 2005 that he'd "never been on a junket in [his] life" and claimed the trips he's taken have been "grueling as hell."[8]

Apparently these trips were so grueling that he had his wife, Vera Davis, accompany him on his trips to St. Kitts, Grand Cayman Island, the Virgin Islands, and several other locations. It takes quite a lot of nerve to claim that is a tough job to visit exotic vacation spots with a spouse.

In the spring of 2005, Davis went on a trip to Sri Lanka paid for by the Tamil Tigers, a group designated by the U.S. government as a terrorist organization.

The Tamil Tigers have, over the decades, wracked up quite a body count of innocent victims, with some of their more notable outrages the Kebithigollewa massacre of sixty-four people,[9] and the Anuradhapura massacre of a hundred and forty-six.[10] The extreme nastiness of the Tamil Tigers is indicated by their use of children to carry out the murders.

Apparently, this wasn't a problem for Davis.

> Davis said he believed that the trip, from March 30 to April 5, 2005, was paid for by the Tamil federation, which in accordance with congressional ethics rules sent him a written statement of the travel expenses, more than $7,000 each for Davis and his aide, Daniel Cantrell. Davis said he knew that the group was "associated" with the Tamil Tigers but did not realize that the trip's costs were covered with funds controlled by the rebel group. ... Davis said he always assumed that the organization had a connection with the Tamil Tigers. "I knew that they were associated with the Tamil Tigers, yes," he said.[11]

He knew the group funding his travel was "associated with" and "connected to" a terrorist organization, but he went anyway.

Rep. Jan Schakowsky insists her travels help her make informed decisions on major policy issues. It is conceivable that traveling to Rome, India, Mexico City, and Hawaii can be very educational. However, such trips can also be very expensive. Her trip to India cost $15,000 for her and her husband.[12]

Massachusetts Rep. John Tierney also enjoys taking privately funded trips to ideal vacation spots like Cancun, Mexico and Montego Bay, Jamaica—allegedly to study education policy. One can only imagine how much studying of education policy Tierney was doing in Cancun during spring break or Montego Bay on Valentine's Day, with his wife in tow.

Each of these trips cost over $6,000 and were paid for by the "nonprofit" Aspen Institute, which has sponsored over six hundred trips—more than any other trip sponsor—nearly 70 percent of which was spent on Democrats.[13]

Tierney took his wife with him on another trip paid for by the Aspen Institute, a ten-day trip to China in April 2005, with a final cost of over $20,000,[14] making it the seventh most expensive trip taken by a member of Congress that year.[15]

Tierney's hometown paper, the *Salem News*, reported in June of 2006 that Tierney took nearly $50,000 worth of privately funded trips during the previous five years. Tierney's spokeswoman defended these trips, claiming they were "related to his committee work," and not the same as "lobbyist-sponsored golf outings and similar junkets that have made headlines in recent months."[16]

Tierney himself was forced to defend these trips after the story was reported in the *Salem News*. According to Tierney, he only participates on trips relevant to his work in Congress.

He attended three Aspen conferences on education reform because he serves on the House Education Committee. He also attended a conference in Finland on political Islam—originally scheduled in Turkey—which he said was relevant to his work on the Intelligence Committee. As for his 2005 trip to China, Tierney said it covered a variety of issues, including education, trade, security, and human rights.[17]

Perhaps someone should ask Tierney how the Finland trip on political Islam he attended, which took place June 27 to July 3, 2003,[18] was relevant to his work on the House Permanent Select Committee on Intelligence (HPSCI) when he wasn't even assigned to that committee until January 26, 2005.[19] Was Tierney so intuitive that he anticipated that hiring Nancy Pelosi's daughter as his chief of staff (see Chapter One) would help him get on the HPSCI a year and half later?

Of course, Tierney says that trips like the ones he's taken are different from the "influence-peddling scandal involving congressional travel," but said he would probably support a proposal to ban all privately funded travel, telling the *Boston Globe*, "In this kind of atmosphere we should probably ban it just so people don't get misperceptions on it."[20]

As Democrats, hoping to claim the high ground on ethics, looked into banning trips paid for by lobbyists, the story broke that another Massachusetts congressman, Representative Michael Capuano, went on such a trip to Brazil, costing over $19,000. Capuano's wife, Barbara, was also on the trip...as well as a few other people who probably shouldn't have been.

The *Boston Globe* reported that the high-priced trip "included several lobbyists and representatives of companies that helped finance the nonprofit business organization that sponsored the trip."[21] Capuano said he was aware that lobbyists were on the trip, saying "I don't think there is anything wrong with it," but claimed he wouldn't have gone on the trip had he known its cost.

In fact, the trip ranks as one of the most expensive privately funded trips taken in 2005 by a member of Congress, ranking as the 14th most expensive out of 535, according to an analysis done for the *Boston Globe*. According to Larry Noble of the Center for Responsive Politics, "This is exactly the type of trip that is causing a problem."[22]

Regardless of whether Democrats claim they want to change the rules or enforce existing ones, they always act as if the rules do not apply to them, as could be seen in the Democrats' attitude towards the filing of travel disclosure forms. A flurry of excuses came from Democrats when their ethical lapses were revealed, yet when the very same transgressions were committed by Republicans, they were considered inexcusable by Democrats, no matter what the circumstance.

When Elizabeth Greer, an aide to Representative F. Allen Boyd, Jr. took a trip to Kenya in December 2004 and failed to file the disclosure forms, she blamed her failure on her messy desk.[23]

Representative Elijah Cummings of Maryland claimed that thirteen travel forms from 2004 had been lost in the House internal mail system.[24]

Twenty trips taken by Rep. Ellen Tauscher of California between 2001 and 2004 remained undisclosed until May 16, 2005, following a review of her travel. Her spokeswoman called it an oversight, not an ethical lapse.

Illinois Democrat Representative Luis Gutierrez, who had been a congressman for seven terms, claimed to have been unaware of his obligation to file reports for the twenty trips he took between 2000 and 2004. Another Illinois Democrat, Representative Bobby Rush, had not filed any trips since 2000 and also claimed to have been unaware of his obligation to do so.[25]

It wasn't until May of 2005, following increased scrutiny of congressional travel—as a result of the Democrats' attacks on Tom DeLay—that Democrats rushed to get their travel forms appropriately filed. In all cases of misfiling or non-filing, Democrats claimed innocence. It seems that the Democrats are babes in the woods—blissfully unaware when their homework is due, but fully prepared to come to class claiming their dog ate it. Republicans' mistakes, on the other hand, were part of an evil and deliberate "culture of corruption." Whether Democrats' travel forms were misplaced on a messy desk, lost in the mail, or their dog ate them, there is always something or someone on which to blame their transgressions. Naturally, they pointed fingers at Republicans.

Representative Steny Hoyer failed to disclose twelve privately-funded trips over an eight-year period, finally reporting them in the spring of 2005. Hoyer's spokeswoman, Stacey Bernards, blamed Republicans for raising the travel issue after doing opposition research to "deflect from their own ethical issues."[26]

Freely translated, Bernards' comment meant that only Republicans would be taking bribes by means of privately funded travel, while Democrats—completely selfless in their desire to participate in these trips—would never fall for such temptations. They would, of course, go on such trips, but were totally impervious to the influence peddling that apparently only happens when Republicans take trips abroad on someone's dime.

As the number two Democrat in the House, Hoyer should have been holding himself to a higher standard, or at least the standard he and his fellow Democrats hold Republicans to.

Rep. Bart Stupak's wife has gained much being married to a congressman. Her job with his campaign has come with many benefits, including the opportunity to travel. Naturally, she's joined her husband on a number of congressional trips to popular vacation spots. One trip in 2003 took them to Barcelona, Spain, and Paris, France. Another took the couple to sunny Florida.

It must have been confusing for Rep. Stupak to discern a personal vacation with his wife from a congressional "fact-finding mission," as he was over two years late in filing disclosure forms for a 2003 trip sponsored by The Nuclear Energy Institute, and a trip to Florida sponsored by the Harvard University Kennedy School of Government. The costs of the trips were $19,778.48, and $3,886.42 respectively, according to the disclosure reports.

Representative Jim McGovern from Massachusetts experienced similar confusion. In February 2005, he took his wife with him to Paris, France, and stayed at the Hotel de Crillon on the Place de la Concorde.

Sounds like the perfect venue for a romantic getaway. However, both their airfare and two nights at the posh hotel were paid for by the nonprofit International Management and Development Institute. McGovern "forgot" to file disclosure reports for the excursion—required within thirty days of the trip—until that May, when he also finally filed reports for four trips taken back in 2003.[27]

Massachusetts Democrats continued to take such questionable trips into 2006, including Representative Barney Frank, who went on a trip to Ft. Lauderdale, Florida, in April paid for by the Family Pride Coalition, a nonprofit organization that advocates gay marriage. But at least he doesn't go on corporate-sponsored junkets, according to his spokesman.[28]

Representative Sheila Jackson-Lee is also quite the traveler. Indeed, she has been described as a house afire in the way she moves from place to place. Her travels seem to leave her little time to take care of constituent business. An example of this is in the rather mundane, but often crucially important, matter of writing the Social Security Administration to clear up problems with the delivery of benefits to citizens.

Normally, a House member would write hundreds of such letters over the years. Between 1997 and 2002, Jackson-Lee's neighboring Democratic House member, Gene Green, wrote 538 such letters. How many did Jackson-Lee write from 1995 to 2002? Seventy-nine.[29]

Jackson-Lee also apparently lacked the time to file disclosure forms for a 2001 trip to Puerto Rico. While many members of Congress were rushing in the middle of 2005 to make sure all the paperwork for their privately funded trips were in order, Jackson-Lee's chief of staff, Leon Buck, said he was not sure why the four-year-old trip was even relevant anymore.[30]

Another frequent flier was Harold Ford Jr., who was first elected in 1996, at the young age of twenty-six, to represent Tennessee's 9th district.[31] The son of a Tennessee political institution, Harold Ford Jr. took a stab at becoming minority leader in 2003 and, in spite of winning only twenty-nine votes from his fellow Democrats, he was seen as a man who could be America's first black president.[32]

Ford took sixty-one privately funded trips between 1998 and 2003, and "failed to file a single travel-disclosure form with the House clerk, as required by the chamber's ethics rules."[33] What makes this worse is that Ford's chief of staff, Mark Schuermann, had previously said that everything had been done by the rules. Schuermann said in a statement, "In every instance, the congressman followed the rules of the House of Representatives and traveled to speak about legislative policies and learn about a subject matter important to his district."[34]

Representative Neil Abercrombie of Hawaii took a two-day trip to Boston in 2001 to speak before the Ancient and Honorable Artillery Company of Massachusetts. His original disclosure forms stated that the Virginia-based lobbying firm Rooney Group International had paid for the trip, which is in violation of House rules. He filed amended travel reports in April 2005, listing the military fraternal organization as the trip's sponsor.

Abercrombie said it was a simple mistake, and even James Rooney, founder of Rooney Group International, said he didn't pay for the trip.

However, Abercrombie himself admitted that when his staff reviewed the matter they learned that the Rooney Group had in fact been reimbursed for Abercrombie's airfare,[35] which suggests they had originally paid the airfare. This, according to Melanie Sloan, of the liberal ethics watchdog group Citizens for Responsibility and Ethics in Washington, is still a violation of House rules.[36]

Representative Maxine Waters of California took nine trips through 2004 that she neglected to disclose until the end of April 2005. Naturally, she considered her late filing unrelated to the problems surrounding Tom DeLay and blamed the trips' sponsors for the late filing.[37]

A staff member of Illinois's freshmen senator Barack Obama took a $2,377 trip to Seattle in March 2005 that was paid for by Microsoft, but wasn't filed until the first week of May.

It took Representative Stephanie Tubbs-Jones nearly *four years* to provide records of the questionable trip she took to Puerto-Rico back in 2001 with other House members, including Nancy Pelosi. For someone who sits on the House Ethics Committee, this was an oversight that should have never happened. Also, according to documents she filed with the House clerk, the trip was paid for by a registered lobbyist firm, something she should have known was against House rules. Jones' spokesman said the listing of the lobbyist firm as the trip's sponsor was a "human error."

The problem of travel and the failure to report it in a timely manner is too widespread to chronicle completely. Other culprits included Representative Bernie Sanders (I-VT.), Delegate Eleanor Holmes Norton (D-D.C.), Representative Diana DeGette (D-Colo.), and Representative Charles Gonzalez (D-Texas).[38]

As previously noted, while some privately funded travel is allowed under House rules, trips paid for by lobbyists are not. Representative Norm Dicks broke the rules by taking a five-day trip to Miami in February 2005, which was sponsored by the defense lobbying firm Spectrum Group. It was only *after* this information was revealed that he decided to pick up the tab. In a letter to Jeff Trandahl, the Clerk of the House, Dicks wrote, "I have subsequently decided to pay for the trip myself and have reimbursed the Spectrum Group for meals and lodging expenses totaling $571.00. I also paid for my transportation costs and returned a check to Spectrum for reimbursement totaling $414.41."[39]

One trip Dicks certainly would not want to pay for was a ten-day trip to China in 2005, sponsored by the Aspen Institute, that cost $17,382—the second-most expensive trip taken by a Washington state congressman since 2001. The most expensive was a six-day trip to India in 2001 taken by Representative Jim McDermott that came to $17,736. McDermott also led his state's delegation in the number of trips taken over a five-and-half-year period, with ninety-eight trips taken by him and his staff, forty-one of which he took himself.[40]

Despite their claims of getting tough on lobbyist-paid travel (which was already prohibited by House rules), a week before Democrats unveiled their lobbying reform proposal, Representatives Gregory Meeks, George Butterfield, Stephanie Tubbs-Jones, and Albert Wynn participated in a trip to Montego Bay, Jamaica.[41] This trip was paid for by the Inter-American Economic Council, a nonprofit group founded in 1999 to "dialogue about current and future economic strategies in the Hemisphere."[42] The stated reason for the trip was to "discuss security and trade issues while visiting tourist sites."[43] We can rest assured that the representatives who visited looked closely at the issue and whatever security problems were discussed have now been solved.

THE DEMOCRATS SO-CALLED LOBBYING REFORM

Despite being the minority party for twelve years, Democrats took more privately-funded trips than Republicans. According to American RadioWorks, Democrats took 54 percent of these paid trips from January 2000 through mid-November 2005.[44]

As it turned out, endless Democratic harping on privately funded travel did generate a backlash against the practice. Privately funded junkets became a target of lobbying reform proposals presented by Democrats and Republicans...with a key difference between them.

On February 9, 2006, Minority Leader Pelosi and Minority Whip Steny Hoyer wrote a letter to the new House Majority Leader, John Boehner.[45] In it, among other proposed reforms, was a demand to ban all travel paid for by *lobbyists* and those who employ them. This was in keeping with Democratic talking points about how bad it was for former Majority Leader DeLay to have traveled using lobbyists' money.

The Republican proposal, however, banned *all* privately sponsored trips.

It was certainly no oversight by the Democrats that their proposal conveniently had an exception for trips sponsored by nonprofits like the Aspen Institute, their number-one sponsor of such trips.[46] Considering trips sponsored by lobbyists were already against House rules, the Democrats' proposal would have changed nothing. But that didn't stop them from claiming that Republican proposals weren't meaningful reforms compared to their own.

The Democrats' plan would not in any way affect the ability of lobbyists to provide travel to members. All a lobbyist need do is donate to a nonprofit with an interest in legislation or create a nonprofit specifically to push whatever issue the lobbyist has been hired to lobby about. All we'll get with this rule, if adopted, is a series of groups with names such as "Concerned Citizens for Mohair Subsidies," and any Fill-in-the-Blank Institute. And this, of course, was the intent all along in the Democrats' so-called reform proposals.

The rules are only as good as the people who enforce them. Honest behavior cannot really be legislated or regulated into existence. A man or woman is either honest or not.

The Democrats focused on a word like "lobbyist" because it has a very negative connotation in the American mind—very convenient to exploit during a period when Republicans controlled the agenda, and thus were more heavily sought after from lobbyists. The word itself brings to mind a slick, backroom wheeler-dealer hired by nefarious special interests to bribe congressmen into passing laws against the will of the people. But in fighting tooth and nail against Republicans corrupted by lobbyists, the Democrats didn't want to lose out on the ability to take trips to Montego Bay to check out the security arrangements.

The Democrats' scandalization of privately funded travel did have an impact on the globetrotting of members of Congress. According to PoliticalMoneyLine, spending on congressional travel dropped from its peak of $33.9 million in 2003 to $1.34 million as of mid-October 2006.[47]

Now back in the majority, it wouldn't be surprising to see the Democrats' views on lobbyists change in order to justify taking more free trips to exotic vacation spots and posh resorts over the next couple years. That, or we'll have to listen to them explain endlessly what makes influence peddling less objectionable when done by nonprofits than when done by lobbyists. No matter how they do it, privately funded trips aren't going to end, because as long as someone else is paying the bill, Democrats won't give up one of their favorite perks of office. It's safe to say that with Democrats back in control, meaningful lobbying reform is officially dead.

CHAPTER TEN

ELECTION LAW VIOLATIONS

"This great center of democracy is truly tainted by money."

—Russ Feingold[1]

WHEN IT COMES to retaining or increasing raw power in Congress, Democrats have demonstrated they will stop at nothing. They certainly haven't let the law stop them, election laws not excluded. And in the matter of Robert Torricelli, the Democrats went right past bending the law to breaking it outright.

Plagued by scandals, Senator Robert Torricelli of New Jersey realized his chances of winning reelection in 2002 were rapidly fading. A scrappy politician his whole life, he seemed determined to fight it out to the end, even at the risk of a loss. That was before the Democratic Powers That Be got to him. Torricelli was eventually persuaded to drop out.

What might have been promised to him remains unknown, but only five days after he was talking like the scandals were behind him, he quit his bid for reelection.[2] In pulling out of the race, Torricelli said, "I will not be responsible for the loss of the Democratic majority in the United States Senate."[3] Once again we saw the Democrats' dedication to the party and its power. Nothing is more important—and if a loyal foot soldier has to be discarded, so be it.

Democrats pushed to place former senator Frank Lautenberg's name on the ballot to replace Torricelli, even though New Jersey law only allowed parties to change nominees if a candidate withdraws at least fifty-one days prior to the election. Torricelli's withdrawal was over two weeks late.

In spite of the law, the New Jersey Supreme Court unanimously ruled on October 2, 2002 that the Democrats could replace Torricelli with Lautenberg. With the election thirty-six days away, the election had technically already started. Approximately sixteen hundred absentee ballots with Torricelli's name were already printed and distributed.[4] Despite Republican efforts to uphold the law, the New Jersey Supreme Court decision prevailed; Frank Lautenberg was put on the ballot, putting Republican candidate Doug Forrester at square one. Lautenberg ultimately prevailed in the election, but neither he nor Torricelli could stop the Republican Party from narrowly regaining majority control of the Senate.

Charles Dickens once wrote "The law is an ass." Democrats, taking note that their symbol is a jackass, seem to have taken Dickens to mean that "the law is a Democrat." For the truly partisan Democrat, the law is whatever works to the Democrats' advantage—and if tomorrow the opposite works better, then the law is automatically changed to fit the new circumstances. This was seen in 2006 when Democrats sued successfully to keep Tom DeLay on the ballot in Texas even after he resigned his seat, announced he wouldn't run for reelection, and moved to another state. In a complete reversal of their 2002 position, Democrats essentially argued that once you are the candidate, you can't cease to be the candidate.

The laws governing elections are vital to the proper functioning of any democratic republic. The Democrats, at least in modern times, seem to have no conception of what law is—or how vital it is for our survival.

When it came to replacing Torricelli with Lautenberg on the New Jersey ballot, the law said one thing, the Democrats said another, and they managed to achieve victory in the courts. That time, they managed to circumvent the law.

Other times, they have not been so successful.

THE MONEY-GO-ROUND

While elected Democrats don't practice what they preach, neither do Democrat candidates, including former Rhode Island Secretary of State Matt Brown, who ran for the U.S. Senate in 2006 on a "clean government" platform. During his campaign, Matt Brown proposed a plan to publicly finance campaigns "to take the influence of money out of politics and get Washington focused on what's right for people."[5] As Brown campaigned on a "taking money out of politics" platform, he was taking money from three state Democratic parties, which appear to have violated campaign finance laws.

Jane Sugimura, the Hawaii Democratic Party's treasurer, told the *Associated Press* that Brown's campaign struck a deal with them that they would give $5,000 to Brown's campaign and, in return, Brown's supporters would donate to the Hawaii Democratic Party, an arrangement that Larry Noble of the Center for Responsive Politics said could violate federal law. Brown also received $10,000 each from the Massachusetts and Maine Democratic Parties.

The donations from the state parties to Brown's campaign were rather uncommon before the Democratic primary, in which Brown faced former state Attorney General Sheldon Whitehouse for the party's nomination.[6]

Brown's campaign denied any wrongdoing, even though they admitted they encouraged donors to make contributions to the Hawaii, Massachusetts, and Maine state parties.[7]

Despite their claims that they had done nothing wrong, Federal Election Commission reports show that one donor who had already reached the legal limit in contributions to Brown's campaign contributed to the Massachusetts state party just days after the state party gave to Brown's campaign.

Joe Sandler, attorney for the Brown campaign, said there was nothing wrong with the donations from the state parties to the campaign. Trying to make everyone believe that it was all a strange coincidence, Sandler claimed, "Based on the facts that we know, this looks like these contributions from the state parties were completely lawful and appropriate and there is nothing untoward about them."[8] Despite this alleged confidence that the donations were on the level, Brown said he would return the disputed contributions and, naturally, blamed both his opponents, saying in a statement from his campaign, "While these contributions are legal, my opponents, Democrat and Republican, have used them to launch negative, personal attacks against me." The Hawaii state party also retracted its earlier claims of a "tit-for-tat" deal—after the *Associated Press* reported that the deal could have violated campaign finance laws.[9] To Brown, the only real crime was getting caught.

With his fundraising practices in question, and facing a lack of funds, Matt Brown had to drop out of the race in April of 2006.[10]

Rep. Cynthia McKinney, the former Georgia congresswoman who had sparked controversy by suggesting that the Bush administration had advance knowledge of the 9/11 attacks, as well as physically assaulting a Capitol Hill police officer, has also had some trouble with the FEC.

First elected to the House in 1992, McKinney lost her reelection bid in the 2002 Democratic primary to Denise Majette, but apparently continued to raise money. She was hit with a $33,000 fine by the Federal Election Commission on October 28, 2005, for accepting excessive contributions in the amount of $106,425. She was also ordered to reimburse over $72,000 to donors.[11] McKinney regained the seat in 2004 after Majette made a run for the Senate.

While a rather bold plan to re-work Florida's election laws post-election failed to deliver the state to Al Gore in 2000, Democrats remain convinced that cutting legal corners is the best tactic.

Democrats took the 2000 loss of Florida and the White House very hard. In spite of their best efforts to eke out a victory with multiple recounts, the law of the land was actually enforced. Nothing in memory so incensed the Democrats. To be robbed of victory by something as pettifogging as the actual law was too much to be borne. Fired up with the conviction they had been cheated, Democrats swore that revenge would be theirs.

Democrats were determined to recapture Florida in 2004, even if it meant skirting election laws. Less than two weeks before the 2004 presidential election, the Republican National Committee and the Florida Republican Party obtained a forty-six-page document called "Florida Victory 2004." The document detail the coordination between the Kerry/Edwards campaign, the Democratic Party, labor unions, and other groups, on a massive get-out-the-vote operation in Florida which appeared to violate federal campaign finance law. While Democrats used their standard tactic of dismissing the charges as baseless, Larry Noble, the executive director of the Center for Responsive Politics and former chief counsel of the FEC, said, "At the very least, this document should lead to an FEC investigation."[12]

The *Washington Post* reported on the allegations:

> Jill Vogel, the RNC's chief counsel, said the document shows "illegal coordination resulting in excessive and prohibited contributions," including the illegal use of "soft" money — unlimited donations from corporations, unions and the wealthy — in a federal election and the making of illegal soft-money contributions to the Kerry campaign. She said the RNC will file a complaint with the Federal Election Commission, but she acknowledged that there is little likelihood of regulatory action in the final 12 days of the campaign.[13]

And right she was, as the Federal Election Commission voted to dismiss the case in January 2006. But, since George W. Bush won Florida and the presidency, the FEC ruling was a bittersweet victory for the Democrats.

The presidential campaign of John Kerry's former running mate, John Edwards, came under fire for receiving donations from twenty-two people linked to the law firm of Geoffrey Fieger, a personal injury lawyer who best known for defending Dr. Jack Kevorkian. These donations amounted to $43,000 *on the same day*. Of those donations, fourteen were from people who had been employed by Fieger's firm, and eight came from their relatives.

Joseph Bird, an attorney at Fieger's Southfield, Michigan firm (who was fired in the summer of 2005) told the *Associated Press* in December 2005 that shortly after he joined the firm in 2003, he was privately informed by partner Ven Johnson that he was expected to donate to John Edwards' presidential campaign and was promised the he would be reimbursed by the firm. He brought in $2,000 in checks and was reimbursed two days later.[14] "I had only been there a week. It was like a condition of my employment," Bird said.[15]

Fieger's firm was not alone in making large simultaneous donations to the Edwards campaign. At least a dozen other law firms nationwide share the strange happenstance of their employees making large, simultaneous contributions to Edwards' presidential campaign. With so much to choose from, federal investigators only focused on donations that were illegally reimbursed.[16] Federal agents raided Feiger's office on November 30, 2005, looking for evidence in the case, and more than twenty attorneys, employees, relatives, and associates of Fieger were subpoenaed by a federal grand jury in January 2006. Fieger, in predicting his federal indictment, insisted he was the victim of a conspiracy, "I fully expect that I will be indicted by a grand jury who will indict a bottle of beer if the Republican U.S. attorney told them to do it."[17]

Why didn't this receive the same amount of attention in the media as Jack Abramoff? Have any of the campaigns he donated to rushed to return the "dirty money," as Republicans who received money from Tom DeLay after he was indicted or from Jack Abramoff were expected to?

There is nothing quite like a Democratic lawyer for believing that the law doesn't apply. In Edwards's case, the thinking would be that if he won, he'd be in the clear. And if he lost, Republicans just wouldn't spend the time coming after him because raking up the past just isn't something a forward-looking party gets into.

MISINFORMATION

In October of 2005, Virginia gubernatorial candidate (now governor) Tim Kaine was sanctioned by the Virginia State Board of Elections for a fraudulent mailer attacking his opponent, Jerry Kilgore. In the mailer, Kaine's campaign used the Republican elephant logo to deliberately deceive voters into thinking the attack on Republican gubernatorial candidate Jerry Kilgore came from Republicans and falsely claimed support from the conservative Virginia Club for Growth. The "Kaine for Governor" disclaimer was cleverly hidden as a photo credit.

Similarly, there was some outrage during the 2004 senate race between former Senate Minority Leader Tom Daschle and John Thune, after Daschle's campaign had sponsored automated phone calls advising listeners to contact Thune and urge him to keep third-party groups out of the state. The calls did not have a disclaimer informing listeners that Daschle had paid for the calls.[18] The supreme irony in this Daschle campaign is that he received very large out-of-state donations—$35,200 from Wisconsin residents alone.[19]

As everyone learned back in 1996, foreign donations to American political campaigns are illegal. This wise and common-sense prohibition is good for America—it prevents wealthy foreigners from unduly influencing the way Americans vote, or the way American politicians in search of campaign cash act. Prior to the revelations that various foreign individuals and entities had donated illegally to the Clinton-Gore reelection effort, the fact that foreign donations were illegal might not have been that well known. Representative Steny Hoyer, (D-MD) a leader in the new Democratic House, ran afoul of this law.

During the 1994 election campaign an Indian-American lawyer named Lalit H. Gadhia, a Democratic activist and fundraiser for the gubernatorial campaign of Parris Glendening (D-MD), made quite a lot of donations. In all, Gadhia donated $46,000 to Congressional candidates who were seen as favorable to Indian interests. A total of twenty such candidates received the donations, the most prominent being former Senator Paul Sarbanes (D-MD), Charles S Robb (D-VA), Benjamin L. Cardin (D-MD) (who was elected to the Senate from Maryland in 2006 to replace the retiring Sarbanes), and, of course, Steny Hoyer. It was just too bad that the money Gadhia donated all came to him via an Indian diplomat stationed in Washington, D.C.

In the end Gadhia was convicted, and Hoyer and the others had to disgorge the illegal funds.[20]

IF ALL ELSE FAILS, CHEAT

For years, there have been questions about the campaign finance irregularities of Bill and Hillary Clinton. Bill Clinton's 1996 reelection effort, with its large amounts of illegal foreign donations, stands as the archetype of a dirty fundraising campaign. After being burned on that, it might be thought that any Clinton would keep his, or her, fundraising efforts squeaky clean.

Not exactly.

In January 2006, following a four-year investigation, the Federal Election Commission determined there was probable cause to believe that Hillary Clinton's 2000 senate campaign had violated the law by not disclosing in-kind contributions totaling over $1.24 million from Peter Paul, the co-host of the infamous Hollywood gala/fundraiser for Hillary Clinton's 2000 senate campaign.

But, as we've seen before, the punishment rarely (if ever) fits the crime, and as the result of a settlement with Hillary's campaign, they only had to pay a $35,000 fine for admitting to not disclosing $721,895 in contributions for the star-studded gala and amend their FEC reports.[21]

Fortunately for Hillary, the media was more interested in covering the Abramoff scandal, providing the perfect smokescreen to keep the public in the dark about her fraudulent ways. Paul filed a civil suit against both Bill and Hillary Clinton, which will go to trial on March 27, 2007. Hillary's name was dropped as a defendant, but she will likely be forced to testify.[22]

Hillary's troubles, ignored by the media, had no effect on her 2006 campaign. She was reelected by a large majority and still had approximately $18 million on hand...that we know about.[23] This amount of money will prove useful now that Senator Clinton has announced a presidential bid.

On May 26, 2005, the Federal Election Commission fined the Democratic National Committee, Reverend Jesse Jackson, the Rainbow/PUSH Coalition, and Jackson's Citizenship Education Fund for campaign finance law violations during the 2000 presidential election.

During the campaign, Jackson stumped for Democrats at more than 120 events during a speaking tour in the fall of 2000. While Jackson's travels were allegedly nonpartisan, the FEC determined they were actually done on behalf of Democratic candidates, and in fact were paid for by the Democratic National Committee. The DNC had agreed to pay nearly half a million dollars for Jackson's travel on their behalf. Because money was tight, the DNC did not pay Jackson upfront, making the payment illegal since Jackson's organizations are nonprofit, tax-exempt corporations.

The FEC determined that Jackson's activities were indeed partisan. "Based on Reverend Jackson's advocacy of specific federal candidates and the fact that his activities were coordinated with the DNC, the purpose of the travel in 2000 was partisan activity conducted in connection with the federal elections," the agreement said, and a $200,000 fine was split. The DNC paid $100,000, and Jackson and his organizations paid another $100,000 fine, plus $5,000 in interest for late payment.[24]

In the summer of 2005, the newly merged *Scranton Times-Tribune* in Pennsylvania began running advertisements that appeared on television, billboards, and buses, featuring a mock newspaper with a banner headline, "Casey to run for Senate." The ads soon came under scrutiny by the National Republican Senatorial Committee, which claimed the ads could be illegal corporate donations for Democrat Bob Casey Jr., son of the former governor of Pennsylvania who eventually defeated Rick Santorum. The NRSC noted Casey's ties to the publisher's family, who have donated over $120,000 to both Bob Casey Jr. and his brother:

> Publisher George V. Lynett and his family have donated at least $85,000 to Casey's state campaigns, according to finance records. The publisher's sister, Cecelia Haggerty, and her husband gave $4,200 to Casey's Senate campaign in March, according to federal records.
>
> Casey's brother Pat received more than $40,000 during his two unsuccessful bids for a Scranton-area congressional seat.
>
> The family's political contributions have been largely limited to the Casey family, the Pennsylvania Democratic Party ($15,000), and past Democratic opponents of Santorum's.[25]

The Republican State Committee of Pennsylvania filed a complaint with the Federal Election Commission to determine the legality of the ads.[26] But the FEC would eventually find that no laws were broken "because the advertising campaign did not expressly advocate the election of Bob Casey," and that there was no coordination between the *Scranton Times-Tribune* and Casey's campaign.[27]

Of course, complaints are frequently filed with the FEC by members of both parties, hoping to nab the other of some violation in order to derail their campaign or simply to have a punishment enforced. Still, we've seen even when the FEC does find that a violation occurred, the punishment usually amounts to a slap on the wrist, giving campaigns little reason to fear being caught and every reason to trivialize the ruling because of a meager fine imposed.

THE LAW AS AN ACROBAT

Law after law is ignored by Democrats in their quest for power. Is there a belief among Democrats that the law is whatever they need it to be? It is a valid question when we discuss the Democratic Party and its systematic efforts to get around any and all laws that inconvenience them. A criminal conspiracy is when two or more people conspire to break the law. The actual breaking of the law doesn't have to happen—all a person has to do is plan to break the law. If what the Democrats have been doing is ever proved to be premeditated, then some people are going to jail for a very long time.

If there isn't collusion among Democrats to violate election laws, then we are forced to conclude that these serial violations are an unfortunate set of accidents. This doesn't seem like a reasonable conclusion, and the Democrats certainly don't see their actions as subverting the American political process. Intentional or happenstance, the Democrats want to make the law follow them rather than make themselves follow the law.

It may be that Democrats, on the whole, are just so entirely self absorbed that they can't see what they are doing as other than right and proper. Whether it was excusing perjury because "it was about sex" back in the '90s, or changing the way ballots are counted post-election in 2000, the Democrats seem to view the law as an endlessly flexible thing, which an army of lawyers can bend any way the Democrats need it to go. The purely partisan Democrat would hotly rejoin that they do nothing of the kind—that everything Democrats do is morally above reproach, and, at any rate, Republicans are worse. Pride and its handmaid, insolence, are prevalent among Democrats, and the farther up the Democratic ranks, the worse it seems to get.

As Winston Churchill once pointed out, facts are stubborn things. It is impossible to look into a person's soul and see what is motivating them to their actions. It could be that the Democrats are so sure of their ends that it blinds them to the means. And it might not be, in the mind of Democrats, that they are using deviltry for honorable ends, but that anything they do cannot be wrong.

It is impossible to give the Democrats a clean bill of health on the matter of election laws. The law enforcement agencies have limited ability to bring sanctions against election law violators, and no sanction will ever undo the ultimate point of violating an election law: getting elected. Once in office, it is nearly impossible to get an election law miscreant out except at the next election, and then there is the daunting task of beating someone who will even go as far as breaking the law to win.

Democrats have learned the system very well, and they know that only the people can call them to account for their disreputable practices. The big trouble is that the results of the 2006 election only confirm the Democrats in their view that they have nothing to fear from the people.

CHAPTER ELEVEN

BRIBES, SHADY DEALS, ILLEGAL ACTIVITIES

"Corruption can also provide opportunities for those who would harness the fear and hatred of others to their agenda and ambitions."

—Senator Barak Obama1

POLITICAL CORRUPTION is not the oldest profession, but it is certainly close to it. Judeo-Christian theology teaches that mankind is fallen and given to sin. Other philosophies hold that our upgbringing determines our morality. Be that as it may, a good number of people have a penchant for deliberately choosing to do the wrong thing. Politicians being people, they are no less afflicted with this than the average man on the street—the difference, however, is that politicians wield power and thus are sought out by others, and some of the seekers are not too scrupulous about how they gain the ear (and the vote) of a politician.

Most of the time when people hear the phrase "political corruption," they think in terms of a politician taking a bribe or some other sort of illegal activity. "Illegal" and "immoral" are not always the same thing.

Real corruption is not mere lawbreaking. The sort of corruption which harms the body politic is when a person or group will do what they know is wrong—even if technically legal—in order to gain particular advantage for a person, group, or cause. Real corruption figures the end justifies any means.

JOHN MURTHA

The famous ABSCAM scandal involved an FBI sting operation in which agents posed as emissaries of an Arab sheik who was offering bribes to U.S. elected officials. At the end of the day, one senator and five House members were convicted of bribery and conspiracy. Since the operation was an FBI investigation, all of the transactions were caught on videotape. The curious thing about these tapes is that some of them were not released for a very, very long time. This is especially true of that part of the tape that has Jack Murtha on it. That was only released in 2006, twenty-six years after the event.

Murtha evaded prosecution in the case by agreeing to testify against two other congressmen involved in the scandal, but the transcript of the tape indicates that Murtha certainly wasn't rock-ribbed in his opposition to bribe taking:

> Unidentified Male: Let me ask you now we're here together, I was under the impression, OK, and I told Howard we were willing to pay. And OK, I went out and got the fifty thousand. From what you're telling me, OK, you're telling me that's not what, you know, that that's not what you...
>
> Murtha: I'm not interested.
>
> Unidentified Male: OK.
>
> Murtha: At this point.
>
> Unidentified Male: OK.
>
> Murtha: You know, we do business for a while, maybe I'll be interested, maybe I won't, you know.[2]

"At this point?" What sort of honorable man makes such a statement? One must wonder if there ever became a point that John Murtha thought that taking a bribe would be acceptable. We can see why the tape was hidden away for so many years—the very powerful Murtha would be offended. As it turns out, the tape was released only because a former agent wanted the truth to get out.

Even with the tape, Murtha cruised to reelection in 2006 in spite of a spirited Republican challenger. It can easily be imagined what the effect of this tape would be had it been a senior Republican House member speaking those words: 'round the clock coverage, demands for resignation, imputations against the honor of all Republicans for allegedly "covering up" the transgressions for years, and all kinds of questions and analysis on how it would impact the coming elections. But because Murtha had a "D" after his name, it might as well have dropped off the earth.

EXPLOITING A TRAGEDY TO RAISE MONEY

As in the aftermath of the Asian tsunami, the American people showed their charitable nature following Hurricanes Katrina and Rita. We were all so determined to help out our suffering fellow Americans that we poured untold billions into disaster relief. This would normally be a time when fundraising for other purposes would be cut back, or eliminated altogether, so as not to compete with the immediate needs of the hurricane victims. This is what Senator Rick Santorum did—he cancelled much of his political fundraising efforts to avoid competition with hurricane recovery donation efforts, including a fundraiser featuring Vice President Cheney.

Very early in the 2006 election cycle, Santorum was considered one of the Republican Party's most vulnerable incumbent senators.[3] He was a very conservative Republican in a largely Democratic state whose chief opponent was running on his politically popular father's legacy. For Santorum to cancel his fundraising events was an actual sacrifice on his part. It was the sort of "people before politics" attitude we should applaud in our public figures.

On the other hand, Bob Casey Jr. went ahead with his fundraising efforts. As it turns out, both Santorum and Casey were scheduled to hold fundraising events in Houston on September 19th, 2005. Santorum cancelled his event. Casey did not, and his campaign brought in $18,000.[4] Bob Casey's financial exploitation of the Katrina tragedy pre-dated his September 19, 2005 fundraiser—on September 7, 2005, Casey sent an e-mail to supporters deploring the federal response to Katrina, and panhandling for donations.

Perhaps we can't place all the blame on Bob Casey, since the whole fundraising ethic of the Democratic Party seems to be like that. The Democratic Senatorial Campaign Committee, chaired by Senator Charles Schumer, also tried to raise money by exploiting Katrina. However, once they were confronted about it they pledged to donate the money to charity.

From immoral to illegal is a fairly short step, but most politicians never make it. In fact, it has become fairly rare for a politician to take or give a direct monetary bribe. Federal law enforcement agencies are too good these days for the old-fashioned envelope of cash in return for a vote to be worthwhile.

BOBBY RUSH

There are a variety of ways to buy your man, if you have an interest. One way that has cropped up often over recent years is via a home mortgage. All you need is a bank that is willing to loan more than a house is worth, and you've got your payoff, and only exceptional diligence will reveal what happened.

Congressman Bobby Rush (D-IL) got into a bit of financial embarrassment when it was revealed in November of 2005 that he hadn't paid his mortgage since July of that year.[5] It was an embarrassing thing, to be sure. On a salary of more than $165,000, Mr. Rush couldn't make the mortgage payment.

Mr. Rush had obtained a $334,600 loan on a house with a market value of $215,000. This is a neat trick, if you can do it—except you can't. If a person tries to borrow more money than a house is worth, then the bank rejects the loan application out of hand…well, unless you're a well-placed congressman. If you are such, then all things are possible.

Of course, Mr. Rush is not the only politician to benefit from such a deal. Randy "Duke" Cunningham (R-CA) also received a bribe by this means. But there is a difference: Given that Cunningham had an "R" after his name, his scandal was front page news; Mr. Rush was protected from such embarrassing scrutiny due to the "D" after his name. And he's not alone.

DON SIEGALMAN

Cunningham's criminal activity, while excellent fodder for scandal-mongering politicians, is rare these days. With so many ways to "legally" obtain money and favors, a corrupt politician on the make normally doesn't resort to the straightforward bribe. But it does happen from time to time, as we saw in the Cunningham case, and that of Don Siegelman.

Elected in 1998 in a landslide, Alabama Governor Don Siegelman lost his 2002 reelection bid to Republican Bob Riley by the smallest of margins. The change from enormously popular new governor to narrow loser was caused by widespread allegations of sweetheart deals for Siegelman supporters during his term of office.

As is quite common for politicians plagued by ethics issues, Siegelman had tried to get out in front of the corruption stories by leading the charge on ethics reform.[6] These efforts of the fox to guard the henhouse proved ineffective, and Siegelman was given his walking papers by the voters of Alabama. As a politician, Siegelman has not been one to admit errors. Even after his defeat, he continued to assert that the charges against him were baseless and only motivated by a desire of his opponents to beat him. Convinced of the purity of his motives, Siegelman tried for a political comeback in 2006, but found that his past actions as governor came back to haunt him.

In 2004, a grand jury began investigating various events of Siegelman's only term in office, including donations made to his 1999 lottery campaign, appointments to a state health panel, and tax breaks and contracts awarded by his administration.[7] Just as he claimed when defeated in 2002, Siegelman said that the continuing investigations are just a smear campaign by his opponents.

Siegelman was indicted in May of 2004 on Medicaid fraud charges, but charges were dropped due to lack of evidence. Siegelman, along with his former chief of staff Paul Hamrick and physician Phillip Bobo, had allegedly tried to rig bids on lucrative contracts sought by Bobo's company.[8]

Siegelman seemed out of the woods, but was indicted *again* in October of 2005[9] on racketeering, bribery, and extortion charges, along with Richard Scrushy. The indictment charged Siegelman with having half a million dollars in debts paid for him by Health-South—a company which runs hospitals in Alabama. The *quid pro quo* for this money was that Scrushy's chosen people were placed on a medical regulatory board.

Governor Siegelman continued to claim that the whole thing was a politically motivated witch-hunt and that he "never put a dime in his pocket that didn't belong there."[10] Such a statement is open to many interpretations—after all, Al Capone never had a dollar in his pocket that didn't belong there, but there is great dispute as to whether or not he should have been earning the dollars he placed in his pocket.

If one wanted a poster boy for Democratic corruption, hypocrisy, and hysterics, Siegelman would be a strong candidate. Back in the days when Alabama was essentially a one-party state ruled by the Democratic Party, Siegelman's activities would likely have gone unnoticed. And this is probably what bothers Siegelman the most—that after a lifetime of watching fellow Democrats commit these sorts of acts, he's the one who had to get caught up in a political system no longer absolutely dominated by friends. But Siegalman's problems did not get national media attention like former Connecticut Governor Rowland's, even when Siegelman and Scrushy were convicted in June of 2006.[11]

Siegelman remains unbowed and still more than willing to go to absurd lengths to try and salvage his life and political career. He has gone as far as to demand the charges against him be dismissed because there weren't enough black jurors on his case.[12] That a white man could make such a charge is flabbergasting—but when you are a crook determined to get back into the feeding trough of the public treasury, nothing is beyond the pale.

ALAN MOLLOHAN

Rep. Alan Mollohan (D-WV) has proven to be another great friend in high places. This has been especially true in regards to the biggest and most talked about bribery scandal during the 2006 campaign season.

The principal of the case was Congressman Cunningham, who took millions of dollars in bribes from defense contractors over the years in return for directing business their way from his committee seat. These actions alone present a massive scandal, but, as in all things corrupt in government, there is more than meets the eye—or, in this case, more than meets the desire of the MSM to report it.

Oddly enough, the House Ethics Committee didn't have much to say on the subject of Cunningham or the scandal he was involved in. The Democrats would say that this is because the "culture of corruption" in Washington is entirely Republican. Democrats are, according to Democrats, unaffected by the moral tone of Washington, D.C. But there might be another explanation as to why the Ethics Committee didn't make a move: Allan Mollohan, the ranking Democrat on the House Ethics Committee at the time, had received $23,000 in campaign contributions from MZM Inc., the company at the center of the Cunningham scandal. Mollohan is not alone, either. Rep. Patrick Kennedy (D-RI), Senator Jay Rockefeller (D-WV), Rep. John Murtha (D-PA), former California Rep. Vic Fazio, and over a hundred other members of both Houses of Congress have received contributions linked to MZM Inc. or ADCS Inc., another company connected to the Cunningham scandal.[13]

It takes a majority vote of the Ethics Committee to initiate an investigation, and no private citizen may bring a possible ethics violation before the Committee.[14] What this means is that unless a House member brings it up and a majority of the Committee decides to move, nothing happens. No harm, no foul, especially when your goose might be cooked along with everyone else's.

Even when Rep. Mollohan attempted to untaint himself by donating $23,000 of his MZM Inc.-linked contributions to charity, the national media took little interest.[15] They also took little interest in other stories about Mollohan's ethical woes.

On April 7, 2006, the National Legal and Policy Center (NLPC) disclosed that in late February it had filed a five hundred-page complaint (the result of a nine-month investigation) with the D.C. U.S. Attorney "detailing hundreds of ethics law violations" of Mollohan. According to the NLPC chairman Ken Boehm, Mollohan "was hiding financial and real estate assets and grossly misrepresenting their value."[16]

It was also reported that Mollohan "used his seat on the House Appropriations Committee to get earmarks directing $250 million in federal funds to five West Virginia nonprofits he helped set up."[17] Employees of these nonprofits in turn donated heavily to his campaign committees and family foundations. With these sorts of series allegations being raised, House Speaker Dennis Hastert called for Mollohan's resignation from the House Ethics Committee.

Of course, Nancy Pelosi was furious. "Republicans destroyed the ethics process in the House to protect their cronies Cunningham, DeLay, Ney, and other Members implicated in the Abramoff scandal—to name only a few," she said. "The Speaker should join me in directing the Ethics Committee to get to work, and not cast aspersions on the independent and distinguished Ranking Member."[18] Apparently Nancy Pelosi thinks the Ethics Committee's only purpose is to investigate Republicans, while ignoring the ethical lapses of Democrats.

It is a curious thing: Was Pelosi trying to protect Mollohan, or was her defense of Mollohan a backhanded way of protecting other Democrats even more directly threatened by scandal? Now that Pelosi is Speaker, it is going to get very hard to find out. As it was, Mollohan temporarily stepped down from the Ethics Committee a couple weeks later, and as the weeks passed, more reports of apparent ethical violations by Mollohan surfaced.

In 2004, Mollohan took his wife on a five-day trip to Spain that was sponsored by a group of government contractors that Mollohan had helped steer tens of millions of federal dollars to.[19]

In June of 2006, it was reported that Mollohan helped steer $179 million in government contracts to a family-run charity named after his father.[20]

Mollohan argued he was the victim of partisan attacks. "Obviously, I am in the crosshairs of the National Republican Party and like-minded entities."[21] Despite his ethical troubles and the apparent anti-corruption climate of the 2006 electorate, 64 percent of the voters in his district voted to reelect Mollohan, and he'll remain a friend in high places for campaign contributors who seek government contracts.

NYDIA VELASQUEZ

Rep. Nydia Velasquez (D-NY) and Judge Margarita Lopez Torres are both originally from Puerto Rico and have been political allies in New York for quite some time. When Lopez Torres needed an endorsement, Velasquez was only too pleased to provide it. The trouble lay in the fact that the way the endorsement went out violated House ethics rules.

In order for representatives to stay in contact with their constituents, we allow them the privilege of sending mail to their districts. The alleged purpose is to keep everyone informed, and this might have made sense back in the days before radio, television, and the Internet, but for whatever reasons we keep it going here in the twenty-first century. Mostly their mailings tend towards telling everyone what a wonderful person their representative is. In Velasquez' case, she wanted to tell everyone what a great person Lopez Torres is, and that is where she ran into trouble.[22]

Under House ethics guidelines, lawmakers may not use official services for purely political purposes—such as endorsing someone in a political race. Naturally for Congress, there is confusion as to whether this violation falls under Ethics Committee jurisdiction or if the House Commission on Congressional Mailing Standards would have charge of it. There is nothing like confusion of jurisdiction to prevent action from being taken. The main thing remains that Velasquez has been using the power of her office for corrupt purposes.

SHERROD BROWN

Sherrod Brown, the newly elected U.S. Senator from Ohio, also has experience abusing his power for corrupt purposes.

In 1985, Secretary of State Brown's office was the subject of a drug probe. Over the course of the nine-month investigation "undercover agents made three buys of marijuana and one buy of a substance purported to be cocaine from the two employees,"[23] but the two employees avoided felony drug prosecution. Brown himself found a bag of marijuana under the seat of his car and turned it over to the highway patrol.[24]

An Ohio State Highway Patrol investigator said Brown tried to end the probe because he feared it would hurt his chances to be reelected.[25] The *Columbus Dispatch* reported on July 8, 1990, that one of the employees who had sold drugs to the undercover agent in 1985 was promoted by Brown and remained on the state's payroll.[26] This scandal did little to hamper his political career, and now he's been elected to the U.S. Senate the same year Democrats made corruption a campaign issue.

ROD BLAGOJEVICH

Advocating a new program in politics is always a gamble. You can never tell in advance how the public will view it, or what sort of opposition an idea might generate. This is why a lot of politicians just tread water while in office—keep things going as they are and hope to God that nothing bad happens while they are in charge. Still, politicians often take the gamble of a new program, and Governor Rod Blagojevich (D-IL) is no different.

Governor Blagojevich wanted to take a gamble on gambling. Specifically, he wanted to introduce a Keno game for the state to pay for school construction. Keno, for those who don't know, is a numbers game in which the player picks a set of numbers out of a large group and hopes that they match what is selected in the game. As in all casino games, the house always wins, so this would be a good money-maker for the state of Illinois.

Two of Governor Blagojevich's aides—John Wyma and Milan Petrovic—are lobbyists for firms that run Keno operations for state lotteries. Wyma was the governor's chief of staff when he was in Congress, while Petrovic was paid thousands of dollars in consulting fees by the Blagojevich campaign.[27] In his defense, a spokesman for Blagojevich has stated that the governor did not know that his former chief of staff worked as a lobbyist for a gaming company. You can lose track of people as time goes on.

Enjoying the perks of a powerful position can also cause you to lose perspective. Solzhenitsyn once observed that there are as many centers of the universe as there are people. Each of us is guilty of all too often thinking of self first, others last.

Rod Blagojevich has certainly been looking out for himself as governor of Illinois, and as a result, has found himself plagued by scandal after scandal. One practically needs a score sheet to keep track of Blagojevich's myriad legal and ethical dilemmas.

Blagojevich was elected governor of Illinois in 2002 after serving three terms in Congress in the seat now held by Rahm Emanuel. Blagojevich was ironically propelled to office on public distaste for the scandals emanating out of the then-GOP governor's office.

But the new Blagojevich administration would usher in a new series of scandals, including: questionable attempts to change the health coverage for Illinois government employees; arranging for kickbacks and sweetheart deals regarding health care, teacher's pensions, and bond issues, as well as other state business; trading political contributions for state jobs and contracts and other questionable hiring practices at state agencies, and a suspicious $1,500 check given to Blagojevich's seven-year-old daughter by a friend whose wife had just been given a state job, just to name a few. So many investigations were ongoing that the impression is that Blagojevich sees his office as a political pork factory for himself and his political cronies.

Indictments and investigations seemed as common for Blagojevich and his administration as ribbon-cutting and bill-signing
ceremonies are for other governors. And despite the fact that corruption was a big issue in the 2006 elections, Blagojevich, with his
scandal-ridden administration, was reelected governor with 49
percent of the vote. If corruption was a factor in the congressional
elections as exit polls claimed, it certainly wasn't a factor in the
gubernatorial election in Illinois.

One is forgiven for thinking that at least Blagojevich is out of
federal office, so he can only damage one state rather than all fifty.
The only problem is that his successor in the House managed to
lower himself to the level Blagojevich had set for his district (see
Chapter Four).

BARACK OBAMA

The scandals of the Blagojevich administration, as we have seen,
extend far and wide in the realm of Illinois politics—so far and
wide, indeed, that they are lapping around the feet of the Democrat's newest star politician, Senator Barak Obama.

Even in the days following his election to the U.S. Senate in
2004, Obama had been floated as a potential presidential candidate. The Democrats clearly believe they have a winner in Obama
and have set their sights on high office for him. And who can
blame them? Obama is wonderfully intelligent, fabulously edu-
cated, articulate and telegenic, with presumably no skeletons in
his closet. Even Senator Joe Biden described him as "clean."[28]

Obama is, on the surface, the ideal standard-bearer, especially
for a party dependent upon image rather than message for its success. Image, however, often fails to live up to reality.

On October 11, 2006, real estate mogul Antoin "Tony" Rezko
was indicted for "trying to collect kickbacks, including a $1.5 mil-
lion contribution 'to a certain public official,' from companies
wanting state business."[29] Unclear in the indictment is the identity
of "a certain public official," though speculation mostly revolved
around Governor Blagojevich.

While Senator Obama sought to downplay his relationship
with Mr. Rezko, the fact that Rezko was part of Obama's financial
team for his 2004 senate campaign, donated a total of $20,000 to
Obama's political campaigns over the years and raised at least

$60,000 for Obama's political campaigns indicated, perhaps, a much closer relationship than Senator Obama would prefer the public to know about.[30]

Obama would like us to believe that his dealings were innocent and that he was unaware of Rezko's history of shady dealings, but even he has to twist logic into some strange circles in explaining his ignorance. "With respect to the purchase of my home, I am confident that everything was handled ethically and above board," he told the *Chicago Sun-Times*, "But I regret that while I tried to pay close attention to the specific requirements of ethical conduct, I misgauged the appearance presented by my purchase of the additional land from Mr. Rezko."[31]

The home in question is adjacent to a vacant lot, which was owned by the same people from whom Obama purchased the house. When that house was on the market, the sellers didn't want to sell only the house—it was buy both, or don't buy either. The reason for this was the vacant lot could only be accessed via the lot featuring the house, and thus would be worthless if not purchased in tandem with the house. Of course, the cost of that vacant lot significantly increased the overall price of the purchase.

The price Obama paid for the house was $1.65 million. The price of the adjacent vacant lot was $625,000. For Obama to purchase his home, he would have had to come up with a total of $2,275,000. That is quite a lot of money. Rezko, from whom Obama now distances himself, agreed to purchase the vacant lot. The lot, it must be remembered, would be useless for Rezko—the only person who could possibly use it was Obama. In fact, so useful was this vacant lot that Obama purchased a ten-foot wide strip of it from Rezko, thus widening Obama's backyard, but also making the vacant lot even more useless for its owner.

Of course, Obama wants us to believe that there was only the *appearance* of impropriety, thinking that we'd be comforted by the fact that he paid higher than the appraised value of a ten-foot strip of land from Rezko.

The outrageous thing about this all was that the story of Rezko's indictment broke less than a month before the 2006 elections and two days prior to the Foley scandal breaking, and yet most Americans have probably never heard of Rezko, his deep connections to the Democratic Party,[32] or the crimes he is accused of. This is the way it is supposed to be: when a scandal breaks—a diligent media is supposed to report the facts fairly and honestly and the people are to pass ultimate judgment. It is just too bad that the media feels protective about the Democratic Party in general and Barak Obama in particular—the people are being prevented from rendering judgment because they are not being fully informed about all of the facts.

Obama has a squeaky clean image and perhaps his brushes against the dishonest have nothing to do with his actual business. In the end, Democrats certainly hope Obama has no ethical issues that could come back to haunt him when and if he embarks on a campaign for the presidency.

The story of Obama's shady land deal, which certainly deserved a national audience, became the tree that fell in the forest without anybody around to hear the crash.

Some might think that the media, with its obsession for scandal, would have been salivating over the opportunity to sully Obama's squeaky clean image, but with the midterm elections around the corner, and with the balance of power in Congress on the line, it didn't make the cut.

After all, it wasn't a Republican scandal and therefore did not play into the Democrats' campaign of vilification. Not only were the Republicans to be cast as the villian in this electoral morality play, the Democrats had to appear as knights in shining armour, come to rescue the fair damsel of the United States from the Republican dragon.

The Democrats, with the help of the media, accomplished this by not only targeting Republicans under investigation or with accusations of ethical lapses, but, to add insult to injury, they also ran candidates who tried to capitalize on the corruption issue by running on clean ethics pledges. When it came to taking Rep. Bob Ney's former seat, this strategy worked very well.

ZACK SPACE

Ohio Democrat Zack Space not only ran on a clean ethics pledge, but also a conservative platform, and taking cues from Nancy Pelosi, he made ethics the centerpiece of his campaign for Ney's congressional seat. [33] He boasted that he was the only candidate in his district to sign an ethics pledge "not to accept dinners, gifts or junkets from lobbyists if elected to Congress."[34] Like Pelosi, Space talked the talk, but didn't walk the walk.

For all his rhetoric about ethics, Space was more than willing to accept dirty money to fund his campaign.

Space accepted a $2,000 donation from John Cafaro who pled guilty in 2001 to bribing Rep. Jim Traficant. Cafaro got fifteen months' probation and a $150,000 fine. Space claimed ignorance, and upon "learning" about the dirty money a staffer claimed he would return it.[35]

Zack Space also broke his clean ethics pledge by accepting money and other favors from political action committees. He received $1,000 from SecureUS PAC a week after he had been invited to an event in Washington hosted by the political action committee... Space egotistically bragged about this on his campaign website,[36] but what he did not brag about was the fact that SecureUS PAC is funded by registered lobbyists and Hollywood liberals.

Zack Space will be in good company in the House of Representatives when he joins other hypocritical Democrats who ran on ethics platforms while running away from their own ethical lapses. Space had said earlier in his campaign "We need honest representation now more than ever, yet our current leaders continue to serve special interests rather than the working families that have elected them."[37] Unfortunately for Ohio's 18th district, that's not what they got in Zack Space.

BILL RICHARDSON

When New Mexico Governor Bill Richardson unveiled a new Augusta Westland A109 Power helicopter for the state police on December 5, 2003, he declared, "It's quick, it's sleek, and the bottom line is it's here to save lives." But he also had other plans for the $3.8 million two-engine helicopter that can seat up to six passengers.[38]

Richardson, who handily won reelection with 68 percent of the vote in November of 2006, has announced a presidential bid for 2008.[39] Presidential ambitions often come with attempts to improve one's image, and Richardson is no exception. For some time now, Richardson has been accustoming himself to luxuries on par with that of a president by lavishly using the state police helicopter, which Richardson had previously claimed was meant "to save lives," to travel to public appearances around his home state.

While it is commonplace for governors to use military or state helicopters to inspect damage from natural disasters and other catastrophes, Richardson, uninterested in waiting in traffic, uses the state police's $3.8 million Augusta helicopter to travel to bill-signing ceremonies, news conferences, and other events. The *Associated Press* surveyed several Western states and "found no governor who regularly flies aboard a state-owned copter as Richardson does to attend meetings, speeches, dedication ceremonies and news conferences."[40]

Between late 2003, when the helicopter went into operation, and October 2005, Richardson flew on forty of the helicopter's 291 trips, averaging two hours of flight time a month, accumulating nearly fifty hours, or 10 percent of the total "passenger hours" logged by the helicopter. The helicopter costs $417 an hour to operate. Richardson's administration says the governor only uses the helicopter when it is not needed by police, but critics claim that his helicopter rides, which have cost New Mexico taxpayers over $20,000 in less than two years, say the helicopter rides are not simply about saving time, but enhancing the governor's image.

> "I can't fathom what would require you to take a helicopter repeatedly from Santa Fe to Albuquerque when it's a 50-minute drive .... And that's driving the speed limit. We all know he doesn't drive the speed limit," said Rep. Dan Foley, R-Roswell, referring to reports that the governor's vehicle has been clocked going more than 100 mph.
>
> Foley likened Richardson's use of the helicopter—what he called "State Police One"—to the president's use of the Marine One helicopter.[41]

Richardson may think that using an expensive state police helicopter as his own personal taxi is a good way to improve his image, but having taxpayers pay for his improved image hardly seems fair.

Richardson's arrogance doesn't start with getting himself a nifty helicopter to make impressive entrances in. With all the experience of a former Energy Secretary, Richardson put himself forward once upon a time as the man to solve the thorny problem of nuclear weapons in North Korea. He's got the helicopter and he's got a failed foreign policy. He's a perfect fit for the next Democratic presidential nominee.

FRANK BALLANCE

If Richardson stands a good chance of being the next Bill Clinton, then former Congressman Frank Ballance might be the next Al Gore. He has acted as if there were "no controlling legal authority."

He was first elected to the North Carolina House of Representative in 1982, then the state Senate in 1988. In 1985, Ballance incorporated a nonprofit charitable group named John A. Hyman Memorial Youth Foundation, for the purpose of "substance abuse education, prevention and rehabilitation services" for poor people in the nearby counties.

During the 1990s, Ballance became chairman of the state Senate Appropriations Committee on Justice and Public Safety. In this position, he was able to secure appropriations for his foundation.

The first appropriation in the amount of $167,000 was made in 1994, another $100,000 came in 1995, and the money just kept rolling in year after year. Despite the inflow of hundreds of thousands of taxpayer dollars, the Hyman Foundation neglected to file a sworn accounting of receipts and expenditures of the state funds. Ballance's control of the foundation combined with his influence in the legislature proved to be very profitable. From 1994 through 2003, the Hyman Foundation received nearly $2.3 million in state funds.

Between 2000 and 2003, Ballance forged (or had forged) the signature of the Executive Director of the Hyman Foundation on ten official disbursement requests to the State of North Carolina and had them falsely notarized in order to conceal those forgeries.

Between 1998 and 2003, Ballance was diverting funds from the Hyman Foundation to his law firm to pay legal fees, purchase a luxury car for his son (a District Court judge in Warren County), pay his daughter for services she never performed, and give money to his mother.

Ballance was elected to the U.S. House of Representatives in November of 2002.

Following an investigation into the Hyman Foundation, Ballance was indicted by a federal grand jury on September 2, 2004, for conspiracy to commit mail fraud and money laundering.

Former Rep. Ballance pleaded guilty in November 2004 and was sentenced a year later to four years in federal prison; his son Garey Ballance was also sentenced to a year of probation, a $5,000 fine, and nine months in prison for failing to report $20,000 he got from the Hyman Foundation to the IRS,[42] and he would also give up his judgeship.

Following Ballance's sentencing, Ferrell Blount, the chairman of the North Carolina Republican Party said, "It's a shame that someone so trusted by the people would betray that trust for their own personal gain and the gain of his family members...The only silver lining to this episode is that Frank Ballance is no longer in a position of public trust."[43] One would think.

Despite the evidence of his guilt and the law finding him guilty, Ballance seems poised to return from his four-year prison sentence with his reputation intact, as Democrats who break the law often manage to do. His supporters seemed more than willing to forgive him, with several hundred gathering for a three-hour farewell luncheon headlined by comedian and activist Dick Gregory on December 3, 2005.[44] Another eighty supporters attended a fundraiser and farewell party for Ballance just days before he had to report to federal prison to begin serving his sentence. Attendees donned orange ribbons and had their fingers dipped in orange paint symbolizing the jail sentences of blacks and "the injustice in the court system toward blacks." The program for the fundraiser asked supporters to not "allow the court system, the news media or any biased force to turn you against Frank and his family. It seems to frustrate the power structure when people of color stand together."[45] It seems that his illegal activities are irrelevant to his supporters since he decided to play the race card. It certainly frustrates the ability for justice to rule when excuses are made for crooks.

Ballance's cunning with money not only benefited him and his family, he also spread some wealth to the Democratic Party. Ballance donated $29,500, to the Democratic Congressional Campaign Committee,[46] which DCCC chairman Rahm Emanuel refused to return, despite his own calls for Republicans to return money connected to Tom DeLay after his indictment (see Chapter Four).

JOHN CONYERS

Ballance's plea for people to stand together would be good advice for John Conyers. Conyers, you see, could use a sense of solidarity with people, especially subordinates.

On the most momentous issues of the day, the people need a tribune who is of sterling character. Someone who is above reproach and whose word will not be doubted even by his foes. John Conyers is not that man—though he has tried to be with his rather obsessive efforts to impeach President Bush; efforts that started even before the liberation of Iraq.

On March 1, 2006, the *Detroit Free Press* reported that Rep. John Conyers made three former aides conduct his personal business while they were supposed to be working in his congressional offices.

According to the story, "Conyers ordered them to act as personal servants, tutoring and baby-sitting his two sons, helping his wife with a law class, and chauffeuring him to political and private events, and picking up tabs at restaurants and motels." The charges were included in complaints filed with the House Ethics Committee.

The complaints were made by the former chief of staff in Conyers's Detroit office, Deanna Maher; his former legal counsel from 1997-2000, Sydney Rooks; and legislative aide Dean Christian Thorton, who had been fired in January.[47]

This is not the first time Conyers has been accused of such violations. The *Detroit Free Press* reported on November 21, 2003, that aides had accused Conyers of assigning campaign work to them on government time:

> Staffers for the 19-term Detroit Democrat [Conyers] told the Free Press they have used government telephones, printers, fax machines and mailing lists to solicit campaign contributions, organize fund-raisers and canvass for votes. It is illegal to raise political funds from any federal office.
>
> This report is based on extensive interviews with six current and former Conyers aides, who asked to remain anonymous for fear of reprisals, and Enid Brown, a Conyers volunteer who said she took notes at a campaign strategy session attended by Conyers and staff members in his down-

town Detroit office. The Free Press also examined congressional payroll and campaign finance records, and schedules
and internal records for Conyers' office.[48]

Maher was revealed to be one of the sources for the November 2003
Free Press story. One staffer denied campaign work was done on
government time. Maher and Rooks provided evidence for the allegations to *The Hill*, including letters, memorandums, e-mails,
handwritten notes, and expense reports.

Rooks said Maher was used by Conyers as a "full-time live-in
nanny for Conyers' young sons for several weeks in 1998, all while
paying her part-time congressional salary. Rooks herself was ordered to tutor one of Conyers' sons, and either her or another
staffer would pick him up from school.[49]

This kind of behavior is actually common, according to an uni-
dentified staffer who worked for two House Democrats. "This type
of behavior is so prevalent, the unofficial duties that members re-
quire you to do off-the-record. Most staffers are subjected to this
unfair treatment. It's the great untold story on Capitol Hill."

Maher had been working for Conyers for seven years when
she quit in May of 2005. She said she was no longer able to tolerate
such an unethical environment. In her letter to House Ethics
Committee, she wrote, "I could not tolerate any longer being involved with continual unethical, if not criminal, practices which
were accepted as 'business as usual.'"[50] Of course, as this book has
demonstrated, unethical and criminal behaviors *are* business as
usual in the Democratic Party. For Conyers, his alleged ethical
lapses go beyond forcing his staffers to babysit, tutor, and chauffer
his children.

In part of Maher's letter to the House Ethics Committee, she
repeated a previous allegation that Conyers allowed former top
aide DeWayne Boyd to obtain a fake passport after being convicted of fraud, making false statements, and government theft.
Boyd used the fake passport to flee to Ghana, where he was eventually recaptured and extradited to the United States.[51]

On December 29, 2006, the House Ethics Committee released a
statement on the matter, revealing that Conyers "acknowledged
what he characterized as a 'lack of clarity' in his communications

with staff members regarding their official duties and responsibilities..."[52]

In other words, Conyers claimed that his staffers doing campaign work, babysitting, and chauffeuring his kids on government time was the result of a miscommunication. But we can all be put at ease because Conyers "accepted responsibility" for his "lack of clarity." The Committee considered the matter "resolved" after Conyers said that he had "begun taking steps to provide clearer guidance to staff regarding the requirement that campaign work and official work be separate."[53]

So, even though this Democrat's "lack of clarity" would have been a Republican's "corruption," Nancy Pelosi, in all her ethical wisdom and moral superiority, said that Conyers would remain chairman of the Judiciary Committee, where he may or may not act on his pledge to start bogus impeachment proceedings against President Bush.[54]

JOE BACA

Conyers is by no means alone in forcing congressional staffers to perform tasks for his personal benefit. In February 2004, Rep. Joe Baca (D-CA) sent six of his staffers from Washington, D.C. to California to campaign for his son, Joe Baca Jr., who had been "locked in an intense primary battle for a seat in the California Assembly." While Baca claims the campaign work was voluntary, two staffers claim they were forced to campaign under pressure from Baca or his chief of staff, Linda Macias.[55]

Not only were staffers forced to volunteer for the campaign during official work time, but taxpayers also footed the bill for their airfare. Macias reportedly spent nearly five weeks in the district leading up to the primary, accumulating $3,000 in hotel bills. During her stay, she kept tabs on Baca's staffers, making sure they were helping with the campaign. She spent a total of ten days in the district throughout the rest of 2004. After their forced campaigning stint, most of the staffers sought new employment, and five had left within a year.[56]

POWER OVER PRINCIPLE

Corruption at any level of government shouldn't be tolerated or excused. When our elected leaders are caught taking bribes or other illegal activities, they must be held accountable. Rep. William Jefferson (D-LA) was under investigation for bribery for well over a year before his fellow Democrats decided to strip him of his powerful committee assignment (see Chapter Five). It simply is not good enough to turn a blind eye to corruption within your own party until it becomes politically expedient to do otherwise.

A sense of shame is necessary in life, and so is a sense of limitations. Shameless people who think that nothing should hold them back always are a problem. People without a sense of inhibition just keep striving until they either get what they want or are destroyed in the process.

People use what power they have. All human beings are gifted with some power or other. It isn't power so much but how it is used that can cause a problem. The greater the power available to a person, the greater the benefit they can bring to everyone, but also the greater destruction they can cause. Some exercises in power, even when corrupt, are rather small beans but still illustrate a larger problem.

In any discussion of political corruption, space has to be made for the mere *arrogance* of power. This is when an elected official starts to view himself or herself as a superior being, not bound by the same rules of conduct required of those poor mortals who haven't managed to get elected to Congress. This is the sort of petty use of power which might make a minor official demand a reserved parking space, or convince a low level elected official that his position demands a good reservation at the new restaurant.

In theory, the MSM should ensure that everyone keeps to a level of honesty. But how are the people to know if the media won't examine Democrats are sternly as they investigate Republicans, and Democrats won't hold themselves to any moral standards at all? Is control of American government going to be determined by who is most successful at hiding scandal? It is to be hoped not.

When Pennsylvania's new senator Bob Casey, Jr. claimed he would donate the money he raised following Hurrican Katrina to disaster relief, it was possible to see what the light of truth can do. But there is a calcification of heart in a person who would even think about raising funds in time of tragedy. The immorality pervading the Democratic Party has hardened a lot of Democratic hearts, and even though what Casey and other Democrats have done isn't always illegal, it has been clearly wrong.

All through the 2006 campaign, even the slightest indiscretion on the part of Republicans was enough to get Democrats fuming and charging ethical violations and corruption. Within their own party, however, it was much easier (and more convenient) to turn a blind eye to the sleaziness and abuses of power by members of their party, especially with their rising stars.

With the Democrats back in the majority, they've discovered that doing what's politically expedient is far more profitable than doing the right thing. While some new laws have been passed—and some, even, which may prove of use in combating corruption—the real cure can only come if the Democrats, as a party, make it their determination that they will no longer break or skirt the law as they feel it necessary to advance their personal and political goals. Institutions are only as good as the men and women who govern them. Right now, the people governing our Congress give much reason for worry.

CHAPTER TWELVE

SEX SCANDALS

"I did not have sexual relations with that woman, Miss Lewinsky."

—Bill Clinton

FOLLOW ME around. I don't care," leading Democrat presidential candidate Gary Hart told The *New York Times* in response to allegations that he was a womanizer early in the 1988 campaign season. "I'm serious. If anybody wants to put a tail on me, go ahead. They'd be very bored."[1]

The interview was published on May 3, 1987. Five days later he dropped out of the race, with his political career in shambles from the revelation of his affair with Donna Rice... a scandal climaxed by the disclosure of a photo showing the twenty-nine-year-old model sitting on the presidential candidate's lap aboard the luxury yacht aptly named *Monkey Business*.[2] His withdrawal from the race paved the way for Mike Dukakis to win the Democratic nomination.

There's nothing like a sex scandal to spice up and change the course of a political campaign. Salacious details leak out, politicians and pundits self-servingly weigh in on the talk shows, and a candidate's career ends up in shambles.

But something different happened during the 2006 midterm elections, when we learned that sex scandals have the potential to do more than take down one political candidate.

The resignation of Florida Republican Mark Foley rocked Capitol Hill after sexually explicit Internet messages between the congressman and a male congressional page surfaced in the media in September of 2006. Democrats saw the opportunity, and we saw a party out of power ride a wave of disgust to political victory.

As devastating as sex scandals can be, there is perhaps no other type of scandal that demonstrates the Democrat's hypocrisy and tolerance for corruption within their party.

"PROTECTING" THE CHILDREN

Democrats, as anxious as ever to take advantage of a Republican scandal, pounced on the Foley story, turning the scandal into a witch-hunt, asking who in the Republican Party knew what and when. Reports that several Republicans had known about inappropriate behavior by Foley for over a year resulted in calls for Dennis Hastert to resign as Speaker of the House and Democrats calling for widespread investigations of Republicans.

Despite various allegations that Hastert and other Republicans knew about Foley's behavior, no Republican ever defended Foley's behavior, or made excuses for it. Still, Democrats had found a new scandal to exploit in order to support their quest to win a majority in the House of Representatives.

In a statement, Nancy Pelosi said, "Republican leaders admitted to knowing about Mr. Foley's abhorrent behavior for six months to a year and failed to protect the children in their trust. Republican leaders must be investigated by the Ethics Committee and immediately questioned under oath."[3]

The question of the moment may have been "what did Republicans know, and when did they know it," but allegations that the media had known about the story for over a year received little attention, as did reports that Democrats had advance knowledge of the allegations as well. In fact, the *American Spectator* reported that not only did Democrats know about Foley's inappropriate behavior before it broke in the media, but they actually wanted it to break closer to the midterm elections.

> According to one political consultant with ties to the DNC and other party organizations, "I'm hearing the Foley story wasn't supposed to drop until ten days out of the election. It was supposed to be the *coup de grace*, not the first shot."

> So why the rush? According to another DNC operative: bad polling numbers across the country. "Bush's national security speeches were getting traction beyond the base, gas prices were dropping, economic outlook surveys were positive. We were seeing bad Democratic numbers in Missouri,

Michigan, Washington, Arizona, Florida, Pennsylvania, even parts of New York," says the operative. "A month before, we were looking at launching an offensive against Republicans who according to polling barely held a five-seat majority if the election were to be held at the end of August. That was doable for Democrats from September 1 to November 7. But by mid-September, Republicans were back to having held seats for a 15-seat majority. In the Senate, it looked like a wash. We held seats in Florida, Nebraska, picked up seats in Pennsylvania, but that that was about it. They were holding in Missouri and possibly within reach of Maryland and Washington. We were looking at a disaster in the making."[4]

Appearing on ABC's *This Week* on October 8, 2006, Rahm Emanuel refused to say whether or not he was aware of explicit messages between Mark Foley and the congressional page. Emanuel was insistent that he had never seen the messages or e-mails; when pressed about whether he was aware of them, he repeatedly responded, "Never saw them."[5]

This stunning inability to admit whether he was aware of the e-mails is particularly surprising since the *Washington Post* reported a few days later that "there [were] indications that Democrats spent months circulating five less insidious Foley e-mails to news organizations before they were finally published by ABC News..."[6] So what did the Democrats know and when did they know it? Who knows? But Rahm Emanuel has some explaining to do.

While Democrats took the opportunity in the aftermath of the Foley scandal to grandstand about "protecting children," and assume a moral high ground, they have a much different attitude when it comes to sex scandals within their own party, a trend also noticed by *Investor's Business Daily*:

> Democrats not only seem OK with the kind of behavior for which Foley is charged, but also they protect and excuse it. Only when it's a Republican do they proclaim themselves shocked—shocked!—when it comes to light.[7]

And not just feigned shock. As Congressman Bob Inglis (R-SC) noted, Nancy Pelosi and other Democrats were very well prepared with talking points when the Foley scandal erupted.[8]

It was another stunning example of the double standard: Whenever a Democrat is caught in a sex scandal, it is quickly dubbed a "private matter" between him and his family, and thus unsuited for political debate, while in the case of Republicans the scandal casts stains on the entire party.

When the Foley scandal broke, coverage given it by the MSM could easily mislead a person to thinking that this was (a) the worst sex scandal that had happened in modern times, and (b) that only a Republican could be so base as to have improper contact with minors and/or subordinates. Indeed, MSM coverage of the Foley scandal prior to the 2006 midterms nearly exceeded coverage of Iraq and terrorism combined.[9] Any reflection at all, of course, reminds that sex and politics all too often go together. What was really disturbing, however, was the way the Democrats hypocritically played up the scandal as if they, themselves, had not in the past had serious sex scandals and behaved infamously in their treatment of the issue.

PAGE SCANDAL HYPOCRISY

On July 20, 1983, following a yearlong investigation by the House ethics committee, the House of Representatives censured two congressmen for having sexual relationships with underage congressional pages: Rep. Dan Crane (R-IL), for a 1980 sexual affair with a female page, and Rep. Gerry Studds (D-MA), for a 1973 sexual affair with a male page. The incident prompted Studds to admit his homosexuality. Studds, in admitting to his involvement with the male page, was adamant that the relationship was "consensual" and claimed that the investigation raised "fundamental questions with respect to privacy and procedural fairness."[10]

There were only three votes against reprimanding Crane and Studds, and it should come as no surprise that all three of the votes came from Democrats.[11] Perhaps these Democrats weren't too concerned that the two congressmen "failed to protect the children in their trust," as Nancy Pelosi would say. At the end of it all, Studds spun his scandal of shame into a badge of honor by claiming that his admission of homosexuality allowed him to "look people in the eye"[12] and that many members of Congress expressed continued friendship and support.

Republican Rep. Newt Gingrich, on the other hand, called for the expulsion of both Crane and Studds, noting that a teacher would never be allowed to continue teaching if he or she had a sexual relationship with a student. "The two Congressmen, like a teacher, must be fired," he said on the floor of the House.[13]

In the end, both let the voters of their districts decide their political fates. Of course, Dan Crane was defeated, while Gerry Studds was apparently forgiven by his constituents and ended up being reelected to six more terms before retiring in 1996.

BARNEY FRANK

While Mark Foley did the right thing by immediately resigning, even he could have prolonged his political career by moving to Massachusetts and registering as a Democrat.

Just ask Rep. Barney Frank; he's still serving. In fact, with the Democrats back in power after the 2006 elections, he became chairman of the House Committee on Financial Services.

Imagine for a moment what would happen if a Republican congressman had a drug-addicted, live-in sex partner who ran a prostitution ring out of the congressman's apartment, all the while being routinely in violation of his parole agreement stemming from a conviction for sex with a minor.[14] How many seconds would it take for the resignation to follow revelation of the scandal?

The Frank prostitution scandal showed one of the primary benefits of being an ultra-liberal Democrat. Liberals can get away with just about anything if their voting record is reliably leftwing. In this scandal, Frank stoutly asserted that he was victimized by Stephen L. Gobie, the male prostitute Frank hired as a personal assistant after Frank had paid him for sex.

The point to remember is that Frank hired Gobie *after* he had paid Gobie for sex. There are lots of things which may be looked for in hiring a competent assistant, but how many people think that selling sexual favors is one of them?

Frank essentially asked the world to believe that he had no clue that Gobie would continue his prostitution activities once Frank hired him and moved him in to his home. Frank was working on the *Pretty Woman* theory—that the prostitute is the good guy and would, of course, immediately cease being a whore upon being hired by a wealthy benefactor. Left unexplained is how

Frank could believe that a man who sells his body for money could behave as an upright citizen. Also unexplained is how Frank remained enough in ignorance of Gobie's character that Frank wrote several letters of recommendation to Gobie's parole board.

The letters Frank wrote were to get Gobie released from parole due to Gobie's 1982 conviction for having sex with a minor. Child molestation didn't become a hot issue in the MSM until it could be tied to the Catholic Church, so this angle in the Frank scandal was left mostly unexplored. But it was and is a serious issue, as Democrats demonstrated when the Foley scandal broke. They believed they had a strong hammer to use against Republicans with Foley's salacious e-conversations with young pages, but what a difference a decade makes.

MEL REYNOLDS

On August 19, 1994, Congressman Mel Reynolds (D-IL) was indicted on statutory rape and child pornography charges as well as witness tampering and obstruction of justice. In what has become typical in American judicial processes, Reynolds, who is African-American, also asserted the charges were racially motivated. Caught by these indictments in the heat of a watershed midterm election (an election that turned Congress over to the Republican Party for the first time in forty years), a person would be forgiven for thinking this spelled the end of the career for the accused. Not quite.

Reynolds was reelected in November of 1994, winning 98 percent of the vote. To add to the astounding nature of this event, Reynolds raised nearly $400,000 for his reelection bid. It is small wonder with that kind of money floating around that Reynolds was also investigated for campaign finance violations.

In the fullness of time, Reynolds did get what was coming to him. In August of 1995 he was convicted on multiple counts of sexual assault, child pornography and obstruction of justice. Icing on the cake was provided when he was convicted in 1997 on various financial fraud charges.

In theory, there should be a limit to what a Democrat can do wrong and still retain friends high up in the Democratic Party. While this is a valid theory, it has yet to be put to the test, at least in the case of Mel Reynolds. In spite of being convicted on twenty-seven felony counts, he still rated a commutation of sentence from President Bill Clinton as he slipped out of office in January of 2001, and while Reynolds failed in his political comeback against Jesse Jackson, Jr., he was given a plum job at Rainbow/PUSH by Jesse Jackson, Sr.

It is a curiosity of politics that Reynolds, a man who had sex with a subordinate, was pardoned by President Clinton, who also had sex with a subordinate, and was then hired by Jesse Jackson, who also had sex with a subordinate. Sex with a subordinate is a sin, which has a long and dishonorable history. It is the classic evil of the powerful exploiting their position over the powerless. Not for nothing have we, as a people, enacted stern laws against such activities. It is just unfortunate that Democrats don't seem to care either about the law, or simple decency.

Gerry Studds may have been censured by the House, but his constituents kept sending him back to Washington until he retired in 1996. Mel Reynolds won reelection in 1994 despite charges of statutory rape and child pornography.

DANIEL INOUYE

Another Democrat who found his political career undeterred by a sex scandal was Hawaii Senator Daniel Inouye. In October 1992, Inouye's Republican opponent ran a campaign ad using audiotape of Inouye's hair stylist saying that Inouye had forced her to have sex with him seventeen years earlier, but didn't consider it rape because she didn't fight back.[15] The tape had been recorded secretly, and the hair stylist, who hadn't intended on going public with the allegations, objected to the ads and threatened to sue Reed unless he pulled the ads.[16] She would later refuse to take part in an investigation because she had forgiven Inouye, whom she described as a sex addict.[17]

Despite the allegations against him, Inouye still won reelection, defeating Reed 58 percent to 28 percent. Inouye even outperformed Bill Clinton, who carried the state with 49 perecent of the vote in Hawaii during his successful run for president.[18]

GARY CONDIT

One Democrat whose political career *was* cut short as the result of a scandal was Congressman Gary Condit (D-CA), who became embroiled in controversy when his young intern, Chandra Levy, went missing in 2001. This story received national attention but the odd thing about it, given Democratic outrage over Mark Foley, is that there was no strong call on the part of Democrats for Condit's resignation, even after Levy's parents claimed that Ms. Levy had told them of an affair between Condit and Levy.[19]

While Condit did lose the Democratic primary in 2002, this still stands as a stark contrast to the immediate and voluntary resignation of Republicans who are much less involved in unsavory sexual activities. Perhaps if Condit had admitted to an affair he would have found more support among his fellow Democrats? At least he might have wound up with a job at Rainbow/PUSH, rather than going bust in Arizona as the owner of a Baskin-Robbins.

JIM MCGREEVEY

On August 12, 2004, the Democratic governor of New Jersey, Jim McGreevey, stood outside the state house in Trenton, New Jersey, surrounded by his wife and parents, and announced to the people of New Jersey and the United States that he was "a gay American," and would resign after it had been revealed that he had a homosexual affair. "I am also here today because, shamefully, I engaged in an adult consensual affair with another man, which violates my bonds of matrimony. It was wrong. It was foolish. It was inexcusable. And for this, I ask the forgiveness and the grace of my wife."

Democrats have an odd understanding of what is inexcusable. How can a man say that his extra-marital affair is inexcusable when he's got his wife standing with him when he admits in public to betraying his wife in the worst possible way? There must have been some excuse offered—and Mrs. McGreevey must have accepted it.

While most wives would have, at least, some problem standing by their adulterous man—regardless of the gender of his lover—Democratic wives seem to have a strong stomach for this sort of thing. As we saw during the Clinton administration, marriage vows often take a backseat to Democratic Party loyalty and the lust for power. By standing with her disgraced husband, Mrs. McGreevey demonstrated, once again, the premium placed by

Democrats on damage control at times of scandal. But the affair was wrong, foolish, and inexcusable for other reasons as well.

While the Clinton years instructed us that, for the Democrats, betraying the sacred oath of matrimony is laudable as long as you lie about it in public to "protect" your wife and family, it was hoped that the safety of the citizens was a serious enough issue to warrant some probity on the part of Democrats. Our hopes were dashed in the case of McGreevey.

When McGreevey took office in 2002, New Jersey was facing a budget crisis. Among the many problems the government faced was a massive increase in payroll costs as between 1998 and 2002 the number of New Jersey employees earning $70,000 or more rose from 3,212 to 10,145. Meanwhile, employees earning $100,000 or more rose from 690 to 1,309 during the same period. McGreevey pledged to bring this under control with a round of layoffs, salary freezes and budget cuts.[20] Still, you can only tighten your belt so far, especially when such a matter as homeland security is at stake. Thus Governor McGreevey had no problem hiring Golan Cipel to be his special counsel on homeland security at a salary of $110,000 per year.[21]

While money is no object when we are talking about the safety of American citizens, the skills and qualifications of people hired to look after public safety should be the main object. Unfortunately, Mr. Cipel was neither qualified for the homeland security job, nor was he an American citizen. In fact, Cipel was not only lacked American citizenship, but he didn't even have a work permit. All of this seemingly slipped McGreevey's mind.[22] Eventually, questions about Cipel's qualifications forced his resignation, first as counsel on homeland security, later as a mere counsel to McGreevey.

In a sad commentary on the current state of American public morality, the fact of the affair was little commented on. There was a day when the revelation of an affair would have in and of itself spelled political doom, but not any more. It took an extra step before McGreevey would realize his political goose was cooked.

While McGreevey specifically referred to the affair as "consensual," Cipel threatened to file sexual harassment charges against McGreevey unless he was paid several million dollars.[23] It was only under such threat that McGreevey came forward to make his announcement of homosexuality and resignation as governor. Betraying your spouse is just one of those things which happen—but sexual harassment? Out you go!

This double announcement caught the country by surprise and made a huge splash in the media. It isn't every day that such an event occurs—but even in the most extraordinary of times, Democrats still must be Democrats. Now that McGreevey was out, the governorship had to be saved for the Party.

In the normal course of events, an announcement like McGreevey's could be expected to result in immediate resignation, with maybe a short period of transition as a successor is brought up to speed. But that would have required a special election to fill McGreevey's seat, and some feared that such a snap election, coming on the heels of scandal, might very well result in the ultimate horror—a Republican taking over the governorship. So, McGreevey's resignation would take effect on November 15, 2004. Had McGreevey resigned immediately, a special gubernatorial election would have taken place on November 2. By waiting three months, the resignation was close enough to the next regular gubernatorial election to void the requirement for a special election. This sly move paved the way ethically challenged former Senator Jon Corzine's successful run for governor.

BOB MENENDEZ

Ironically, Corzine's handpicked replacement for his Senate seat, Bob Menendez, also has been accused of sexual misconduct. Menendez reportedly had a long-term extramarital affair with a novice lobbyist and political consultant (and his former chief of staff) and then steering over $200,000 in fundraising and political consulting contracts her way as she lobbied him in Congress (see Chapter Five). Menendez being a New Jersey Democrat, all of that didn't matter as the senator went on to win reelection with fifty-three percent of the vote.

Even outside of New Jersey, it seems that more often than not, sex scandals (or scandals of any kind) rarely become political liabilities for politicians on the Democratic side of the aisle. Whether your name is Bill Clinton, Daniel Inouye, Gerry Studds, or Mel Reynolds, faithful Democrats seem willing to overlook even the most serious of allegations out of party loyalty.

In other words, they get away with it because their liberal constituencies easily forgive them and demonize those who dare criticize them.

KENNEDY SEX SCANDALS

Oftentimes you don't have to be in Congress to get away with having sex with a minor—you just have to be a Kennedy.

Michael Kennedy, son of the late Robert Kennedy and nephew to Ted Kennedy, would make headlines in 1997, when it was revealed that he had a sexual affair with the family's fourteen-year-old babysitter. Kennedy's wife had allegedly caught the two in bed together. Ironically, Michael had been considering running for Gerry Studd's vacated congressional seat the previous year.[24] He wasn't the only Kennedy to get away with serious sexual misconduct.

William Kennedy Smith, nephew of Ted Kennedy, was accused of rape in 1991. Ironically, the incident occurred some time after Kennedy took his son Patrick and his nephew out for a night of drinking, when William met the woman who would later accuse him of rape. The senior senator from Massachusetts would testify in his nephew's defense,[25] and the star power of the Kennedy name went a long way towards helping his nephew be acquitted.

In fact, the bringing up of the deviant sexual proclivities of Democrats has become passé in American politics, while attacking the sexual activities of Republicans (especially when those activities turn out to be homosexual in nature) cannot be exploited enough. Even today, Clinton's lack of candor about his sexual transgressions has become mere bumper sticker slogans for his apologists who argue, "no one died when Clinton lied."

Democrats can be accused of sexual misconduct, but ultimately Republicans are at fault for having the audacity to take advantage of the scandal. In other words, "Don't look at me, it's the Republicans, stupid."

Democrats are the party that blandly ignores Senator Kennedy's extensive sexual misconduct, including driving off a bridge and leaving a girl—a subordinate who worked on Kennedy's political campaigns—to die.

Voting for things like a higher minimum wage and tax increases apparently clears up more sins for Democrats than saying the rosary does for Catholics. When Bill Clinton wagged his finger at the American people and asserted he didn't have sex with "that woman," no one ever dreamed that Democrats would shortly thereafter be asserting that oral sex isn't really sex, and so Clinton wasn't lying. Furthermore, this sex on public property with a subordinate was translated by Democrats in to a purely private affair, which only a peeping-Tom pervert would have any interest in.

True enough, when Bill Clinton admitted to "inappropriate" behavior with Monica Lewinsky, *Newsweek* contributing editor Eleanor Clift said, "I think people are disappointed in this president that he behaved this way. But, they are also putting it in perspective and [understand] that it is largely a private matter."[26] Clinton ultimately survived and so did the "private matter" talking point—carefully stored for use by later Democrats, but off limits to Republicans.

Sex scandals are nasty business, and sexual misconduct on either side of the aisle should not be tolerated. Too often Democrats and their allies show us that it is more important for them to hold onto power than to preserve the integrity of the offices they hold. The sexual tendencies of elected officials aren't simply private matters. A politician's sexual indiscretions reflect not only a lack of moral temperament, but also a potential to exercise poor judgment in making decisions that affect the safety of their constituents.

CONCLUSION

AFTER the Democrats won control of the House in 2006, the soon-to-be House Speaker Nancy Pelosi, like a wolf in sheep's clothing, declared "Democrats intend to lead the most honest, the most open and the most ethical Congress in history."[1]

While exit polls showed that corruption was a big issue with the voters in 2006, clearly Republican candidates were held to a much higher standard, as many corrupt Democrats featured in this book were elected or reelected (in some cases in landslides). These same people are really going to lead "the most honest, the most open and the most ethical Congress in history?"

When Bill Clinton was asked by Dan Rather why he had his affair with Monica Lewinsky, the former president answered, "I think I did something for the worst possible reason—just because I could."[2] It is a telling answer and one, we think, that is indicative of the broader Democratic attitude toward the world.

If Democrats were asked why they behave so corruptly, a truthful answer would echo Clinton's—"Because we can."

People will use power for their own personal pleasure when they do not feel the weight of their obligations to others. As we pointed out in the introduction, the Democratic dearth of ideas seems to have diminished their sense of responsibility to the greater good.

As a result, Democratic leaders ultimately pursue politics for personal gain, and enact policies *only when they are politically expedient,* which keeps them in power. This mercenary approach to politics seems to have bled into their ethical decisions.

But now they have been given additional powers. And we are asked to believe that the corruption that is so deeply embedded in the Democratic Party is going to disappear. Ethical decisions and cultures, however, do not work that way. A person or a group's ethics stem from the way they view the world, and that will not change immediately. Democrats have not recovered the vision of

JFK, of Woordow Wilson, or of FDR, and so there is little reason to think that they will have any guide to their moral instincts other than their own immediate political futures.

"Just because I could." And unfortunately, the Democrats can. Scandals have done little to stop Democrats from getting re-elected. The media has done little to report on the Democrats' corruption. And their supporters are unwilling to recognize or accept that any corruption even exists in the Democratic Party. The lesson of the mainstream media and of modern politics is that, for Democrats, their immediate political futures very rarely depend upon whether they act appropriately or not.

Democrats have been given every reason to believe that no matter what they do, they will not be held accountable for it. They have seen firsthand that even when they are plagued by a scandal that they are more likely to get a standing ovation than get the boot.

Before we can have an open, honest, and ethical Congress, Democrats must be held accountable for their own corruption. The Democrats need to prove they are serious about cleaning up Washington by first ridding their party of its most corrupt members. If they were to apply to themselves the same standards Republicans hold themselves to, they would be vastly improved. If they were to apply to themselves the same standards *they* hold Republicans to, then we would have an exceptionally clean government, and probably significantly fewer of the current Democrats in office.

The Democrats had their chance to dominate the debate about corruption. But the tables have now turned. With this book, you are now armed with an inconvenient truth about the Democratic Party. If left unchecked, corruption has a corrosive effect on both government and society, so it must be brought to light. It is time to expose the corruption and hypocrisy of the Democratic Party, not just for the sake of removing Democrats from office, but for the sake of the health and proper functioning of our government, and of the United States of America.

ABOUT THE AUTHORS

Matt Margolis, 27, graduated *summa cum laude* from the University of Hartford in 2002, earning a degree in architectural engineering technology.

In November 2003, Matt founded Blogs for Bush, which quickly became one of the top blogs during the 2004 presidential campaign. Matt runs a number of other blogs, and he has been an invited guest on CNN and other television and radio programs.

Matt is currently pursuing a master's degree in architecture and works full-time as an architectural designer. He lives near Boston, MA.

Mark Noonan is originally from New Jersey but grew up in San Diego, California. He spent four years in the U.S. Navy after completing high school. He served extensively in Europe and the Middle East. Self-educated in history, philosophy, and politics, he remains astounded by how much he doesn't know. After September 11, 2001, Mark attempted to reenlist, but was unable to serve again on account of his age.

After meeting Matt Margolis in the fall of 2003, Mark joined Blogs for Bush as a regular contributor. Mark has been an invited guest on MSNBC and other television and radio programs. Mark is married and currently lives in North Las Vegas, Nevada.

Authors' Websites:

Blogs for Bush: http://www.blogsforbush.com
GOP Bloggers: http://www.gopbloggers.org
No Agenda: http://blog.noagenda.org
Hub Politics: http://www.hubpolitics.com
Battle Born Politics: http://www.battlebornpolitics.com
Caucus of Corruption: http://www.caucusofcorruption.com

NOTES

Preface

1. "Dean: Bin Laden guilt best determined by jury," CNN.com, December 26, 2003.
2. Raphael Lewis and Frank Phillips, "Dean rips DeLay at convention," *Boston Globe*, May 15, 2005.

Introduction

1. Theodore Roosevelt, Speech, Cambridge, Massachusetts, March 11, 1890.
2. Howell Raines, "7 Vying to Lead the Democrats Somewhere," *New York Times*, January 13, 1985.
3. Glen Johnson, "Democrat to Offer Social Security Plan," *Associated Press*, May 14, 2005.
4. Dan Balz, "Pelosi Hails Democrats' Diverse War Stances," *Washington Post*, December 16, 2005, p. A23.
5. E.J. Dionne Jr., "Vision Check for the Democrats," *Washington Post*, November 8, 2005, p. A19.
6. http://www.housedemocrats.gov/news/librarydetail.cfm?library_content_id =780 Accessed July 22, 2006.
7. Charles Hurt, "'Miracle' needed to win back Senate," *Washington Times*, April 29, 2005.
8. From points that surfaced on National Review Online's blog, The Corner.
9. http://www.democrats.org/a/2005/09/dean_on_delay_i.php.
10. http://www.democrats.org/a/2005/10/gop_culture_of.php.
11. http://www.nytimes.com/2005/10/21/politics/21delay.html.
12. Todd J. Gillman, "Bush says he thinks DeLay is innocent. President praises Texan's effectiveness as House GOP leader," *Dallas Morning News*, December 15, 2005, p. 11A.
13. George Archibald, "Gephardt Socked with Ethics Charges," The *Washington Times*, 3 February 1996, 3, http://www.questia.com/PM.qst?a=o&d=500050021.
14. Ibid.
15. Brian Blomquist, "Republicans Seek to Lessen Sanctions against Gingrich: Point to Gephardt, McDermott Cases," The *Washington Times*, 16 January 1997, 18, http://www.questia.com/PM.qst?a=o&d=5001608719.
16. Lynn Sweet, "Obama's online pitch gives Byrd's campaign a big boost," *Chicago Sun-Times*, April 11, 2005.

17. http://salon.com/news/feature/2006/09/24/allen_football/index.html; accessed November 7, 2006.

18. http://www.allenhq.com/2006/09/25/webbs-dirty-tricksters-salon; accessed November 7, 2006.

19. http://www.allenhq.com/2006/09/20/jewish-leaders-blast-anti-semitic-webb-campaign-tactics/; accessed November 7, 2006.

20. "How Do I Repair Reputation?" *Chicago Tribune*, May 27, 1987, page C4.

21. R. G. Ratcliffe, "DA Absolves Richards in Phone Probe," The *Houston Chronicle*, August 27, 1994, page A1.

Chapter 1: Nancy Pelosi

1. http://democraticleader.house.gov/press/releases.cfm?pressReleaseID=1197.

2. "Carter Names Delegation on Aid to Italian Earthquake Victims," *Associated Press*, December 11, 1980.

3. "California Democratic Party Fined $7,000," *Associated Press*, December 31, 1981.

4. David S. Broder, "Opposition Without a Voice," *Washington Post* Op-Ed, June 7, 1981.

5. *United Press International*, Washington News, December 3, 1982.

6. *United Press International*, Domestic News, January 14, 1983.

7. Eleanor Randolph, "Democrats Fear Protestors Will Offer TV Cameras a Better Show," *Washington Post*, July 12, 1984.

8. Analysis of data from OpenSecrets.org

9. Ethan Wallison, "Pelosi's PAC Stirs Questions," *Roll Call*, October 24, 2002.

10. http://www.nlpc.org/view.asp?action=viewArticle&aid=167; accessed July 22, 2006.

11. "Affiliated Leadership PACs Fined," FEC Press Release, March 26, 2004.

12. Brody Mullins, "Pelosi PAC Hit With $21K Fine," *Roll Call*, February 9, 2004.

13. http://www.nlpc.org/view.asp?action=viewArticle&aid=168; accessed July 22, 2006.

14. Edward Epstein, "Pelosi accused of pork-barrel politics," *San Francisco Chronicle*, February 21, 2003.

15. Fox News broadcast, 3/17/05.

16. Juliet Eilperin, "House Members Assigned to Committees," *Washington Post*, January 10, 2003, p. A07.

17. "Texas lawmaker tight with Pelosi gets coveted seat," *Houston Chronicle*, March 30, 2005.

18. "Date Nancy's Daughter, Get Hot Seat," *Washingtonian*, April, 2003.

19. Han Nichols, "Matsui widow to get Rules seat," The *Hill*, February 9, 2005.

20. Ibid.

21. Ibid.

22. http://www.democrats.reform.house.gov/Documents/

20050927102957-66023.pdf.

23. http://www.house.gov/tierney/press/intell12605.shtml.

24. "Pols & Politics: Prez Sox it to Hub heroes," *Boston Herald*, February 27, 2005, p. 23.

25. Charles Babington, "Harman May Get Boot in '07," *Washington Post*, September 27, 2005.

26. Stephan Dinan, "Pelosi helped donor to PAC," *Washington Times*, April 5, 2005.

27. Ibid.

28. http://www.house.gov/pelosi/press/releases/March03/HuntersPT033104. html.

29. "GOP Lawmakers Float Ethics Probe of Murtha," *Roll Call*, November 18, 2005.

30. http://democraticleader.house.gov/press/releases.cfm?pressReleaseID=928; accessed March 6, 2006.

31. Charles Hurt, "Lobbyist paid for Jones' '01 trip," *Washington Times*, April 20, 2005.

32. Ibid.

33. Charles Hurt, "Jones provides records of '01 trip," *Washington Times*, April 28, 2005.

34. Ibid.

35. Charles Hurt, "Pelosi pressed for trip records," *Washington Times*, April 22, 2005.

36. http://transcripts.cnn.com/TRANSCRIPTS/0504/26/ip.01.html; accessed March 5, 2006.

37. http://www.nationalreview.com/pfeiffer/pfeiffer200504111009.asp; accessed January 26, 2006.

38. John Bresnahan, "Travel Scandal Fallout Ensnares Both Parties," *Roll Call*, May 5, 2005.

39. Mike Allen, "Pelosi Turns In Delinquent Report for 3 Sponsor-Funded Trips," *Washington Post*, July 5, 2005, p. A03.

40. Ibid.

41. Elana Schor, "34 took Taiwan trips," The *Hill*, June 8, 2005.

42. Charles Hurt, "GOP hits Pelosi's 'hypocrisy' on wage bill," *Washington Times*, January 12, 2007.

43. Ibid.

44. Ibid.

45. http://johnshadegg.house.gov/News/DocumentSingle.aspx?DocumentID= 55404; accessed January 12, 2007.

46. Mary Ann Akers, "Culture of Something," *Roll Call*, March 1, 2006.

47. "High Gas Prices Linked to Oily White House," *People's Weekly World*, April 29, 2006.

48. Information obtained from opensecrets.org, run by the Center for Responsive Politics.
49. Nancy Pelosi, "Smoke Screen From Big Tobacco on Treaty," *San Francisco Chronicle*, February 27, 2003.
50. Peter Schweizer, *Do As I Say (Not As I Do): Profiles In Liberal Hypocrisy.* (New York: Doubleday) p. 147-149.
51. Joseph Klein, "Nancy Pelosi: Anatomy of a Trainwreck," FrontpageMagazine.com, October 9, 2006.
52. Ibid.
53. "Republican Record on Border Security a 'Catastrophic Failure,'" *US Newswire*, July 27, 2006.

Chapter 2: Harry Reid

1. "Reid on the Attack," *Pahrump Valley Times* online, December 23, 2005.
2. Stephen Elliott, "Searching for Harry Reid," The *Progressive* online, March 2005.
3. *New York Times*, Information Bank Abstracts, November 5, 1974, page 22, column 4.
4. According to the American Conservative Union, Reid votes conservative only 20 percent of the time.
5. Sen. Harry Reid on *Fox New Sunday*, Fox News online, December 18, 2005.
6. Ibid.
7. Ibid.
8. Ibid.
9. Jeffrey H. Birnbaum and Derek Willis, "Democrats Also Got Tribal Donations," *Washington Post*, June 3, 2004, p. A01.
10. Tony Batt, "Reid Won't Be Returning Lobbyist Contributions," *Las Vegas Review-Journal* online, June 4, 2005.
11. Information obtained from opensecrets.org, run by the Center for Responsive Politics.
12. Ibid.
13. Jeffrey H. Birnbaum and Derek Willis, "Democrats Also Got Tribal Donations," *Washington Post*, June 3, 2004, p. A01.
14. Rebecca Adams, "The Game's The Thing: Reid Has Been A Ready Ally To Abramoff-Linked Interests," *Congressional Quarterly Weekly*, January 16, 2006.
15. *Associated Press* Online, February 11, 2006.
16. Tony Batt, "Tribes gave to Reid after hiring Abramoff," *Las Vegas Review-Journal*, February 3, 2006.
17. *Investor's Business Daily*, Editorial, January 31, 2006, page A14.

18. John Solomon, and Sharon Theimer, "Lawmakers Pressured Interior While Getting Large Donations," *Associated Press*, November 18, 2005.

19. Amanda B. Carpenter, *Human Events* Online, January 17, 2006.

20. Letter to Interior Secretary Gale Norton dated November 8, 2002.

21. Letter to President George W. Bush dated January 17, 2006.

22. Ibid.

23. Tony Batt, "Reid Won't Be Returning Lobbyist Contributions," *Las Vegas Review-Journal* online, June 4, 2005.

24. Jon Kamman and Billy House, "Hayworth Will Keep Tribal Gifts Despite Scandal," The *Arizona Republic* online, December 23, 2005.

25. Steve Tetreault, "Reid, Ensign show no worry," *Las Vegas Review-Journal*, January 4, 2005.

26. http://blogs.abcnews.com/theblotter/2006/11/abramoff_report.html; accessed November 15, 2006.

27. Ibid.

28. Steve Sebelius, "Ambition plus Ambition Equals Dario Herrera," *Las Vegas Review-Journal*, December 12, 2000, page 7B.

29. Information obtained from opensecrets.org, run by the Center for Responsive Politics.

30. Raven Tyler, "Clark Cty. Commissioner Dario Herrera (Democrat)", *PBS Online Newshour*, undated.

31. Steve Miller, "Corruption in Nevada? (Part Twenty-Five)," *Twisted Badge* online, November 28, 2004.

32. Information obtained from opensecrets.org run by the Center for Responsive Politics.

33. Kathleen Hennessey, "FEC; Reid, Herrera Donors Broke Campaign Finance Laws," *Associated Press* State and Local Wire, March 10, 2006.

34. John Solomon and Kathleen Hennessy, "Reid Got $1M in Land Deal," *Associated Press*, October 11, 2006.

35. Ibid.

36. Chuck Neubaeur and Tom Hamburger, "A Deal in the Desert for Reid?" *Los Angeles Times*, January 28, 2007.

37. "Sen. Reid Backed Funding for Bridge Near Property Holding," *Associated Press*, November 13, 2006.

38. Chuck Neubauer and Richard T. Coope, "In Nevada, Reid is the Name to Know," *Los Angeles Times*, June 23, 2003.

39. Harry Reid biography, official Senate Web site, undated.

40. S.2612, "A Bill to Establish Wilderness Areas, Promote Conservation, Improve Public Land, and Provide for High Quality Development in Clark County, Nevada and for Other Purposes," The Library of Congress—Thomas, summary as of October 8, 2002.

41. Chuck Neubauer and Richard T. Coope, "In Nevada, Reid is the Name to Know," *Los Angeles Times*, June 23, 2003.

42. Information obtained from opensecrets.org, run by the Center for Responsive Politics.

43. "The Reid Connections," *Los Angeles Times* online PDF document, June, 2003.

44. Michael Weissenstein, "Staking a Claim to Searchlight," *Las Vegas Review-Journal*, October 18, 2000, Page 1B.

45. John Solomon, "Reid to Reimburse Campaign for Donations," *Associated Press*, October 16, 2006.

Chapter 3: Chuck Schumer

1. "Schumer Says Bush Hurting GOP Prospects in 2006," *Bulletin News Network* quoting from the *Hill*, November 3, 2005.

2. http://en.wikipedia.org/wiki/Charles_Schumer.

3. The *New York Times*, March 13, 1979, Section 2, page 4.

4. Frank Lynn, "Reagan Easily Defeats Carter, Republicans Gain in Congress, D'Amato and Dodd," *New York Times*, November 5, 1980, page A1.

5. "Post Says Government May Seek Indictment of New York Congressman," *Associated Press*, January 6, 1983.

6. Ibid.

7. Leslie Maitland, "Federal Officials Won't Prosecute In Schumer Case," *New York Times*, January 10, 1983.

8. Eileen Putman, "FEC Closes Books On Alleged Schumer Campaign Violations," *Associated Press*, May 1, 1986.

9. Ibid.

10. Tracey Tully and Joel Siegel, "Al's Defeat A Shakeup for State's GOP, Dems," *New York Daily News*, November 5, 1998.

11. Douglas Turner, "Schumer Puts Big Dent In State GOP Machine Built By D'Amato," *Buffalo News*, November 4, 1998.

12. Brian Blomquist, "Feds Slap Chuck for '98 Campaign Violations," *New York Post*, April 21, 2001.

13. Amy Keller, "FEC Looks at Schumer's Books Report Reveals $1 Million in Errors; Democrat Blames Sloppy Accounting," *Roll Call*, April 23, 2001.

14. Elaine S. Povich, "Audit Urges Schumer to Refund Donations," *Newsday*, April 21, 2001.

15. Douglas Turner, "Schumer's Lawyer Says Not To Return Contributions," *Buffalo News*, April 25, 2001.

16. Douglas Turner, "Schumer Agrees To Pay Fine For '98 Fund Raising," *Buffalo News*, April 16, 2003.

17. Peter Lyman, "Schumer to GOP: Reveal Ties to Abramoff," *Post-Standard* (Syracuse, NY), January 20, 2006, p. A8.

18. http://www.gop.com/media/PDFs/021606ReidAllAboutIt.pdf; accessed March 6, 2006.

19. http://www.senate.gov/~schumer/SchumerWebsite/pressroom/ press_releases/2006/PR67.AG%20Abramoff.021606.html; accessed July 22, 2006.

20. Ibid.

21. "Schumer's Shame," *New York Post*, September 10, 2005, p. 18.

22. Lukas I. Alpert, "Chuck Sparks Storm," *New York Post*, September 9, 2005, p. 11.

23. Ibid.

24. Jonathan Kaplan, "Schumer: Election is about Bush," The *Hill*, April 6, 2006.

25. Chuck Schumer, "2006 is going to be the year for Democrats," The *Hill*, November 3, 2005.

26. http://schumer.senate.gov/SchumerWebsite/pressroom/press_releases/2005/ PR41520.ID%20Theft.030905.html ; accessed December 21, 2005.

27. John Wagner and Matthew Mosk, "FBI Investigates Democrats on Steele's Credit Report," *Washington Post*, September 21, 2005, p. B05.

28. Deborah Orin, "Schumer Staffers Eyed In Probe of Political ID Theft," *New York Post*, September 22, 2005.

29. http://www.newsday.com/news/nationworld/nation/ ny-usschu024451742 oct02,0,2622724.story?coll=ny-nationalnews-headlines.

30. Glenn Thrush, "Schumer's consumer crusade tarnished by his own staffers," *Newsday*, October 2, 2005, p. A25.

31. Ibid.

32. http://www.foxnews.com/story/0,2933,177617,00.html.

33. Both would eventually resign.

34. Glenn Thrush, "Schumer's consumer crusade tarnished by his own staffers," *Newsday*, October 2, 2005, p. A25.

35. Ibid.

36. S. A. Miller, "Steele supporters call Democrats' credit probe 'racist'," *Washington Times*, October 18, 2005, p. B01.

37. Ibid.

38. Letter To Charles Schumer, September 26, 2005.

39. Raymond Hernandez, "Democrats Are on Defensive In Maryland Senate Race," *New York Times*, October 6, 2005 p. A20.

40. http://www.usdoj.gov/usao/dc/Press_Releases/2006_Archives/Mar_2006/ 06122.html; accessed July 22, 2006.

41. "Woman pleads guilty in Steele credit report case," *Associated Press*, March 24, 2006.

42. http://www.steeleformaryland.com/

SteeleLettertoCardinDeanSchumerLier man.htm; accessed November 6, 2006.

Chapter 4: Rahm Emanuel

1. John Heilemann, "The Dems' Newt Ideas," *New York Magazine*, November 21, 2005.
2. Ibid.
3. Lloyd Grove, "Clinton's Lean Green Machine," *Washington Post*, July 7, 1992, page C1.
4. One of the House Democrats instrumental in setting the stage for the savings and loan crisis in the 1980s.
5. Mark Hornung, "40 Under 40: Rahm Emanuel," *Crains Chicago Business*, October 1, 1990, Sec. 1, page 29.
6. Ibid.
7. Info accessed at Open Secrets.
8. Rostenkowski was at the center of the House "check kiting" scandal. His own take from that scandal was about $1 million—and seventeen months in jail.
9. Steve Warmbir, Tim Novak and Fran Spielman, "Bagman Pleads to Hired Truck Role," *Chicago Sun Times* online, May 3, 2005.
10. Ben Bradley, "Tomczak Pleads Guilty," ABC 7 Chicago online, July 29, 2005.
11. Steve Warmbir, Fran Spielman and Tim Novak, "Feds Probe Young Inspectors' Hiring," *Chicago Sun Times* online, February 21, 2006.
12. Fran Spielman, "Feds Take Files From Streets and Sanitation Offices," *Chicago Sun Times* online, May 4, 2005.
13. Ibid.
14. Ibid.
15. http://www.ipsn.org/hired_truck_scandal/wesolowski/Wesolowski_plea.pdf (p. 13).
16. Ibid.
17. Jeff Zeleny, Mike Dorning and Michael Tackett, "Join Congress, See The World," *Chicago Tribune*, May 8, 2005 p. C1.
18. Ibid.
19. Maher had disgraced himself by comparing the acts of the 9/11 terrorists to the acts of American military pilots. He was booted off network television and hired by HBO, which lives off of intense controversy.
20. http://www.dccc.org/campaignforchange/petitions/armpac/default/; accessed December 23, 2005.
21. Chris Fusco, Dave McKinney, Abdon Pallasch and Steve Warmbir, "Feds Charge 3 in Kickback Scheme," *Chicago Sun-Times*, August 4, 2005.
22. Andrea Stone, "Republicans May Return DeLay's PAC Funds," *USA Today*, September 29, 2005.

23. Patrick Crowley, "Davis Fires Back," NKY.com, December 22, 2005.

24. Information obtained from opensecrets.org, run by the Center for Responsive Politics.

25. Stephen Dinan, "Extortion Case Hits Contributions," The *Washington Times*, September 1, 2005.

26. Alison Vekshin, "Boozman Will Keep DeLay Funds," *Arkansas News Bureau*, October 1, 2005.

27. Stephen Dinan, "Extortion Case Hits Contributions," *Washington Times*, September 1, 2005.

28. The *Charlotte Observer*, http://www.charlotte.com/mld/observer/news/local/12888303.htm.

29. Liz Hester, "GOP cites Ballance case as hypocrisy," *Herald-Sun* (Durham, NC) October 31, 2005, p. A1.

Chapter 5: Dishonorable Mention

1. Erin P. Billings and Lauren W. Whittington, "Jefferson Begins To Fight Charges," *Roll Call*, September 15, 2005.

2. Vice President Albert Gore, White House News Conference, March 3, 1997.

3. The *Record*, Bergen County, New Jersey, October 19, 1997, Page A01.

4. The *New York Post*, October 1, 2002, Page 007.

5. *Associated Press* State and Local Wire, July 31, 2002.

6. The *Pittsburg Post-Gazette*, October 1, 2002, page A-12.

7. *Philadelphia Inquirer*, May 6, 2004, page A01.

8. *New York Daily News*, January 20, 2004, page 24.

9. "Corzine Campaign Gets Boost From CWA," Jon Corzine for Governor press release, June 27, 2005.

10. David Kocieniewski, "Corzine Forgave $470,000 Loan To Friend Who Runs State Union," *New York Times*, August 4, 2005, p. A1.

11. Eric Pfeiffer, "State of Corruption," *National Review* Online, August 12, 2005.

12. Carl Mayer, "Ethics Charges Filed Against Corzine," The Untouchables Group (blog), August 31, 2005.

13. John P. McAlpin and Clint Riley, "Corzine Vote Aided Investment Deal," NorthJersey.com, September 15, 2005.

14. Ibid.

15. Ibid.

16. Howard Dean, "What 2005 Means," Democrats.org, November 9, 2005.

17. Angela Delli Santi, "Corzine bailed out lobbyist accused of stalking party chairman," *Associated Press*, March 8, 2006.

18. Josh Margolin, "Ethics panel finds no violation in Corzine bail loan to lobbyist," *Star-Ledger*, March 23, 2006.

19. The *New York Sun*, August 20, 2004, page 4.

20. Jeffrey Gettleman, "A Swift Climb Up the Ladder, From Lowly Assistant to a Highly Paid Lobbyist," *New York Times*, July 17, 2005.

21. Bill Albers, "Menendez Letter Aides Public Contracts for Big Campaign Donor," PoliticsNJ.com, March 7, 2006.

22. *Associated Press*, September 8, 2006.

23. Renshaw, Jarrett. "Doc's Suit Links Menendez to Scheme," the *Jersey Journal*. March 25, 2006.

24. "N.J. Senator Accused Of Kickbacks," *Associated Press*, September 29, 2006.

25. Ibid.

26. Renshaw, Jarrett. "Doc's Suit Links Menendez to Scheme," the *Jersey Journal*. March 25, 2006.

27. Stephen Spruiell, "Culture of Corruption: The special case of Bob Menendez," *National Review*, October 31, 2006.

28. David Kocieniewski, "Report Finds Patronage Rife at NJ University," *New York Times*, April 4, 2006.

29. About $2.1 million to the DNC over the years.

30. Herb Jackson, "Officials kept Kushner's cash after guilty plea," *[Bergan County] Record*, April 24, 2006.

31. Ibid.

32. The amount cited by the Federal Elections Commission as having been donated illegally.

33. Ibid.

34. Ibid.

35. Amy Fagan, "Senate Democrats to keep Menendez on N.J. ballot," *Washington Times*, September 29, 2006.

36. David Kocieniewski and Ray Rivera, "Waterfront Project Reflects 2 Images of a Senator," *New York Times*, October 29, 2006.

37. Ibid.

38. Amy Fagan, "McDermott Ethics Probe Blocked, GOP Aide Says," *Washington Times*, April 15, 2005.

39. Brian Blomquist, and Laurie Kellman, "McDermott Quits Gingrich Probe: FBI Focuses on Democrat in Tape Case," *Washington Times*, January 15, 1997.

40. Ibid.

41. *Boehner v. McDermott*, United States District Court for the District of Columbia, August 20, 2004.

42. Charles Pope, "McDermott to Appeal Judge's Order to Pay $600,000 in Cell Phone Case," *Seattle Post-Intelligencer*, November 19, 2004.

43. Matthew Daly, "Court to Hear Arguments in Taped Call Case," *Associated Press*, June, 26, 2006.

44. "Appeals Court Hears New Arguments in McDermott-Boehner Tape Case," *Bulletin News Network*, November 1, 2006.

45. http://www.house.gov/ethics/McDermott_Report.pdf; accessed December 12, 2007.
46. "Panel: McDermott Violated Ethics Standards," *Associated Press*, December 12, 2006.
47. McDermott's legal defense fund was created to help pay the legal bills for his defense from Rep. John Boehner's lawsuit.
48. James Varney and Martha Carr, "FBI raids Jefferson's car, homes, treasurer; Feds are mum on reason for searches," *Times-Picayune*, August 4, 2005, p. 1.
49. Allan Lengel, "FBI Sting Targeted Louisiana Lawmaker," *Washington Post*, August 13, 2005, p. A01.
50. Ibid.
51. Bill Walsh and Bruce Alpert, "Jefferson probe focus is Nigeria telecom deal; Investors sought to deliver broadband," *Times-Picayune*, August 25, 2005.
52. The *Hotline*, (National Journal) February 16, 2006, National Briefing.
53. Matthew Barakat, "Former political aide pleads guilty to bribery, implicates congressman," *Associated Press*, January 11, 2006.
54. Jake Tapper, ABC News, September 13, 2005.
55. Cunningham, a Republican Congressman from California, was convicted of taking very large bribes from defense contractors.
56. "CREW Drafts Ethics Complaints Against Rep. William Jefferson (D-LA),",Citizens for Responsibility and Ethics in Washington, Press Release, April 12, 2006.
57. Mark Sherman, "FBI Searches Office of LA. Congressman," *Associated Press*, May 20, 2006.
58. http://democraticleader.house.gov/press/releases.cfm?pressReleaseID=1583; accessed November 4, 2006.
59. Matthew Barakat, "Filing: Tape Shows Lawmaker Taking Money," *Associated Press*, May 21, 2006.
60. Ibid.
61. Ibid.
62. Allan Lengel and Charles Babington, "Congressman Tried to Hide Papers, Justice Dept. Says," *Washington Post*, May 31, 2006, p. A04.
63. Pelosi to Jefferson: Resign from Ways and Means Committee, Press Release, May 24, 2006.
64. "House takes away Jefferson committee seat," *Associated Press*, June 16, 2006.
65. Janet McConnaughey, "What Does Congressional Power Shift Mean for Louisiana?" *Associated Press* State and Local Wire, November 8, 2006.
66. Democratic Incumbent William Jefferson Wins House Runoff Election Despite Federal Bribery Probe," *Associated Press*, December 10, 2006.
67. When Congress reconvened on January 4, 2007, the Congressional Black Caucus gave Jefferson a standing ovation.

68. Andrew Miga, "Kennedy Confirms Car Crash Near Capitol," *Associated Press,* May 4, 2005.
69. Susan Mulligan, "Rep. Kennedy in 3 a.m. crash near Capitol," *Boston Globe,* May 5, 2006.
70. David Wedge, "Pat cites pills in car wreck," *Boston Herald,* May 5, 2006.
71. Michael King, "Report: McKinney Punches Cop," News11Alive, March 30, 2006; accessed March 30, 2006.
72. "McKinney Statement," WSB-TV Atlanta, March 30, 2006; accessed March 30, 2006.
73. Josephine Hearn, "McKinney is distraction, say the Dems," the *Hill,* April 4, 2006.
74. http://www.wsbtv.com/news/8343403/detail.html; accessed July 22, 2006.
75. "Grand Jury Won't Indict Rep. McKinney," *Associated Press,* June 16, 2006.
76. Jackie Kucinich, "Union seeks ethics probe of McKinney," the *Hill,* June 20, 2006.
77. "McKinney Defeated in Georgia Runoff," *Associated Press,* August 9, 2006.
78. Carlos Campos, "McKinney Alleges Voting Irregularities," *Atlanta Journal-Constitution,* August 8, 2006.
79. Michael King, "McKinney Supporters Blaming Jews," News11 Alive, August 10, 2006.
80. Erick Stakelbeck, "Will the Peach State give America its first significant electoral victory for a champion of the radical Muslim cause?" *Jewish World Review,* July 15, 2003.
81. "McKinney Staffer Claims He Was Fired for Being Jewish," *Hannity & Colmes.* August 18, 2006. Transcript.

Chapter 6 : Botched Jokes

1. Josh Gerstein, "Kerry Retreats From His Denial on Vietnam Meet," *New York Sun,* March 19, 2004.
2. Ibid.
3. Ibid.
4. Keith Love and Dan Morain, "Pelosi Wins Democratic Contest for Burton Seat," *Los Angeles Times,* April 8, 1987.
5. Letta Taylor, *States News Service,* January 25, 1988.
6. Paul Kengor, "The Crusader: Ronald Reagan and the Fall of Communism," pg 205-210.
7. Ibid.
8. Ibid
9. Senator Ted Kennedy, speech, July, 1987.
10. Jill Zuckerman, "Score in Congress Dissent Over Iraq," *Chicago Tribune,* October 9, 2002, page 1.

11. Jay Bookman, "Big Stories Not Always Tied to Truth," the *Atlanta Journal-Constitution*, Editorial, December 29, 2003, page 11A.

12. Amy Keller, "McDermott Finds New Controversy," *Roll Call*, February 24, 2003.

13. Jim Brunner, "Aide Says McDermott Wasn't Aware of Saddam Link," *Seattle Times*, April 17, 2004.

14. Steve Miller, "Iraqi-born American has funded Democrats; Businessman seeking end to sanctions denies he supported Saddam," *Washington Times*, May 6, 2003, p. A04.

15. Ibid.

16. Inigo Gilmore and Charles Laurence, "Saddam attempted to bribe Ritter with gold Documents show Baghdad was desperate to influence ex-arms inspector's film project," *Sunday Telegraph*, May 4, 2003.

17. "Impact: Did Saddam Bribe Former U.N. Weapons Inspector, Scott Ritter?" *The O'Reilly Factor* (FOX News Channel), May 28, 2003. Transcript.

18. "Rangel Introduces Bill to Reinstate Draft," *CNN.com*, January 8, 2003.

19. Michael S. Gerber, "Rangel Votes Against Own Draft Measure," the *Hill*, October 6, 2004.

20. "A Key Test for Pelosi," *San Francisco Bay Guardian*, December 12, 2006.

21. Doug Ireland, "Pelosi's Problems," *LA Weekly*, November 13, 2002.

22. Representative Nancy Pelosi, *Press Release*, April 12th, 2003.

23. Brian Skoloff, "San Francisco Shuns Retired USS Iowa," *Associated Press*, August 20, 2005.

24. Joetta Sack-Min, "San Francisco School Board Eliminates JROTC Program," *School Board News*, December 12, 2006.

25. *USA Today*, October 8, 2001.

26. Christian Lowe, "Murtha: Marines Killed Haditha Civilians in Cold Blood," *Army Times*, May 18, 2006.

27. Senator Barak Obama, "Escalation is Not the Answer," e mail, December 28, 2006.

28. "Appeals Court Upholds Disputed Military Ballots in Florida Election," CNN, December 11, 2000.

29. "Soldiers Worried About Ballots Getting Back in Time," NBC10.Com, October 27, 2004.

30. Ibid.

31. All information on campaign spending obtained at OpenSecrets.org

Chapter 7: Abramoff Democrats

1. DNC Chairman Howard Dean, CNN Late Edition with Wolf Blitzer, January 8, 2006.

2. "Hoyer Leads Democrats' Effort to Pressure Lobbyists for Additional Funds," the *Frontrunner*, December 7, 2005.

3. Josephine Hearn, "Pelosi Calls for Investigation into Ney Dealings with Wireless Firm," the *Hill*, October 20, 2005.

4. Josephine Hearn, "Harkin pays tribe for use of skybox," the *Hill*, October 20, 2005.

5. DNC Chairman Howard Dean, *Today Show*, January 26, 2006.

6. DNC Chairman Howard Dean, *Fox News Sunday*, January 29, 2006.

7. John Solomon and Sharon Theimer, "Lawmakers Helped Abramoff Tribes Get Federal Money, Collected Donations," *Associated Press*, November 24, 2005.

8. Ibid.

9. Josephine Hearn, "Harkin Pays Tribe for His Use of Skybox," the *Hill*, October, 2005.

10. Alexander Bolton, "GOP links tribe funds to Dem sens.," the *Hill*, April 26, 2006.

11. Mary Clare Jalonick, "Baucus Will Return Abramoff Donations," *Associated Press*, December 19, 2005.

12. Jim Drinkard, "In Congress, 'we simply have too much power,'" *USA Today*, January, 9, 2006.

13. Philip Shenon and Anne E. Kornblut, "Lobbyist Paid by Pakistan Led U.S. Delegation There," *New York Times*, May 8, 2005.

14. Larry Margasak and Sharon Theimer, "Lobbyist Paid for Lawmakers Travel," *Associated Press*, May 3, 2005.

15. Byron York, "Hillary, Saipan, Sweatshops, Campaign Cash—and Abramoff," *National Review* Online, March 10, 2006.

16. Peter H Stone, "K Street Stumble," *National Journal*, March 27, 2004.

17. Josephine Hearn, "Harkin Pays Tribe for His Use of Skybox," the *Hill*, October, 2005.

18. John Solomon and Sharon Theimer, "Abramoff Tied to Dorgan Donation, Tribe Says," *Associated Press*, November 29, 2005.

19. John Solomon and Sharon Theimer, "Abramoff Investigator Aided Mashpee Tribe," *Associated Press*, December 1, 2005.

20. Ibid.

21. John Solomon, "Sen. Dorgan Returns Tribes' Donations," *Associated Press*, December 13, 2005.

22. Charles Rangel, "Native American Tribal Contributions To Rangel Political Committees," Press Release, January 5, 2006.

23. Ian Bishop, "Rangel's Wampum Linked To Scandal," *New York Post*, December 27, 2005.

24. "Jack Abramoff Lobbying and Political Contributions 1999-2006," *Capital Eye*, January 13, 2006.

25. *Associated Press*, January 6, 2006.

26. Michael Kranish, "Patrick Kennedy to Keep Tribal Donations," *Boston Globe*, January 6, 2006.
27. Derek Willis and Laura Stanton, *Washington Post*, Dec. 12, 2005.
28. Patrick Kennedy, Letter to the Editor, *Washington Post*, December 18, 2005.
29. "Jack Abramoff Lobbying and Political Contributions 1999-2006," *Capital Eye*, January 13, 2006.
30. David Ammons, "Returning Abramoff cash 'taints' tribes, Murray says," *Associated Press*, January 21, 2006.
31. Shay Totten, "Jeffords, Leahy Received Funds From Donors Linked to Abramoff," *Vermont Guardian*, January 24, 2006.
32. Ibid.
33. Ibid.
34. Information obtained from opensecrets.org, run by the Center for Responsive Politics.
35. Maeve Reston, "Casey's Abramoff-Linked Donations Draw Flak From GOP, Santorum," *Pittsburgh Post-Gazette*, February 16, 2006.
36. William Tate, "Dean's Abramoff Tie," *The American Thinker*, February 24, 2006.
37. Ibid.
38. Ibid.
39. Jeffrey H. Birnbaum and Derek Willis, "Democrats Also Got Tribal Donations," *Washington Post*, June 3, 2005.
40. Tory Newmyer, "Democrats Court Lobbyists Heavily," *Roll Call*, September 7, 2006.
41. Michael Forsyth and Christine Jensen, "Democratic Lobbyists Relish Return to Power Elite," *Bloomberg*, November 11, 2006.

Chapter 8: Family Hiring & Nepotism

1. 2004 Democratic Party Platform, Page 19.
2. Philip Shenon, Eric Lipton and Monica Brokowski, "Political Groups Paid 2 Relatives of House Leader," *New York Times*, April 6, 2005.
3. "The Jackson 3," the *Hill*, November 29, 1995.
4. Steve Miller and Jerry Seper, "Jackson's Income Triggers Questions: Minister Says Money Not His Objective," the *Washington Times*, February 26, 2001, page A1.
5. Dennis Conrad, "Freshman Democrat Raises Nearly $1 Million for 2006 Re-election," the *Associated Press* State and Local Wire, July 15, 2005.
6. Campaign finance information obtained from Open Secrets.
7. Marc Sandalow and Carolyn Lochead, "Capitol Heat," the *San Francisco Chronicle*, July 19, 2003, page A1.
8. "Lawmakers With Relatives on Payroll," *Associated Press*, April 13, 2005.
9. Ibid.

10. Ibid.
11. J. Jioni Palmer, "All In The Political Family," *Newsday*, April 5, 2005.
12. Ibid.
13. Ibid.
14. Richard Simon, Chuck Neubauer and Rone Tempest, "Political Payrolls Include Families," *Los Angeles Times*, April 15, 2005.
15. Ibid.
16. http://www.forward.com/issues/2003/03.07.18/news.extra.html.
17. "Culprits in the Kerry Camp,", *New York Post*, November 5, 2004, page six.
18. Information obtained from opensecrets.org, run by the Center for Responsive Politics.
19. Ibid.
20. Chuck Neubauer and Ted Rohrlich, "Capitalizing on a Politician's Clout," *Los Angeles Times*, December 19, 2004.
21. Ibid.
22. Ibid.
23. Associated Press, "Report Cites Fees Paid To Family of Lawmaker," *Washington Post*, December 19, 2004, p. A04.
24. Information obtained from opensecrets.org, run by the Center for Responsive Politics.
25. Associated Press, "Report Cites Fees Paid To Family of Lawmaker," *Washington Post*, December 19, 2004, p. A04.
26. Ibid.
27. "GOP Lawmakers Float Ethics Probe of Murtha," *Roll Call*, November 18, 2005.
28. Ibid.
29. Ibid.
30. Jerry Lynott, "Unpaid Bills Plague Cornerstone," *Wilkes Barre Times Leader*, March 20, 2005, Page 1D.
31. http://metroactive.com/feinstein/index.html; accessed January 26, 2007.
32. Ibid.
33. Ibid.
34. Ibid.
35. Ibid.
36. Ibid.
37. Ibid.

Chapter 9: Privately Funded Travel

1. Deirdre Shesgreen, "Members of Congress get away, courtesy of special interests," *St. Louis Post-Dispatch*, June 5, 2005.
2. However, accepting trips paid for by registered lobbyists is prohibited.
3. http://americanradioworks.publicradio.org/features/congtravel/b1.html.

4. Jeffrey H. Birnbaum, "Privately Funded Tripps Add up on Capitol Hill," *Washington Post*, June 6, 2006.
5. http://americanradioworks.publicradio.org/features/congtravel/b1.html.
6. Jeff Zeleny, Mike Dorning and Michael Tackett, "Join Congress, See the World," *Chicago Tribune*, May 8, 2005, p. 1.
7. Ibid.
8. Ibid.
9. "Australia Condemns Kebithigowella Attack," *Lankanewspapers.com*, June 17, 2006.
10. "Sri Lanka Tamil Terror," *Time*, May 27, 1985.
11. Andrew Zajac and Mike Dorning, "Davis' Tamil trip scrutinized," *Chicago Tribune*, August 24, 2006.
12. Jeff Zeleny, Mike Dorning and Michael Tackett, "Join Congress, See the World," *Chicago Tribune*, May 8, 2005, p. 1.
13. http://americanradioworks.publicradio.org/features/congtravel/ sponsor_by_cost_report.php?limit=10 ; accessed March 4, 2006.
14. http://americanradioworks.publicradio.org/features/congtravel/ member_report.php?member=7356.
15. Michael Kranish, "Capuano, wife given a $19,000 trip to Brazil," *Boston Globe*, January 9, 2006.
16. Ben Casselman, "Tierney's free trips add up: Private group sends Tierney to China, Cancun, Jamaica," *Salem News*, June 7, 2006.
17. Ben Casselman, "Tierney defends trips paid for by nonprofit," *Salem News*, June 9, 2006.
18. http://americanradioworks.publicradio.org/features/congtravel/member_ report.php?member=7356; accessed July 22, 2006.
19. http://www.house.gov/tierney/press/intell12605.shtml; accessed July 22, 2006.
20. Michael Kranish, "Capuano, wife given a $19,000 trip to Brazil," *Boston Globe*, January 9, 2006.
21. Ibid.
22. Ibid.
23. Larry Margasak, "Lawmakers Belatedly Disclose Trips," *Associated Press*, May 31, 2005.
24. Ibid.
25. Jeff Zeleny, Mike Dorning and Michael Tackett, "Join Congress, See the World," *Chicago Tribune*, May 8, 2005, p. 1.
26. Larry Margasak, "Lawmakers Belatedly Disclose Trips," *Associated Press*, May 31, 2005.
27. Michael Kranish, "Lawmakers' privately financed trips face scrutiny," *Boston Globe*, May 11, 2005.

28. David Wedge, "Mass. Pols get a free ride; Firms foot bill for exotic trips," *Boston Herald*, May 13, 2006.

29. Karen Masterson, "Catering to Voter," *Houston Chronicle*, September 1, 2002, Page A1.

30. Charles Hurt, "Lobbyist paid for Jones' '01 trip," *Washington Times*, April 20, 2005.

31. http://www.house.gov/ford/about/; accessed March 10, 2006.

32. James W. Brosnan, "Harold—In the Wings," the *Commercial Appeal*, December 14, 2003, p. A1.

33. Charles Hurt, "Lawmakers dash to correct records of trips," *Washington Times*, June 7, 2005.

34. Josephine Hearn, "Groups paid $16M for trips, report says," the *Hill*, April 27, 2005.

35. Dennis Camire, "Abercrombie denies violating House ethics rules in 2001 trip," the *Honolulu Advertiser*, April 29, 2005.

36. Tory Newmyer, "Abercrombie Asks Ethics to Investigate His Travel," *Roll Call*, April 21, 2005.

37. Larry Margasak, "Lawmakers Belatedly Disclose Trips," *Associated Press*, May 31, 2005.

38. Josephine Hearn, "Rush to file late travel reports," the *Hill*, May 10, 2005.

39. Kate Ackley, "Dicks Decides to Pay for February Trip," *Roll Call*, May 2, 2005.

40. Charles Pope, "98 Trips by McDermott led way for the state," *Seattle Post-Intelligencer*, June 6, 2006.

41. Mike Forsythe and Alison Fitzgerald, "U.S. Lawmakers Flock to Tropics as Montego Bay Trumps Abramoff," *Bloomberg News Service*, January 20, 2006.

42. http://www.inter-american.org/index2.cfm?catID=15; accessed March 9, 2006.

43. "Members of Congress Arrive in Jamaica for Five Day Trip", *Associated Press* State and Local Wire, January 12, 2006.

44. http://americanradioworks.publicradio.org/features/congtravel/party_report.php; accessed February 3, 2007.

45. "Democratic Leaders Letter to Boehner on Lobbying Reform," *States News Service*, February 9, 2006.

46. http://www.democrats.org/a/2006/01/the_democratic.php; accessed March 10, 2006.

47. Kimberly Geiger, "Steep drop in travel spending after congressional scandals," *San Francisco Chronicle*, October 15, 2006.

Chapter 10: Election Law Violations

NOTES

1. http://feingold.senate.gov/speeches/02/03/2002320C54.html; accessed November 12, 2006.
2. Owen Moritz with Thomas M DeFrank, "Ethics Flap Gettin' Old, Says Torch," *New York Daily News*, September 28, 2002, page 9.
3. "Lautenberg Replaces Torricelli," *Washington Post* , October 6, 2002.
4. Iver Peterson, "In New Jersey Senate Race, Another Day Spent in Court," *New York Times*, October 5, 2002, p. 6.
5. http://www.mattbrown.org/index.php?option=com_content&task=view&id=166&Itemid=99999999; accessed March 6, 2006.
6. Whitehouse went on to defeat incumbent Republican Senator Lincoln Chafee in the general election.
7. M.L. Johnson, "AP NewsBreak: Hawii Democrat says party traded money with Brown," *Associated Press*, March 1, 2006.
8. Lauren Whittington, "Party Donor Had Maxed Out to Brown," *Roll Call*, March 2, 2006.
9. Lauren Whittington, "Brown to Repay State Committees," *Roll Call*, March 6, 2006.
10. M.L. Johnson, "Brown drops out of Senate race," *Boston Globe*, April 26, 2006.
11. Jeffrey McMurray, "Georgia Congresswoman Fined $33,000," *Associated Press*, October 28, 2005.
12. Thomas B. Edsall, "GOP Accuses Democrats of Violating Campaign Law in Fla.," *Washington Post*, October 22, 2004, p. A07.
13. Ibid.
14. Sara Karush, "Lawyer says Fieger partner told him to contribute to Edwards," *Associated Press*, December 2, 2005.
15. Brad Heath, "Fieger's firm not alone in donations to Edwards; Many attorneys' offices made big contributions, but feds probe possible illegal reimbursements," *Detroit News*, December 4, 2005.
16. Ibid.
17. Joe Swickard, "Fieger expects federal indictment over fundraising for Edwards," *Detroit Free Press*, January 17, 2006.
18. "Thune Camp Blasts Daschle's Phone Calls," *Roll Call*, April 29, 2004.
19. Open Secrets, search done March 8, 2006.
20. Paul W Valentine, "Md. Political Fundraiser Sentenced," The *Washington Post*, August 7, 1996, page D01.
21. Michael McAuliff, "Sen. Clinton fundraising committee to pay fine," *New York Daily News*, January 6, 2006.
22. Art Moore, "Trial set in civil suit against Bill Clinton," WorldNetDaily.com, April 8, 2006.
23. Information obtained from opensecrets.org, run by the Center for Responsive Politics.

24. Lynn Sweet, "Jackson, PUSH fined for campaign violations; Dems also pay $100,000 penalty for 'nonpartisan' speaking tour in 2000," *Chicago Sun-Times*, May 27, 2005.

25. Carrie Budoff, "GOP accuses newspaper of boosting Casey with ad blitz," *Philadelphia Inquirer*, August 14, 2005.

26. Kimberly Hefling, "State Republicans file complaint against newspaper ad campaign," *Associated Press*, August 19, 2005.

27. http://www.fec.gov/press/press2006/20061103mur.html; accessed November 7, 2006.

Chapter 11: Bribes, Shady Deals, Illegal Activities

1. Barak Obama, "An Honest Government, A Hopeful Future," Speech given at the University of Nairobi, Kenya, August 28, 2006.

2. "FBI Tape Reveals John Murtha's Role in ABSCAM Scandal," Fox News *Hannity and Colmes*, transcript, October 3, 2006.

3. The authors had the opportunity to discuss the 2006 midterms with GOP political strategists early in 2006. The best they could offer on Santorum was his proven ability to come from behind and win.

4. Carrie Budoff, "Casey's Fund-Raising in Texas Brings in $18,000 Post-Katrina," Philly.com, October 7, 2005.

5. *Chicago Sun-Times*, November 29, 2005.

6. Ken Chandler, "Ethics Placed Atop Agenda," *Birmingham News*, August 29, 2001.

7. Kim Chandler, "Probe of Siegelman's administration may go into summer," *Birmingham News*, May 18, 2005, p. 2B.

8. "Fraud Case Against Ex-Governor Dropped," *Los Angeles Times*, October 6, 2004, p. 11.

9. "Former Alabama Governor Indicted," *Associated Press*, October 26, 2005.

10. Ibid.

11. Kim Chandler, "Siegelman, Scrushy Guilty of Bribery Charges," *Birmingham News*, June 30, 2006.

12. Phillip Rawls, "Siegelman Challenges Racial Makeup of Juries," *Associated Press* State and Local Wire, January 27, 2006.

13. Dana Wilke, "Lawmakers Shed Cash Tied to Two Contractors," Sign On San Diego.com, December 8, 2005.

14. Rules, House Committee on Official Conduct, adopted May 4, 2005.

15. John Bresnahan, "Mollohan To Donate MZM Funds," *Roll Call*, December 13, 2005.

16. http://www.nlpc.org/view.asp?action=viewArticle&aid=1346; accessed November 4, 2006.

17. "Step Aside, Mr. Mollohan," *Washington Post*, April 15, 2006.

18. "Pelosi: Republicans Destroyed the Ethics Process to Protect Their Cronies," Press Release, April 7, 2006.
19. John Bresnahan, "W.Va Firms Footed Mollohan Trip," *Roll Call*, May 8, 2006.
20. Michael Forsythe, "Mollohan Helped Steer U.S. Contracts to Family-Charity Donors," *Bloomberg News Service*, June 22, 2006.
21. Jodi Rudoren, "Congressman's Special Projects Bring Complaints," *New York Times*, April 8, 2006.
22. Josephine Hearn, "Velazquez Press Advisory Faces Ethical Questions," the *Hill* online, March 9, 2006.
23. Roger Snell and Mike Curtin, "Reviving Drug Case Branded As Politics Probe Centered On 2 In Secretary Of State's Office," *Columbus Dispatch*, June 23, 1990.
24. Mary Beth Lane, "Sherrod Brown Denies Halting Drug Probe," *Plain Dealer*, June 23, 1990.
25. "Brown Wanted Probe Halted, Ex-Officer Says," *Plain Dealer*, July 5, 1990.
26. Roger Snell and Mike Curtin, "Suspect In Drug Case Promoted, Still On Payroll," *Columbus Dispatch*, July 8, 1990.
27. *Associated Press* report, January 13, 2006.
28. Fredreka Schouten, "Biden burned by 'clean' language," *USA Today*, February 1, 2007.
29. Deanna Bellandi, "Topinka could get bump from indictment of Blagojevich fundraiser," *Associated Press* State and Local Wire, October 12, 2006.
30. John O'Connor, "Blagojevich Not Only Politician to Benefit From Rezko," *Associated Press* State and Local Wire, October 13, 2006.
31. Dave Mckinney and Chris Fusco, "Obama spells out 'regret' after land deal with Rezko," *Chicago Sun Times*, November 5, 2006.
32. Rezko and his companies and associates have made some $400,000 in political donations over the past sixteen years, almost all of it to Democrats.
33. Ney would eventually drop out of the race in August 2006 and plead guilty to corruption charges as a result of the Abramoff scandal.
34. http://www.zackspace.org/content/view/102/55/; accessed April 26, 2006.
35. Sabrina Eaton, "Cafaro conviction was lost on Space," *The Plain Dealer: Openers*, April 27, 2006.
36. http://www.zackspace.org/content/view/101/55/; accessed April 26, 2006.
37. http://www.zackspace.org/content/view/102/55/; accessed April 26, 2006.
38. Kate Nash, "Gov. Hails New State Copter," *Albuquerque Journal*, December 6, 2003, p. E3.
39. Chris Cillizza, "N.M. Governor Joins Presidential Race," *Washington Post*, January 22, 2007.
40. Barry Massey, "AP Enterprise: Busy governor relies on sleek police copter for journeys across New Mexico," *Associated Press*, December 13, 2005.

41. Ibid.

42. Dan Kane, "Balance gets 4 years for misuse of money," The *News & Observer* (Raleigh, NC) October 13, 2005, p. A1.

43. Lance Martin, "Supporters: 'He will rise again,'" *Roanoke Daily Herald*, October, 13, 2005.

44. "Former N.C. congressman gets send-off before prison," *Associated Press*, December 4, 2005.

45. "Fundraiser held for former NC congressman sentenced to prison," *Associated Press*, December 28, 2005.

46. Liz Hester, "GOP cites Ballance case as hypocrisy," the *Herald-Sun* (Durham, NC), October 31, 2005, p. A1.

47. Joel Thurtell and Ruby L. Bailey, "Former aides to Conyers say they were used as personal servants," *Detroit Free Press*, March 1, 2006.

48. Joel Thurtell, Chris Christoff and Ruby L. Bailey, "Conyers Staff Broke Rules For Campaign Work, Aides Charge; But Others Deny That Fundraising Was Done On Government Time," *Detroit Free Press*, November 21, 2003.

49. Joel Thurtell and Ruby L. Bailey, "Aides: Conyers Made Us Babysit; Former Staffers Airing Complaints," *Detroit Free Press*, March 2, 2006.

50. Jonathan Kaplan, "Former Conyers aides press ethics complaints," the *Hill*, March 1, 2006.

51. Ibid.

52. http://www.house.gov/ethics/Press_Statement_Conyers.htm; accessed December 30, 2006.

53. Ibid.

54. Jonathan E. Kaplan and Jackie Kucinich, "Conyers accepts responsibility for possible ethics violations," the *Hill*, December 30, 2006.

55. Josephine Hearn, "Former staff accuse Baca of 'forced volunteering,'" the *Hill*, May 18, 2006.

56. Ibid.

Chapter Twelve: Sex Scandals

1. E.J. Dionne Jr., "Gary Hart The Elusive Frontrunner," *New York Times*, May 3, 1987.

2. Deborah Mesch, "Hart Ends Campaign With Attack on Media," *Associated Press*, May 8, 1987.

3. Nancy Pelosi, "Pelosi Statement on Speaker's Comments Regarding Foley Matter," Press Release, October 02, 2006.

4. The Prowler, "Saved By Foley," the *American Spectator*, October 10, 2006.

5. "Foley Fallout," ABC's *This Week*. October 8, 2006. Transcript.

6. Jonathan Weisman, "History of Foley Messages' Release Clarified by Players," *Washington Post*, October 11, 2006.

7. "Did Democrats Page Mark Foley?" *Investor's Business Daily*, October 2, 2006.
8. Katrina A Goggins, "Inglis, Griffith Debate on Budget, Challenges Abroad," *Associated Press*, October 12, 2006.
9. Peter Johnson, "Heavy Coverage at Midterm Favors Democrats, Study Says," *USA Today*, January 29, 2007.
10. "House Panel Finds Sexual Misconduct," *Facts on File News Digest*, July 15, 1983.
11. "Move Opposed By 3 Democrats," *Associated Press*, July 21, 1983.
12. "Censured Studds Says He Will Probably Run Again", *United Press International*, July 29, 1983.
13. Steven V. Roberts, "Congressman Asks Expulsion of Two," *New York Times*, July 19, 1983.
14. Enrique J Gonzales and Vincent McGraw, "Frank Aid May Have Violated Probation on Sex Charge," *Washington Times*, August 28, 1989.
15. "Hair Stylist Accuses Sen. Inouye of Sexual Attack," *Associated Press*, October 19, 1992.
16. Barbara Vobejda, "Inouye's Challenger Pulls Ad on Woman's Allegation," *Washington Post*, October 19, 1992.
17. "Senator's Accuser Says She Won't Be Part Of Any Investigation," *Associated Press*, November 21, 1992.
18. "Inouye Overcomes Sex Charges; Clinton Carries Hawaii," *Associated Press*, November 4, 1992.
19. "Levy's Parents Say Chandra Admitted Affair", CNN, August 1, 2001.
20. *Associated Press* State and Local Wire, April 10, 2002.
21. *Associated Press* Worldstream, February 21, 2002.
22. *Associated Press* State and Local Wire, March 22, 2002.
23. Jeff Pillets, "McGreevey resigns; reveals gay affair; Onetime lover and aide demanded money, sources say; Codey, Senate president, will assume office on Nov. 15," the *Record*, August 13, 2004.
24. "Kennedy kin allegedly had affair with sitter," *Boston Globe*, April 5, 1997.
25. Robin Toner, "In Glare of Latest Scandal, Kennedy Defends the Dynasty," *New York Times*, December 7, 1991.
26. "White House Scandal," Hannity & Colmes, August 17, 1998. Transcript.

Conclusion

1. Calvin Woodward, "Democrats Sweep Into Power in House," *Associated Press*, November 8, 2006.
2. http://www.cbsnews.com/stories/2004/06/16/eveningnews/main623570.shtml; accessed February 4, 2007.